D1737460

Border Patrol Exam

3rd Edition

Border
Patrol
Exam
3rd Edition

80025 75540 x

LEARNINGEXPRESS®

NEW YORK

Copyright © 2006 LearningExpress, LLC.

All rights reserved under International and Pan-American Copyright Conventions.
Published in the United States by LearningExpress, LLC, New York.

Library of Congress Cataloging-in-Publication Data:
Border patrol exam.—3rd ed. / [Joseph N. Dassaro].
        p. cm.
    Rev. ed. of: Border patrol exam [Byron Demmer, Valerie Demmer, Shirley Tarbell].
2nd ed. New York : LearningExpress, © 2001.
    In English, Spanish, or an undetermined artificial language.
ISBN 10 1-57685-575-9
ISBN 13 978-1-57685-575-1
    1. United States. Immigration Border Patrol—Examinations—Study guides. 2.
Civil service—United States—Examinations—Study guides. I. Dassaro, Joseph N. II.
Demmer, Byron. Border patrol exam. III. LearningExpress (Organization)
    JV6483.B66 2006
    363.28'5076—dc22

                                                    2006018759

Printed in the United States of America

9 8 7 6 5 4 3 2 1

For information or to place an order, contact LearningExpress at:
or bulk sales, please write to us at:
    LearningExpress
    55 Broadway
    8th Floor
    New York, NY 10006

Or visit us at:
    www.learnatest.com

About the Contributor ▶

Joseph N. Dassaro entered on duty with the U.S. Border Patrol in 1992 and served 13 years as a senior border patrol agent in Imperial Beach, California. During his career, he worked as a field agent and an intelligence agent and was a member of the Border Patrol Criminal Alien Program (BORCAP). He is currently a labor relations consultant and holds a master's degree in legal and ethical studies.

Contents ▶

Border Patrol Exam
3rd Edition

Becoming a Border Patrol Agent

CHAPTER SUMMARY

If you think you might like to pursue a career as a United States Border Patrol Agent, this chapter is the starting point for your journey. It provides a glimpse into the exciting and dangerous world of federal law enforcement with the U.S. Border Patrol. You'll also find out how to locate and apply for job openings, what the job requirements are, and what training you will need.

The Border Patrol is a highly trained and extremely mobile uniformed federal law enforcement organization that relies on the latest law enforcement training techniques and operational technologies to prevent terrorists and illegal aliens from entering the country. It also prevents smuggling activities and the deportation of criminal aliens. The organization is statutorily authorized to enforce myriad federal laws anywhere in the United States and its possessions, which makes it the premier uniformed federal law enforcement agency. Border Patrol Agents operate in all types of environments—from remote areas of the southern border to the highly urbanized downtown areas of cities such as San Diego, CA. Today more than ever, the men and women of the U.S. Border Patrol are relied on to protect the borders of the United States. Today's Border Patrol Agent represents the convergence of tradition, modern technology, advanced training, and unique skills.

▶ A Short History of the U.S. Border Patrol

In order to fully understand all aspects of the Border Patrol Agent position, it is necessary to briefly review its proud tradition. As early as 1904, the U.S. Immigration Service assigned a token force of mounted inspectors to patrol the southern border of the United States to prevent illegal crossings. The officers were untrained and few in numbers, and authorities were unable to stem the rising tide of illegal aliens. In March 1915, Congress authorized a separate group of inspectors called mounted guards, or mounted inspectors, who operated from El Paso, TX. These guards, who never numbered more than 75, rode on horseback and patrolled as far west as California.

On May 28, 1924, Congress established the U.S. Border Patrol as part of the Immigration Bureau, a division of the Department of Labor. In 1925, patrol areas were expanded to include over 2,000 miles of seacoast extending along the Gulf and Florida coasts.

Initially, the Patrol recruited many of the early force of 450 officers from the Texas Rangers and local sheriffs and their deputies. These officers knew the land and the dangers it presented. Appointees from the Civil Service Register of Railroad Mail Clerks supplemented this rough and ready crew. The U.S. government initially provided the Border Patrol Agents a badge, a revolver, and an annual salary of $1,680.

Since its inception, the Border Patrol has achieved an almost legendary status in the law enforcement community. As in the past, Border Patrol Agents today continue to provide a critical service as their duties have evolved to encompass much more than preventing illegal entry into the United States.

▶ What the Work of a Border Patrol Agent Is Really About

Even today, the work of a Border Patrol Agent is difficult, diverse, and, more often than not, extremely hazardous. This position is best suited to the rugged individualist who is self-assured, well educated, and well trained. The important task of protecting our sovereign borders in a humane and compassionate way, consistent with American ideals and security needs, has assumed an entirely new dynamic in a post-9/11 environment. So if you think this type of occupation is for you and you are prepared for the challenge of your life, read on!

Important Website Addresses

To find the latest information on all available federal law enforcement positions, including U.S. Border Patrol Agent, visit www.usajobs.gov.

To determine if you are veterans' preference eligible, visit www.dol.gov/elaws/vets/vetpref/mservice.htm.

▶ Salary and Benefits

As a Border Patrol Agent, you will receive all the benefits of federal employment. This includes a generous benefits package that includes vacation and sick leave, health and life insurance, and a special law enforcement retirement plan (also referred to as 6c) that offers retirement at age 50 after at least 20 years of service or retirement at any age after 25 years of service. Although not as generous as many law enforcement packages (which provide 3% retirement multiplied by the number of years of service), this retirement plan is generally competitive with the private sector and includes pension and savings plans to form a multitiered diversified retirement portfolio.

New Border Patrol Agents are always recruited at the GS-5 or GS-7 level unless they are transferring from another federal agency. Where you start on the General Service (GS) pay scale will depend on your previous education and experience in law enforcement. Salaries are significantly higher in certain metropolitan areas (like San Diego, CA.). However, in general, annual starting salaries begin at around $35,000 and rapidly increase. Senior Patrol Agents routinely earn in excess of $70,000 per year, while Supervisory Patrol Agents routinely earn in excess of $80,000 per year. Keep in mind that special overtime provisions known as AUO (Administratively Uncontrollable Overtime) increase the pay of Border Patrol Agents by 25%. Additionally, Border Patrol Agents, like many other law enforcement positions, receive FLSA pay (Fair Labor Standards Act), which also increases pay depending on the number of hours by which you exceed the normal workweek.

▶ Education and Experience Requirements for Border Patrol Agent Positions

The following table shows the amounts of education and/or experience required to qualify for Border Patrol Agent Positions.

Grade	Education	or Experience	
		General	Specialized
GS-5	four-year course of study above high school leading to a bachelor's degree	one year equivalent to at least GS-4	none
GS-7	one full academic year of graduate education or law school *or* superior academic achievement	none	one year equivalent to at least GS-5
GS-9	none	none	one year equivalent to at least GS-7
GS-11	none	none	one year equivalent to at least GS-9
GS-12 and above	none	none	one year equivalent to at least next lower grade level

Equivalent combinations of education and experience are qualifying for grade levels for which both education and experience are acceptable. Note that academic study may be prorated to allow combinations of education and experience that total one year for GS-5, e.g., one year of college study is equivalent to three months of general experience, two years of study to six months of general experience, and three years of study to nine months of general experience.

Source: Office of Personnel Management

Under the accelerated promotion program, after $6\frac{1}{2}$ months at the GS-5 entry level, you will be eligible for promotion to GS-7; individuals hired at the GS-7 level are eligible for promotion to GS-9. Thanks to a relatively recent legislative lobbying effort by their Union, Border Patrol Agents are now promoted noncompetitively to the GS-11 Journeyman level grade. However, these promotions are contingent upon new agents successfully completing their six- and ten-month probationary exams as well as the field training segment of the training program.

▶ Where the Jobs Are

Due to overwhelming illegal immigration originating from our southern borders, first duty stations of new Border Patrol Agents are almost always along the Southwest United States/Mexico border in Arizona, California, New Mexico, and Texas. Many initial assignments are located in small, isolated communities, and transfers from initial duty assignments are limited and normally at your own expense. It is important that prospective agents consider the impact on their families of moving to an isolated community along the border where healthcare access, educational resources, entertainment, and housing may be extremely limited. This cultural shift is most prevalent in families relocating from highly urbanized areas such as New York City to remote locations like Eagle Pass, TX. In cases in which agents are first assigned to large metropolitan areas such as San Diego or Riverside County, CA, prospective agents should consider the cost of housing in local markets to avoid "sticker shock." It is always a good idea to first visit the location where you may be assigned prior to formally accepting a position. Trainee agents are not routinely assigned to their hometowns or within commuting distance of their hometowns. Accordingly, when considering a position, be prepared for a complete household move. This move will be at your own cost (certain expenses may be tax deductible; check with your accountant).

The task of a Border Patrol Agent is vital to the security of our country, inherently interesting, and exciting for the adventurous among us. If you are disciplined, physically fit, and up for a challenge, this position may be for you. Men and women leaving the military, recent college graduates, and current law enforcement officers are particularly good candidates for this position. Finally, since many local and federal law enforcement agencies seek the traits and training inherent in a Border Patrol Agent position and actively recruit agents, the U.S. Border Patrol often serves as an entry-level law enforcement position. Many Border Patrol Agents routinely move on to other positions throughout the federal government including U.S. Marshal, Federal Air Marshal, Drug Enforcement Agent, Naval Criminal Investigative Service, Special Agent, Federal Bureau of Investigation, U.S. Secret Service, and even the Central Intelligence Agency.

▶ Duties of a Border Patrol Agent

Border Patrol Agents are employed by the Department of Homeland Security's Bureau of Customs and Border Protection. Agents predominantly work to deter terrorism and prevent smuggling and illegal entry of aliens into the country. The duties of an agent include the following: patrolling urban and remote areas to apprehend persons seen or suspected of crossing the border illegally, conducting train checks, examining vehicles both at the border and in interior checkpoints, conducting surveillance of areas of the border, preparing intelligence reports and assessments, and conducting drug interdiction efforts. Agents also serve on Joint Terrorism Task Forces, joint operations with other law enforcement agencies, surveillance teams, extradition teams, and various intelligence operations. Many Border Patrol Sectors utilize watercraft for patrol activities, particularly in California and Florida.

Although most people normally associate a Border Patrol Agent's duties with the external boundaries of the United States, Border Patrol Agents are authorized to engage in federal law enforcement activities anywhere in the United States, including Hawaii, Guam, Alaska, and Puerto Rico. Subsequently, Border Patrol Agents can be found in many interior locations of the United States at permanent and temporary checkpoints, major cities, airports, and even attached to some local law enforcement agencies. Following the tragic events of September 11, 2001, Border Patrol Agents were deployed nationwide at U.S. airports as well as aboard commercial flights. Finally, Border Patrol Agents are one of the few law enforcement positions authorized to carry firearms anywhere in the United States and aboard commercial aircraft in flight. Border Patrol Agents are also considered a quasi-national police force capable of rapid full-scale deployment anywhere in the country to represent the interests of the U.S. government. Agents have been deployed in desegregation efforts during the Civil Rights Era, in Los Angeles during the riots that followed the Rodney King trial, and even in the Elian Gonzalez reunification operation.

An example of one of the most routine daily activities of a Border Patrol Agent is linewatch. This activity involves the detection, prevention, and apprehension of undocumented aliens and smugglers of aliens at or near the land border by maintaining strict surveillance from predominantly covert positions; following up on intelligence; responding to electronic sensor alarms; using infrared scopes during night operations; operating low-light level television systems; responding to aircraft sightings; and interpreting and following tracks, marks, and other physical evidence. Some of the other major responsibilities are farm and ranch check, traffic check, traffic observation, city patrol, and transportation check. Duties may be administrative, intelligence related, undercover operations, or anti-smuggling activities.

An agent's job normally involves significant physical exertion under harsh environmental conditions, often requiring exposure to extreme weather for extended periods of time. Border Patrol Agents are well known for their ability to engage suspects in protracted foot chases as well as their ability to track suspects over extended terrain. In recent years, agents have apprehended a million or more illegal aliens per year with as few as 5,200 agents nationwide. Most agents rarely work in pairs, and it is not uncommon for a single agent to arrest 20 or more illegal aliens without assistance at one time. It is routinely noted that Border Patrol Agents single-handedly operate in an environment that most law enforcement agencies consider a riot situation. Agents may routinely encounter an illegal alien looking for work or criminal aliens evading arrest warrants. In recent years, Border Patrol Agents have begun encountering extreme foreign criminal elements including terrorists and violent gang members. Most recently, Border Patrol Agents have even engaged in "running gun battles" with elements of the Mexican military suspected of conducting screen operations drug cartels.

Border Patrol Agents make critical decisions—often in split seconds—that require excellent reasoning and critical decision-making skills. As with any law enforcement officer, decisions made by Border Patrol Agents in split seconds are subject to years of scrutiny and legal analysis. On occasion, Border Patrol Agents find themselves working in a highly politicized environment that brings even harsher scrutiny. Therefore, as an agent, you will be required to study and demonstrate comprehension of various types of laws and regulations as well as legal commentary. You will be trained to apply those laws and regulations in dynamic and confrontational situations and to later testify in court proceedings in defense of your decisions. It is critical that Border Patrol Agents are able to articulate and justify their actions in criminal, civil, and administrative proceedings. Prospective agents must have the ability to project a positive and confident image in the field as well as in the courtroom. Public speaking courses are highly recommended for Border Patrol Agent candidates.

There is a great deal of unofficial sources of information for those considering the position of Border Patrol Agent. These sources of information are primarily Internet based and managed by current or former Border Patrol Agents. There is even a moderated Internet message board where you can talk to real Border Patrol Agents and ask questions. Here are a few sources recommended by Border Patrol Agents:

- **www.nbpc1613.org.** This is the official website of the largest Border Patrol Agents association. It provides information on the latest workplace issues affecting Border Patrol Agents, pay, legislation, and general inside information regarding the work of agents.
- **www.honorfirst.com.** This unofficial Border Patrol recruiting website is managed by a highly regarded former Border Patrol Agent. Current and former Border Patrol Agents recommend this site because it consolidates real-world information regarding testing, positions, academy schedules, and pay and benefits, and even includes an online message board (moderated by active Border Patrol Agents) to talk to real agents or with other applicants.

▶ Requirements and Qualifications

Preemployment requirements consist of a thorough background investigation, medical examination, fitness test, and drug test. If your background includes past or present arrests, convictions, dismissals from previous jobs, debts and financial issues, excessive use of alcohol, use of illegal drugs, or the sale or distribution of illegal drugs, you most probably will be rated unsuitable for this position. You may also be subject to a polygraph examination.

    Job requirements: Border Patrol Agents must wear a uniform, carry a weapon, work overtime and shift work (sometimes under arduous conditions), and be subject to random drug testing. Agents undergo extensive background checks every three to five years.

▶ General Qualifications

- **Must be a U.S. citizen.** U.S. Customs and Border Protection (CBP) also has a residency requirement that applies to all applicants other than current CBP employees. If you are not a current CBP employee, CBP requires that for the three years prior to filing an application for employment, individuals must meet one or more of the following primary residence criteria:

1. Applicant resided in the United States or its protectorates or territories (short trips abroad, such as vacations, will not necessarily disqualify an applicant); **or**
2. Applicant worked for the U.S. government as an employee overseas in a federal or military capacity; **or**
3. Applicant was a dependent of a U.S. federal or military employee serving overseas.

- **Must possess a valid state driver's license at the time of appointment.**

- **Must be under age 40 to apply.** This position is covered under law enforcement retirement provisions. Therefore, candidates must be referred for selection prior to their 40th birthdays unless they presently serve or have previously served in a position covered by federal civilian law enforcement retirement. (Note: In April 2006, the 40-year limit was raised from the former 37-year limit.)

- **To qualify for a GS-5 level position, you must have the following:**

  1. Substantial work experience that demonstrates an ability to (1) take charge, make sound decisions, and maintain composure in stressful situations; (2) learn law enforcement regulations, methods, and techniques through classroom training and/or on-the-job instruction; and (3) gather factual information through questioning, observing, and examining documents and records. Examples of qualifying experience include interviewing in a public/private service agency or working as a claims adjuster, journalist, building guard, jail guard, or certain customer relations positions, **or**
  2. Earned a bachelor's or higher degree, **or**
  3. A combination of education and experience.

- **To qualify for a GS-7 level position**, you must meet the basic entry qualification requirements for the GS-5 plus have superior academic achievement, or one year of graduate level education, or one full year of specialized experience equivalent to the GS-5 level, or a combination of education and experience. Specialized experience is law enforcement experience that has demonstrated the ability to (1) make arrests and exercise sound judgment in the use of firearms; (2) deal courteously, tactfully, and

effectively on law enforcement matters with individuals or groups; (3) rapidly analyze information and take appropriate action in accordance with applicable laws, court decisions, and law enforcement procedures; and (4) develop and maintain contact with the network of informants.

Applicants relying in whole or part on educational qualifiers should verify, beforehand, the accreditation status of their institutions. If you gain employment by relying on educational qualifiers from an unaccredited educational institution, you may be subject to severe disciplinary action and debarment from government service for a period of not less than five years. Applicants who are unsure of the accreditation status of their educational institutions should visit the following Department of Education website for more information (www.ed.gov/admins/finaid/accred/index.html) or check with the registrar of their educational institutions.

Disqualifying Misdemeanor

If you have ever been convicted of a misdemeanor crime of domestic violence, it is a felony for you to possess any firearm or ammunition. A misdemeanor crime of domestic violence is defined as any offense that has, as an element, the use or attempted use of physical force or the threatened use of a deadly weapon, committed by a current or former domestic partner, parent, or guardian of the victim. The term *convicted* does not include anyone whose conviction has been expunged or set aside or who has received a pardon. As a condition of employment, individuals selected for Border Patrol Agent positions are required to carry weapons and ammunition as part of their official duties. Therefore, an individual with a conviction of a misdemeanor crime of domestic violence may not be employed in a Border Patrol Agent position.

▶ General Conditions of Employment

In addition to these qualifications, you must be willing to:

- Undergo an extensive background investigation
- Accept appointments at any location on or near the Mexican border
- Work rotating shifts, primarily at night
- Work long and irregular hours, including weekends and holidays
- Work alone
- Learn the Spanish language
- Adhere to strict grooming and dress standards
- Carry, maintain, and use a firearm in compliance with applicable laws and regulations
- Work under hazardous conditions such as inclement weather, rough terrain, heights, moving trains, high-speed chases, physical assaults, and armed encounters
- Operate a wide variety of motor vehicles including SUVs, Police Crown Victorias, and Hummers
- Submit to a thorough physical examination
- Fly as a passenger/observer in various types of aircraft including helicopters
- Maintain composure and self-control under stressful conditions
- Bear initial travel costs to your duty location
- Undergo intensive physical and academic training, including an 18-week course of study at the Border Patrol Academy and subsequent probationary exams
- Work on operational details away from home for extended periods—35 days or more; some details may last up to a year

▶ A Word about the Federal Career Intern Program (FCIP)

Border Patrol Agent positions are full-time positions filled under the FCIP. This hiring program is a program that helps federal agencies recruit talented individuals for entry-level government positions. FCIP appointments are designed with a two-year internship, during which time you will be learning the job and the organization, attending formal training programs, and developing job-related skills. If your performance and conduct are satisfactory, your appointment will be made permanent after the two-year internship. However, since the FCIP is an "excepted service" appointing authority, you may be removed from your position anytime during this two-year period for any reason. This is a significant departure from past hiring practices, which provided only a one-year probationary period. The probationary period is extended to two years under this FCIP program.

▶ How to Apply

USA Jobs (Office of Personnel Management Online)

Applications for Border Patrol Agent (trainee) positions are primarily submitted through the Internet. This departure from traditional paper-based methods provides the applicant with a speedier and more reliable application process. To apply online, visit the Office of Personnel Management's website at www.usajobs.gov to check for open positions, or go directly to https://cbpmhc.hr-services.org/BPA. Additionally, many Border Patrol Sectors maintain recruiters you can personally talk with to guide you through the process. Here is a current list of contact numbers or e-mail addresses for Border Patrol Sectors that conduct hiring.

Sector Office	Contact Information
Blaine Sector	360-752-0104
Buffalo Sector	315-342-7017 ext. 239
Del Rio Sector	888-590-2559
Detroit Sector	586-307-2011
El Centro Sector	760-353-7627
El Paso Sector	915-834-8848
Grand Forks Sector	701-775-6654
Harve Sector	HVM_Recruitment@dhs.gov
Houlton Sector	207-868-3900
Laredo Sector	956-764-3676 or 3677
Marfa Sector	432-729-3298
Rio Grande Valley Sector	956-984-3804
Miami Sector	954-965-6300 option #5
New Orleans Sector	504-376-8021
Ramey Sector	787-882-3560 ext. 601
San Diego Sector	619-216-4211
Spokane Sector	bpnw.recruit@dhs.gov
Swanton Sector	866-240-8354 802-868-5167
Tucson Sector	520-584-4075
Yuma Sector	928-341-6519

▶ A Word about Truthfulness in the Application Process

Throughout this chapter, we will continually mention the importance of truthfulness and full disclosure. Applicants who gain federal employment through material falsification in the application process or through simple omission of key facts are subject to administrative, civil, and/or criminal penalty. If you fail to disclose all your speeding and parking tickets or lie about a credit card payment you did not make, you will be subject to immediate removal from federal employment and could possibly be barred from future federal employment for a period of five years or more. In addition, if your falsification or omission is discovered even five years after you are hired, you will most likely be removed from your position. When in doubt, always disclose the information. In many instances, waivers may be attainable to overcome what appears to be an obstacle to employment.

Both U.S.-born and foreign-born applicants will be required to disclose all foreign family ties and business interest, no matter how insignificant they may seem. Disclosing this information will actually protect you should your integrity ever be questioned. Be sure to have the most recent contact and financial information available in this regard.

▶ The Next Steps in the Application Process

Following are the next important steps you must take in order to be considered for a Border Patrol Agent position.

The Written Exam

Each year, tens of thousands of people nationwide take the Border Patrol Exam, which is offered when current lists of eligible applicants are depleted and Congress authorizes additional hiring. At most, less than 800 of these candidates will be selected. Tests are normally scheduled at the nearest location to your home and could be administered in a federal building, civic hall, or library. You will be notified where to report for your written exam. When you receive the test notification packet, be sure to read all the material carefully! Test results are normally available in two weeks.

You must pass a written exam like the exams contained in this book. The exam consists of the following sections: Logical Reasoning and a language test consisting of **either** the Spanish Language Proficiency Test **or** (if you don't speak Spanish) the Artificial Language Test (which tests your ability to learn languages). There is also an assessment of job-related activities and achievements.

The test takes about four and a half hours. You can practice taking the exam with sample questions in Chapters 10 and 11. Once you have taken the Border Patrol Agent test, you should receive a Notice of Results in the mail within four weeks following the test.

Compressed Testing

For candidates who register to take the written test at a compressed testing location, CBP, in cooperation with the Office of Personnel Management (OPM), utilize a compressed testing process that requires approximately eight hours on the day of your test. Compressed testing is normally conducted in Buffalo, NY; San Diego, CA; San Antonio and El Paso, TX; and Tucson, AZ. The initial step in the process is the test itself. After completing the test, a Border Patrol Agent will present an orientation session about the agent position. You will be given a copy of your test results (Notice of Results). If you successfully pass the written exam, you will be given a packet of forms to complete and mail to the Minneapolis Hiring Center, as well as a date

(within two weeks of the examination date) for an oral board interview.

If you are unable to attend your scheduled test date and you are unable to reschedule your test date with OPM, you will need to reregister during the next Border Patrol Agent open application period.

Logical Reasoning Test

This section of the test measures your vocabulary, reading comprehension, and critical thinking skills, which are necessary to prepare and perform the duties required of a Border Patrol Agent. Good written and oral communication skills are crucial to succeed in the academy and on the job. You should know that Border Patrol Agents are often called upon to testify in legal proceedings, and it is imperative to understand the legal reasoning process. The logical reasoning questions were designed with this application in mind. The logical reasoning questions are also designed to test your ability to understand complicated written material and derive conclusions. You will be required to make logical conclusions based on various facts in the written material.

Language Testing

If you speak Spanish, you may take a proficiency test that measures that ability. However, if you do not speak Spanish, then you will take an Artificial Language aptitude test that measures your ability to learn the Spanish language. Whether you are a native or near-native speaker of Spanish, you learned Spanish in school, or you don't speak Spanish at all, you'll benefit from the test-preparation materials in this book. The official sample questions for language will show you what the language section of the test will be like. (Even if you're a native speaker, the Spanish section might surprise you. It focuses on grammar, which may not be your strongest suit.) Then you can decide to use either "Using the Artificial Language Manual" or "Checking Your Spanish Proficiency" to help you improve your performance.

The Structured Oral Interview

After you pass the written exam, your name is added to a register of eligible persons. As an eligible candidate, you will be called for an oral interview where you must demonstrate the abilities and characteristics important to a Border Patrol Agent. The oral interview is a panel of at least three experienced Border Patrol Agents who will present scenarios that test your ability to think quickly and respond to stressful situations. The oral interview tests your judgment, emotional maturity, and problem-solving skills. You will receive advance notice of the date and place of your interview, and you must appear at your own expense. Business dress is appropriate (i.e., suit and tie for men, suit for women).

The Medical Exam

After passing the oral interview, you will immediately be fingerprinted. A preemployment medical examination is also necessary and is provided at no expense. This exam is normally provided within a month of passing the oral interview. Candidates must be medically able to perform the full duties of a Border Patrol Agent efficiently and without hazard to themselves and others. Also, you must be physically able to perform all of the strenuous duties, sometimes under harsh environmental conditions. Duties require:

- physical stamina
- running long distances
- climbing
- jumping
- withstanding exposure to extreme weather conditions for extended periods
- standing/stooping for long periods of time

In addition, irregular and protracted hours of work are required. The medical examination is designed to find out if you are medically suited for these duties. The exam is given by a medical examiner and paid for by the U.S. government. You will have to pay for any travel to the exam. Also, as a Border Patrol

Agent, you will have to pass a urinalysis test to screen for illegal drugs prior to final appointment and then again randomly throughout your career. It is important to note that a positive drug test will, without exception, terminate your current application process and prohibit you from future employment with the Border Patrol.

The Fitness Test

Due to the strenuous nature of Border Patrol Agent duties and the associated training programs, fitness tests are required for entry-level Border Patrol Agent positions. Although fitness tests are a separate preemployment requirement, they are conducted at the same time and location as the medical examination. The fitness tests include a push-up test, sit-up test, and five-minute cardiovascular endurance step test.

The preemployment fitness tests are as follows:

1. **Push-up test** is a timed test that requires you to complete 20 proper-form push-ups in 60 seconds. The depth of the push-up will be measured using a foam block. If needed, rests between push-ups must be taken in the "up position." The test administrator will evaluate your form during the test and will instruct you when to start and stop.

2. **Sit-up test** is a timed test that requires you to complete 25 proper-form sit-ups in 60 seconds. The test administrator will hold your feet during this test and instruct you when to start and stop.

3. **Step test** is a timed test that requires you to step up and down on a 12-inch-high step at a rate of 30 steps per minute for a total time of five minutes. To maintain the cadence, an audiotape is used that maintains a constant beat and gives verbal cues. The audiotape also contains instructions to switch your lead leg every minute to avoid local muscle fatigue.

In order to graduate from the required training at the CBP Border Patrol Academy, all trainees must pass a fitness test that includes running 1.5 miles in 13 minutes or less, running a 220-yard dash in 46 seconds or less, and completing the confidence course in 2 minutes and 30 seconds or less. If a trainee fails the test, he or she will be provided only one additional chance to pass.

The Background Investigation

Your appointment is subject to a thorough background investigation to ensure you have the loyalty, honesty, and integrity expected of a Border Patrol Agent. This can take three months or more, and you can be disqualified for evidence of any of the following:

- Habitual use of intoxicants
- Disloyalty to the U.S. government
- Moral turpitude
- Disrespect for law (excessive moving violations, prior arrests)
- Failure to honor just financial obligations
- Unethical dealings
- Misstatement of material fact on the application for employment and any related documents. Note: Misstatement of material fact or material falsification of employment application discovered at any time in your career is justification for immediate termination without appeal. Furthermore, you will be barred from all government service for no less than five years.

During your background investigation, investigators will examine every part of your life, including schools, jobs, military service, civic organizations, and social groups. Just about everyone you ever knew will be contacted for references and, in many cases, interviews. Additionally, your credit and arrest reports will be collected by the investigator, as well as bank records and financial holdings. The investigator has wide latitude in evaluating your suitability for employment

with the U.S. Border Patrol. Even after you are approved by the investigator, your suitability for employment will be further reviewed by agency suitability specialists. Following your acceptance into the Border Patrol, you will undergo periodic background checks no less than every five years and upon each successive promotion.

Once the background investigation is successfully completed and all other phases of the application process are complete, you will receive your first duty station assignment offer (normally six to eight months). Normally, it is not wise to turn down the offer in anticipation of a better location. However, if it is imperative, you may request another duty station assignment in lieu of the one offered.

Once selected, you may have only a short amount of time to report to your station, and Border Patrol practice requires that you relocate at your own expense. You will need funds to cover travel, lodging, and expenses for three to four days. This is commonly referred to as Entrance on Duty (EOD). You should not bring your family or loved ones with you during your EOD, since you will be busy for no less than 10–12 hours a day. Additionally, you will report right to the Border Patrol Academy from your EOD. If, during the EOD process, any significant errors or omissions are discovered, you may be rejected at that time. It is therefore very important that you have been truthful throughout the entire process. When your EOD is completed, you have successfully been accepted as a Border Patrol Agent trainee.

► The Border Patrol Academy

Following your EOD process, you will be detailed to the Border Patrol Academy at the Federal Law Enforcement Training Center (FLETC) in Glynco, GA; Charleston, SC; or the new training facility in Artesia, NM. At the academy, trainees undergo 20 weeks of intensive instruction and receive full pay and benefits. Part of the curriculum includes:

- Immigration and Nationality Law
- Criminal Law and Statutory Authority
- Legal Processes
- Intensive Spanish
- Physical Training
- Care and Use of Firearms
- Operation of Motor Vehicles
- Report Writing
- Self-Defense
- Ethics
- Civil Rights
- Border Patrol Operations
- National Threat Assessment Training

▶ A Word on "Recycles" or "Retreads"

The U.S. Border Patrol Academy has historically had an unusually high washout rate; many trainees wash out for personal reasons or injury, while others simply cannot perform academically or physically. If a trainee drops out of the academy, he or she will have the opportunity to "recycle" from the beginning. In other words, if a trainee drops out of the academy in week 20, he or she will have to repeat the entire program to graduate. To accomplish this, trainees will require the approval of the chief of the Border Patrol Academy as well as their instructors.

After graduation from the academy, you will continue formal training to prepare for probationary examinations at $6\frac{1}{2}$–10 months. Post-academy training is predominantly conducted by designated classroom instructors and field training officers in a field training unit. The unit will train as a group in the field and attend regular classroom training when not in the field. Trainees are required to attend all training sessions, both classroom and field. The use of sick or

annual leave should be severely limited until the probationary period ends. The classroom component of the post-academy training requires the successful completion of numerous exams in addition to the formal $6\frac{1}{2}$- and 10-month exams.

All Border Patrol Agents must successfully complete a one-year probationary period concurrent with successful completion of the two-year stipulated FCIP. The Border Patrol probationary period expires at the one-year anniversary date of EOD, whereas the FCIP period expires at the two-year anniversary. Probationary exams consist of essentially three components: law, Spanish, and field assessment (ratings by experienced Agents). Failing any of the three exams will result in immediate removal from your position as a Border Patrol Agent. During the FCIP period, you may also be removed from your position for virtually any reason prescribed by your supervisor. Removal from your position under either of these circumstances is generally unappealable.

Information for a Border Patrol Agent's Spouse

If you have a spouse who would like to talk to spouses of current Border Patrol Agents, he or she should visit www.bpspouses.com. This free site, managed by the spouse of a current Border Patrol Agent, provides just about all information any spouse would need regarding life as a spouse of a Border Patrol Agent.

▶ A Special Word on Post-Academy Training

Formal training and evaluation and all its inherent stresses continues well after the academy graduation ceremony. This stress, combined with the stress of relocating oneself or a family, coupled with the ongoing possibility of failing a critical exam, can be burdensome not only for the new agent, but also for the entire family. Many trainees succumb to this stress and fail to prioritize adequately. It is extremely important that new agents continue studying and preparing for their new jobs and the continuing assessments without neglecting their family obligations.

Expenses

Living quarters and meals are provided free at the Border Patrol Academy. Additionally, towels, linens, and physical training clothing (except athletic shoes) are provided and are laundered free of charge. As a trainee, you are paid a small per diem for incidental expenses in addition to your salary. The government pays costs to and from the training academy and the first duty station. However, the first year of service with the Border Patrol can be costly, so you should have adequate resources before entering.

Uniforms

On arrival at the academy, trainees must buy official Border Patrol uniforms. A $1,000 allowance offsets this cost; however, you are encouraged to have an addi-

tional $300 on hand for the purchase of additional uniform items required while attending the academy. Thereafter, an annual uniform allowance of $680 is provided toward additional or replacement uniforms, but a complete set of official and rough duty uniforms costs approximately $1,600. Border Patrol Agents, particularly trainee agents, wear through a lot of uniforms due to harsh environmental conditions.

Other Tips

The Border Patrol recommends that trainees **not** move households and families to permanent posts of duty until completion of training. Trainees are required to live on campus at the academy, which has no facilities for family members. It is recommended that you not bring your car, since parking is at a premium at the academy. And, since you must fly from the academy to your first duty station, having a car could prove problematic. While at the academy, you will receive breaks on occasion. These could prove a good opportunity for you to receive visitors. Visitors will not be allowed to stay on campus. Therefore, hotel reservations should be made early. Additionally, there are a number of rental car companies available near all three academies.

CHAPTER

2 ▶ Other Opportunities with the DHS

CHAPTER SUMMARY

This chapter describes the requirements and hiring procedures for immigration-related entry-level jobs with the Department of Homeland Security (DHS) for positions other than Border Patrol. You will learn the advantages offered by these jobs, how to find the jobs, and what to expect in the application and selection process. Let's take a closer look at what it means to work for the immigration-related component of the DHS.

Following the establishment of the Department of Homeland Security in 2003, a number of agencies were consolidated. Among them, the former Immigration and Naturalization Service (large parts) and U.S. Customs Service were combined into the newly formed Bureau of Customs and Border Protection (CBP) within the DHS. As a result, many former positions have been and still are being restructured. Many nonenforcement positions (primarily adjudicatory, asylum, and informational) of the former INS were transferred to a newly formed component of the DHS called U.S. Citizenship and Immigration Services (USCIS). Most enforcement positions such as U.S. Border Patrol Agent were combined into Customs and Border Protection (CBP) or Immigration and Customs Enforcement (ICE). This section focuses on entry-level immigration enforcement-related positions in CBP and ICE.

The DHS expends significant effort ensuring that immigration to the United States is done legally and that prospective immigrants are treated fairly. The DHS has over 22,000 employees to handle these important tasks. Besides Border Patrol Agents, entry-level jobs include:

- Criminal Investigator (Special Agent) ICE
- Deportation Officer

- Immigration Inspector
- Immigration Agent
- Detention Enforcement Officer
- Adjudications Officer

▶ Why Work for the DHS?

As a member of the DHS team, your work will be absorbing and diverse. You'll also enjoy a competitive salary, advancement opportunities, and good benefits. Even at the entry level, you'll earn a respectable income. It's hard to beat the advantages of working for the federal government. Although the benefits may vary slightly from job to job, most career employees are entitled to:

- 10 paid holidays per year
- 13–26 days of paid vacation per year
- 13 days of sick leave per year
- regular cost of living adjustments
- death and disability insurance
- group life insurance
- healthcare (medical and dental benefits)
- a government pension
- special employee programs available only to government workers.

One of the greatest additional advantages of working for the federal government is job security. Once you've completed the three-year probationary period, you become a career employee who is not only eligible for full benefits, but who is also protected from layoffs by several layers of employees. This, in addition to the pride of doing a job that is intrinsically important to the nation, makes working for the DHS an excellent career choice.

Jobs other than Border Patrol Agent require different exams. However, once a candidate becomes a U.S. Border Patrol Agent, it is possible to transfer without further testing; although most Border Patrol

Agents choose to take the specific agency tests anyway, as it is sometimes a faster route to getting hired by the other agency.

▶ DHS Programs

As part of the Department of Justice, DHS has both law enforcement and service-oriented positions. Responsibilities include admitting, excluding, investigating, and deporting aliens as well as guiding and assisting them in gaining entry to the United States. Employers may be fined if they knowingly hire aliens not authorized to work in the United States; however, aliens may temporarily reside in the country to meet agricultural labor needs.

The CBP patrols more than 6,000 miles of border with Canada and Mexico, as well as the Gulf of Mexico and the coastline of Florida. Along with ICE, CBP conducts in-depth criminal investigations dealing with illegal aliens and alien-smuggling rings. In addition, the CBP and ICE work with the Department of State, FBI, CIA, DHS, United Nations, and the Department of Health and Human Services in the admission and resettlement of refugees.

Law Enforcement Positions

The primary immigration enforcement missions of the DHS are to prevent aliens from entering the country illegally and to find and remove those who are living or working here illegally. These functions are performed by the following enforcement programs, namely:

- Border Patrol
- Inspections
- Investigations
- Intelligence
- Detention and Deportation

Inspections

Inspections is responsible for screening all travelers arriving in the United States by air, land, or sea through some 250 ports of entry. This screening includes the examination and verification of travel documents for every alien seeking to enter the country. Last year, hundreds of millions of travelers passed through immigration inspection.

Investigations

Investigations focuses on enforcement of immigration laws within the United States and in territorial possessions. Plainclothes special agents investigate violations, and agents often participate in multiagency task forces against narcotics trafficking, violent crime, document fraud, terrorism, and organized crime. They also identify incarcerated aliens who are deportable because of criminal convictions. Agents monitor and inspect places of employment to apprehend unauthorized alien workers and to impose sanctions against employers who knowingly employ them. The anti-smuggling branch of Investigations is responsible for detecting, apprehending, and prosecuting sophisticated alien smuggling operations.

Intelligence

Intelligence collects, evaluates, analyzes, and disseminates information relating to all DHS missions, both Enforcement and Examinations. Intelligence also directs the Headquarters Command Center, which maintains communications with other offices and agencies 24 hours a day.

Detention and Deportation

Detention and Deportation (D&D) is charged with taking criminals and illegal aliens into custody pending proceedings to determine their status or to expedite their removal from the United States after they have exhausted all relief available to them under due process. D&D operates DHS detention facilities, known as Service Processing Centers, and when necessary, places detainees in Bureau of Prisons institutions, approved contract facilities, or state and local jails.

▶ Jobs Available

The DHS expects to increase and expand its hiring over the next several years as the federal government expands its efforts to curtail illegal immigration and guard against terrorism. Last year, the DHS hired 4,100 employees. The following section details certain key immigration law enforcement positions available within DHS. Other law enforcement and non-law enforcement jobs also exist. (For further information on such positions, follow the instructions in "Finding Job Openings" on page 18.)

Law Enforcement Jobs

Salaries and benefits for the jobs listed in this section are based on the federal government's special rates for law enforcement officers at the GS-5 through GS-7 levels. Entry-level salary ranges change with time, of course, but those listed here can be used as a rough guide. Exact pay information, including special pay for high cost of living areas, can be found in specific vacancy announcements.

GS-5: $31,000–$39,000
GS-7: $35,000–$45,000

The benefits are as outlined in the beginning of this chapter and may also include dependent care, employee support programs, and cost of living/ geographic locality pay for some jobs. Please note that for enforcement jobs, you must not have passed your 40th birthday, although exceptions to the maximum entry age requirement may be granted for persons who have prior federal civilian law enforcement experience or pending legislative change. You must be in qualifying physical condition based on a special medical examination. It should also be noted that education may be substituted for all or part of the experience required. The following are a few of the jobs you might consider.

Criminal Investigator (Special Agent)

These positions start at the GS-5 or GS-7 level, with promotion potential to GS-13. Special Agents conduct investigations under the criminal and statutory provisions of the immigration and nationality laws.

Deportation Officer

Like Special Agents, Deportation Officers start at GS-5 or GS-7, with potential promotion to GS-12. Deportation Officers provide for the control and removal of persons who have been ordered deported or otherwise required to depart from the United States.

Immigrations Inspector

Immigration Inspectors start at GS-5 and can progress to GS-9. The primary function of Immigrations Inspectors is to determine whether an applicant for admission to the United States may enter. Immigrations Inspectors are required to detect false claims or fraudulent documents. Inspectors must have extensive knowledge of laws, regulations, and policies.

Detention Enforcement Officer

Detention Enforcement Officers start at GS-4 through GS-7 level, with the potential of progressing to GS-7. Detention Enforcement Officers perform duties related to the custody and care of aliens who have been detained in Service Processing Centers for violations of U.S. immigration laws. Duties include maintaining surveillance over aliens, escorting detained aliens to hearings, and performing administrative duties.

Non-Law Enforcement Jobs

These jobs are primarily found in USCIS. For these jobs, you must be in qualifying physical condition based on medical examination. Education may be substituted for all or part of the experience required. Adjudications Officers, Asylum Officers, and Immigration Information Officers generally start at the GS-5 through GS-7 levels, with varying potential for promotion.

Adjudications Officer

Adjudications Officers review and make determinations regarding the eligibility of aliens requesting benefits, including permanent residence and citizenship, provided under the immigration and nationality laws of the United States. District Adjudications Officers are located in District Offices nationwide. Center Adjudications Officers are located in one of the four Service Centers.

Asylum Officer

Asylum Officers decide if applicants for asylum meet the requirements of the Immigration and Nationality Act. These officers interview applicants and therefore must have insight into human behavior to determine an applicant's credibility. They work in Asylum Offices throughout the United States.

Immigration Information Officer

Immigration Information Officers administer the many benefits available under the Immigration and Nationality Act. They provide information about immigration and nationality law, assist in completing forms, and answer questions. Immigration Information Officers work in District Offices, Sub-Offices, and Service Centers throughout the United States.

▶ Finding Job Openings

In order to qualify for an appointment to most positions in the any of the components of DHS, applicants must have current eligibility on an appropriate OPM (Office of Personnel Management) register or have been previously appointed to a federal job on a career or career-conditional basis. If you do not meet these requirements, you should contact your nearest OPM office regarding the application procedures. Phone numbers for OPM offices can be found in the telephone directory or at www.opm.gov.

Job Vacancy Announcements

When a civil service job opens within the DHS, that department will normally issue a *Competition Notice, Exam Announcement, Vacancy Announcement,* or *Civil Service Announcement.* These are four names for essentially the same thing with the predominant name being *Vacancy Announcement.* Application procedures and eligibility requirements for each vacancy are outlined in the respective announcement. It is important for applicants to carefully study and understand the vacancy announcement, since any deviation from the published instructions will automatically render an applicant ineligible.

Employee Registers/Eligibility Lists

If the position is one in which there are often regular openings or in which several vacancies are expected before the next job announcement, the agency will keep a list of eligible candidates called a *register,* or *eligibility list.* With such a register, the agency doesn't have to look for new applications but can call on a list of candidates it already knows is qualified. This makes it all the more important that you be aware of application windows, as it may be some time before there's another filing period. Generally, however, registers are considered old after three years, and most registers have an average life span of one year.

Job Listings through the OPM

The OPM updates a list of federal job vacancies daily. You can access the list 24 hours a day, seven days a week by visiting the OPM job vacancy website at www.usajobs.gov. Using the USAJOBS website will enable applicants to search the entire database of available jobs by occupation type, geographic location, salary, grade level, and agency or department.

Contacting the DHS Directly

Because the OPM is no longer responsible for overseeing hiring in most agencies, you can also get detailed job information directly from the DHS. They have their own personnel offices that publish their own job lists through the USAJOBS website (www.usajobs.gov). You can also look in your local blue pages for names and addresses to contact. A list of available positions and job descriptions within DHS can be obtained by visiting the DHS website at www.dhs.gov.

▶ How to Apply

The federal government has recently simplified the general application process considerably, and the streamlined process is detailed in this section.

Filing Period

Again, keep in mind that all openings have a *filing period* or *application window,* a specific period during which applications will be accepted. Be sure to find out the dates because there are no exceptions.

Application Forms and Resume

You may fill out the rather lengthy Standard Form (SF 71) or the Optional Application for Federal Employment (OF 612). These forms are available at any of the websites previously provided. You may also submit a resume instead of an OF 612 or SF 171, but if you do, be sure to include all the information requested on the OF 612 and in the job vacancy announcement or *you will not be considered* for the job. Keep your resume brief, and be sure to include your Social Security number and current federal position (if held).

Test Scheduling Information

For government jobs that require a written exam, you will receive information by mail. It is critical you read, understand, and strictly follow the instructions. Late arrivals at testing centers are not normally permitted. Late arrivals at structured interviews will guarantee ineligibility.

Veterans' Preferences and How to Apply

If you've served on active duty in the military, you may be eligible for veterans' preference, an addition of 5 points—or 10 points, if you are a disabled veteran—to your rating in the job selection process. For information, visit www.usajobs.gov or www.opm.gov/veterans. Veterans can also take an online preference advisor questionnaire that will determine eligibility. To take the questionnaire, go to www.dol.gov/elaws/vets/vetpref/mservice.htm.

▶ The Next Steps in the Application Process

If you are selected for further consideration, there are additional steps in the selection process. These may include:

- a written exam (which usually may be retaken after a six month waiting period if you fail),
- a physical exam, and/or
- one or more structured interviews (which will most likely be scheduled only after your agency has determined you are qualified for the job).

Depending on the position, there may be other requirements you might not expect of a private employer. For instance, you may be asked to fill out a Declaration for Federal Employment (OF 306) to determine your suitability as an employee of the federal government and to authorize a:

- background investigation
- drug screening test
- psychological evaluation or personality test

These checks may significantly lengthen the hiring process, but they're important to ensure the well-being of all the citizens who interact with these employees.

▶ How to Prepare for the Application Process

The best way to prepare for any hiring process is to talk to people who work in the position you desire. They can best tell you about job demands, the hiring process, and on-the-job information. You can learn what qualities are most valued by those departments and what techniques successful candidates have used to get in shape (both physically and mentally) for exams and interviews. You can use the practice exams in this book to help you get ready for the parts of your test that include reading and language skills.

▶ Other Methods of Searching for Jobs

Although most federal job information has been consolidated on www.usajobs.gov, most federal buildings also maintain listings of available jobs. Some locations also maintain job kiosks that provide access to the Internet job databases. Additionally, many agencies and departments utilize internal recruiters to provide information.

CHAPTER

3 ▶

The LearningExpress Test Preparation System

CHAPTER SUMMARY

Taking the Border Patrol Exam can be tough. It demands a lot of preparation if you want to achieve a top score and reach the next step of the hiring process. The LearningExpress Test Preparation System, developed by leading test experts, gives you the discipline and attitude you need to be a winner.

First, the bad news: Taking the Border Patrol Exam is no picnic, and neither is getting ready for it. Your future as a Border Patrol Agent depends on your getting a passing score, but all sorts of pitfalls can keep you from doing your best on this all-important exam. Here are some of the obstacles that can stand in the way of your success:

- being unfamiliar with the format of the exam
- being paralyzed by test anxiety
- leaving your preparation to the last minute
- not preparing at all
- not knowing vital test-taking skills, such as how to pace yourself through the exam, how to use the process of elimination, and when to guess
- not being in tip-top mental and physical shape
- working through the test on an empty stomach or shivering through the exam because the room is cold

What's the common denominator in all these test-taking pitfalls? One word: *control*. Who's in control, you or the exam?

Now the good news: The LearningExpress Test Preparation System puts you in control. In just nine easy-to-follow steps, you will learn everything you need to know to make sure that you are in charge of your preparation and your performance on the exam. Other test takers may let the test get the better of them; other test takers may be unprepared or out of shape, but not you. You will have taken all the steps you need to take to get a high score on the Border Patrol Exam.

Here's how the LearningExpress Test Preparation System works: Nine easy steps lead you through everything you need to know and do to get ready to master your exam. Each step is part of a plan that takes a mere three hours. It's important to follow each step thoroughly, or you won't be getting the full benefit of the system. The activities in each step take a small amount of time, but they pay off in big benefits to you.

Step 1. Get Information	30 minutes
Step 2. Conquer Test Anxiety	20 minutes
Step 3. Make a Plan	50 minutes
Step 4. Learn to Manage Your Time	10 minutes
Step 5. Learn to Use the Process of Elimination	20 minutes
Step 6. Know When to Guess	20 minutes
Step 7. Reach Your Peak Performance Zone	10 minutes
Step 8. Get Your Act Together	10 minutes
Step 9. Do It!	10 minutes
Total	**3 hours**

We estimate that working through the entire system will take you approximately three hours, though it's perfectly OK if you work faster or slower than the time estimates assume. If you can take a whole afternoon or evening, you can work through the entire Learning-Express Test Preparation System in one sitting. Otherwise, you can break it up, and do just one or two steps a day for the next several days. It's up to you—remember, *you're* in control.

▶ Step 1: Get Information

Time to complete: 30 minutes
Activities: Read Chapter 1, "Becoming a Border Patrol Agent," Chapter 2, "Other Opportunities with the DHS," Chapter 4, "Logical Reasoning," Chapter 5, "Official Sample Questions for the Logical Reasoning Section," and Chapter 6, "Official Sample Questions for Language."

Knowledge is power. The first step in the LearningExpress Test Preparation System is finding out everything you can about the Border Patrol Exam. Reading the introductory chapters in this book will give you a good overview. Taking advantage of the contact numbers or websites noted in those chapters will be helpful, too.

Once you have your information, follow the next steps in the LearningExpress Test Preparation System.

Part A: Straight Talk about the Border Patrol Exam

Why do you have to take this exam, anyway? This exam is mandated by the federal government for all applicants for the position of Border Patrol Agent. Border Patrol Agents must speak Spanish at a level rated from good to excellent by the end of their one-year probationary period. Besides including a Spanish test, this exam tests the ability of non-Spanish-speaking applicants to learn a language other than English. The test also emphasizes English-language skills. If an applicant cannot communicate in writing or readily understand written communications, then that applicant simply cannot handle the important duties inherent in positions with the Border Patrol. Fortunately, with the help of this book, you can vastly improve your communications and language skills.

It's important for you to remember that your score on the Border Patrol Exam does not determine how smart you are or even whether you will make a good Border Patrol Agent. There are all kinds of things a written exam like this can't test: whether you are likely to show up late or call in sick a lot, whether you can keep your cool under pressure, whether you can be trusted to enforce the law with integrity. Those kinds of things are hard to evaluate, but the DHS can get a good idea during the oral interview.

This is not to say that filling in the right little circles is not important! The knowledge tested on the written exam is knowledge you will need to do your job. And your opportunity to become a Border Patrol Agent depends on your passing this exam. And that's why you're here—using the LearningExpress Test Preparation System to achieve control over the exam.

Part B: What's on the Test

If you haven't already done so, stop here and read Chapters 1 and 2 of this book, which give you an overview of federal government hiring procedures, and take a quick look at Chapters 4, 5, and 6 for an overview of the content of the test.

The Border Patrol exam consists of two parts.

1. **Logical Reasoning:** You must demonstrate the ability to read, understand, and apply critical thinking skills presented in real-life situations.

2. **Spanish or Artificial Language:** You must demonstrate a good to excellent ability to understand, speak, and write Spanish, **OR** if you do not know Spanish at the time you take the exam, you must take the Artificial Language Test, which requires you to demonstrate a good ability to learn a foreign language.

Stop now and read Chapter 4 to unlock the secrets of the Logical Reasoning section. Then decide which part of the language exam you want to take. If you are fluent in Spanish, opt for that section. If you are not, then the Artificial Language section is for you. See Chapters 7 and 8 for language preparation.

▶ Step 2: Conquer Test Anxiety

Time to complete: 20 minutes
Activity: Take the "Test Stress Test."
Having complete information about the exam is the first step in getting control of the exam. Next, you have to overcome one of the biggest obstacles to test success: test anxiety. Test anxiety can not only impair your performance on the exam itself, but it can also even keep you from preparing. In Step 2, you'll learn stress management techniques that will help you succeed on your exam. Learn these strategies now, and practice them as you work through the exams in this book. Then they'll be second nature to you on exam day.

Combating Test Anxiety

The first thing you need to know is that a little test anxiety is a good thing. Everyone gets nervous before a big exam—and if that nervousness motivates you to prepare thoroughly, so much the better. It's said that Sir Laurence Olivier, one of the foremost British actors of the twentieth century, was ill before every performance. His stage fright didn't impair his performance; in fact, it probably gave him a little extra edge—just the kind of edge you need to do well, whether on a stage or in an examination room.

On the next page is the "Test Stress Test." Stop here and answer the questions on that page to find out whether your level of test anxiety is something you should worry about.

Stress Management before the Test

If you feel your level of anxiety getting the best of you in the weeks before the test, here is what you need to do to bring the level down again:

- **Get prepared.** There's nothing like knowing what to expect. Being prepared for the test puts you in control of test anxiety. That's why you're reading this book. Use it faithfully, and remind yourself that you're better prepared than most of the people taking the test.
- **Practice self-confidence.** A positive attitude is a great way to combat test anxiety. This is no time to be humble or shy. Stand in front of the mirror and say to your reflection, "I'm prepared. I'm full of self-confidence. I'm going to ace this test. I know I can do it." Say it into a tape recorder and play it back once a day. If you hear it often enough, you'll believe it.
- **Fight negative messages.** Every time someone starts telling you how hard the exam is or how it's almost impossible to get a high score, start telling them your self-confidence messages. If the someone with the negative messages is you, telling yourself *you don't do well on exams, you just can't do this*, don't listen. Turn on your tape recorder and listen to your self-confidence messages.

- **Visualize.** Imagine yourself boarding the plane that will take you to your first duty station. Think of yourself coming home with your first paycheck as a Border Patrol Agent. Visualizing success can help make it happen—and it reminds you of why you're going to all this work in preparing for the exam.
- **Exercise.** Physical activity helps calm your body down and focus your mind. Besides, being in good physical shape can actually help you do well on the exam and will be essential to your success on the job. Go for a run, lift weights, go swimming—and do it regularly.

Stress Management on Test Day

There are several ways you can bring down your level of test anxiety on test day. Decide which ones work best for you. Then practice them in the weeks before the test.

- **Deep breathing.** Take a deep breath while you count to five. Hold it for a count of one, then let it out on a count of five. Repeat several times.
- **Move your body.** Try rolling your head in a circle. Rotate your shoulders. Shake your hands from the wrist. Many people find these movements very relaxing.
- **Visualize again.** Think of the place where you are most relaxed: lying on the beach in the sun, walking through the park, or whatever. Now close your eyes and imagine you're actually in that place. If you practice in advance, you'll find that you need only a few seconds of this exercise to experience a significant increase in your sense of well-being.

When anxiety threatens to overwhelm you right there during the exam, there are still things you can do to manage the stress level:

- **Repeat your self-confidence messages.** You should have them memorized by now. Say them quietly to yourself, and believe them!

Test Stress Test

You only need to worry about test anxiety if it is extreme enough to impair your performance. The following questionnaire will provide a diagnosis of your level of test anxiety. In the blank before each statement, write the number that most accurately describes your experience.

0 = Never   1 = Once or twice   2 = Sometimes   3 = Often

_____ I have gotten so nervous before an exam that I simply put down the books and didn't study for it.

_____ I have experienced disabling physical symptoms such as vomiting and severe headaches because I was nervous about an exam.

_____ I have simply not showed up for an exam because I was scared to take it.

_____ I have experienced dizziness and disorientation while taking an exam.

_____ I have had trouble filling in the little circles because my hands were shaking too hard.

_____ I have failed an exam because I was too nervous to complete it.

_____ **Total: Add up the numbers in the blanks above.**

Your Test Stress Score

Here are the steps you should take, depending on your score. If you scored:

- **Below 3,** your level of test anxiety is nothing to worry about; it's probably just enough to give you that little extra edge.

- **Between 3 and 6,** your test anxiety may be enough to impair your performance, and you should practice the stress management techniques listed in this chapter to try to bring your test anxiety down to manageable levels.

- **Above 6,** your level of test anxiety is a serious concern. In addition to practicing the stress management techniques listed in this chapter, you may want to seek additional, personal help. Call your local high school or community college and ask for the academic counselor. Tell the counselor that you have a level of test anxiety that sometimes keeps you from being able to take the exam. The counselor may be willing to help you or may suggest someone else you should talk to.

- **Visualize one more time.** This time, visualize yourself moving smoothly and quickly through the test, answering every question right and finishing just before time is up. Like most visualization techniques, this one works best if you've practiced it ahead of time.

- **Find an easy question.** Skim over the test until you find an easy question, and answer it. Getting even one circle filled in gets you into the test-taking groove.

- **Take a mental break.** Everyone loses concentration once in a while during a long test. It's nor-mal, so you shouldn't worry about it. Instead, accept what has happened. Say to yourself, "Hey, I lost it there for a minute. My brain is taking a break." Put down your pencil, close your eyes, and do some deep breathing for a few seconds. Then you're ready to go back to work.

Try these techniques ahead of time to find out which ones work best for you.

▶ Step 3: Make a Plan

Time to complete: 30 minutes
Activity: Construct a study plan.
Maybe the most important thing you can do to get control of yourself and your exam is to make a study plan. Too many people fail to prepare simply because they fail to plan. Spending hours on the day before the exam poring over sample test questions not only raises your level of test anxiety, but also is simply no substitute for careful preparation and practice.

Don't fall into the cram trap. Take control of your preparation time by mapping out a study schedule. On the following pages are four sample schedules, based on the amount of time you have before you take the Border Patrol Exam. If you're the kind of person who needs deadlines and assignments to motivate you for a project, here they are. If you're the kind of person who doesn't like to follow other people's plans, you can use the suggested schedules here to construct your own.

Even more important than making a plan is making a commitment. You can't improve your comprehension and language skills in one night. You have to set aside some time every day for study and practice. Try for at least 20 minutes a day. Twenty minutes daily will do you much more good than two hours on Saturday.

Don't put off your study until the day before the exam. Start now. A few minutes a day, with half an hour or more on weekends, can make a big difference in your score.

▶ Step 4: Learn to Manage Your Time

Time to complete: 10 minutes to read, many hours of practice!
Activities: Practice these strategies as you take the sample tests in this book.
Steps 4, 5, and 6 of the LearningExpress Test Preparation System put you in charge of your exam by showing you test-taking strategies that work. Practice these strategies as you take the sample tests in this book, and then you'll be ready to use them on test day.

First, you'll take control of your time on the exam. The Border Patrol Exam has a time limit, which may give you more than enough time to complete all the questions—or may not. It's a terrible feeling to hear the examiner say, "Five minutes left," when you're only three-quarters of the way through the test. Here are some tips to keep that from happening to you.

- **Follow directions.** If the directions are given orally, listen to them. If they're written on the exam booklet, read them carefully. Ask questions *before* the exam begins if there's anything you don't understand. If you're allowed to write in your exam booklet, write down the beginning time and the ending time of the exam.
- **Pace yourself.** Glance at your watch every few minutes, and compare the time to how far you've gotten in the test. When one-quarter of the time has elapsed, you should be a quarter of the way through the test, and so on. If you're falling behind, pick up the pace a bit.
- **Keep moving.** Don't waste too much time on one question. If you don't know the answer, skip the question and move on. Circle the number of the question in your test booklet in case you have time to come back to it later.
- **Keep track of your place on the answer sheet.** If you skip a question, make sure you skip on the answer sheet too. Check yourself every five to ten questions to make sure the question number and the answer sheet number are still the same.
- **Don't rush.** Though you should keep moving, rushing won't help. Try to keep calm and work methodically and quickly.

Schedule A: The Leisure Plan

If you have six months or more in which to prepare, you're lucky! Make the most of your time.

Time	Preparation
Exam minus 6 months	Read Chapter 4 for an overview of logical reasoning questions. Practice the Official Sample Questions in Chapter 5.
Exam minus 5 months	Read Chapter 6, and work through the sample questions. Find other people who are preparing for the test and form a study group.
Exam minus 4 months	Read Chapters 7 and 8, and work through the exercises if you do not speak Spanish. Set aside some time every day for some serious reading of books and magazines.
Exam minus 3 months	Read Chapter 9 if you speak and read Spanish. If you will be taking the Artificial Language Test, you should review Chapters 6 and 7. In fact, the glossary of grammatical terms in Chapter 7 may help you even if you're taking the Spanish test.
Exam minus 2 months	Take the first practice test in Chapter 10. Review the relevant chapters, and get the help of a friend or teacher.
Exam minus 1 month	Take the second practice test in Chapter 11, and again review the areas that give you the most trouble.
Exam minus 1 week	Review both exams in this book, as well as the sample questions in Chapters 5 and 6. Choose one area to review this week.
Exam minus 1 day	Relax. Do something unrelated to the exam. Eat a good meal and go to bed at your usual time.

Schedule B: The Just-Enough-Time Plan

If you have three to five months before the exam, that should be enough time to prepare for the written test. This schedule assumes four months; stretch it out or compress it if you have more or less time.

Time	Preparation
Exam minus 4 months	Read Chapter 4 and complete the sample logical reasoning questions in Chapter 5.
Exam minus 3 months	Read Chapter 6, and work through the exercises. Start a program of serious reading to improve your vocabulary and reading comprehension.
Exam minus 2 months	Read Chapter 9 if you speak and read Spanish, or Chapter 7 if you do not. If you will be taking the Artificial Language Test, you should also review Chapter 8. In fact, the glossary of grammatical terms in Chapter 7 may help you even if you're taking the Spanish test.
Exam minus 1 month	Take the first practice test in Chapter 10. Review the relevant chapters, and get the help of a friend or teacher.
Exam minus 1 week	Take the second practice test in Chapter 11. See how much you've learned in the past months? Review the chapter on the area that gives you the most trouble.
Exam minus 1 day	Relax. Do something unrelated to the exam. Eat a good meal and go to bed at your usual time.

Schedule C: More Study in Less Time

If you have one to three months before the exam, you still have enough time for some concentrated study that will help you improve your score. This schedule is built around a two-month timeframe. If you have only one month, spend an extra couple of hours a week to get all these steps in. If you have three months, take some of the steps from Schedule B and fit them in.

Time	Preparation
Exam minus 8 weeks	Read Chapters 4 and 5. Evaluate your performance to find the one area you're weakest in. Choose one chapter from among Chapters 7–10 to read in these two weeks. When you get to that chapter in this plan, review it again.
Exam minus 6 weeks	Read Chapter 6, and work through the exercises.
Exam minus 4 weeks	Read Chapter 9 if you speak and read Spanish, or Chapter 7 if you do not. If you will be taking the Artificial Language Test, you should also review Chapter 8. In fact, the glossary of grammatical terms in Chapter 7 may help you even if you're taking the Spanish test.
Exam minus 2 weeks	Take the first practice test in Chapter 10. Review the areas where your score is lowest.
Exam minus 1 week	Take the second practice test in Chapter 11. Review Chapters 7–10, concentrating on the areas where a little work can help the most.
Exam minus 1 day	Relax. Do something unrelated to the exam. Eat a good meal and go to bed at your usual time.

Schedule D: The Short-Term Plan

If you have three weeks or less before the exam, you really have your work cut out for you. Carve half an hour out of your day, *every day*, for study. This schedule assumes you have the whole three weeks to prepare; if you have less time, you'll have to compress the schedule accordingly.

Time	Preparation
Exam minus 3 weeks	Read and complete the sample questions in Chapters 4 and 5. Read Chapter 6, and work through the exercises.
Exam minus 2 weeks	Read Chapter 9 if you speak and read Spanish, or Chapter 7 if you do not. If you will be taking the Artificial Language Test, you should also review Chapter 8. Take the first practice test in Chapter 10.
Exam minus 1 week	Take the second practice test in Chapter 11. Evaluate your performance on the practice tests. Review the parts of Chapters 5–6 that you had the most trouble with. Get a friend or teacher to help you with the section you had the most difficulty with.
Exam minus 1 day	Relax. Do something unrelated to the exam. Eat a good meal and go to bed at your usual time.

▶ Step 5: Learn to Use the Process of Elimination

Time to complete: 20 minutes
Activity: Complete worksheet on "Using the Process of Elimination."

After time management, your next most important tool for taking control of your exam is using the process of elimination wisely. This standard test-taking wisdom tells you that you should always read all the answer choices before choosing an answer. This helps you find the right answer by eliminating wrong answer choices. And, sure enough, that standard wisdom applies to your exam, too.

Let's say you're facing a reading comprehension question that goes like this:

When a suspect who is merely being questioned incriminates himself, he might later seek to have the case dismissed on the grounds of not having been apprised of his Miranda rights when arrested. So police officers must read suspects their Miranda rights upon taking them into custody.

1. When must police officers read Miranda rights to a suspect?
   a. while questioning the suspect
   b. before taking the suspect to the police station
   c. before releasing the suspect
   d. while placing the suspect under arrest

You should always use the process of elimination on a question like this, even if the right answer jumps out at you. Sometimes, the answer that jumps out isn't right after all.

So you start with answer choice **a**—*while questioning the suspect*. This one is pretty easy to eliminate. The first sentence states that a suspect might incriminate himself while being questioned, so obviously, his Miranda rights should be read to him before ques-

tioning begins. Mark an **X** next to choice **a** so you never have to look at it again.

Move to the next choice—*before taking the suspect to the police station*. This looks like a possibility, although you can imagine situations in which a suspect might incriminate himself before being taken to the police station. Still, if no better answer comes along, you might use this one. Put a question mark beside choice **b**, meaning "pretty good answer; this could be the right choice."

Choice **c** has the same problem as choice **a**—*before releasing the suspect* can cover a long time period, certainly long enough for the suspect to incriminate himself. So you place an **X** beside this answer choice, meaning "no good, I won't come back to this one."

Choice **d**—*while placing the suspect under arrest*. Look quickly back at the passage and notice the second sentence, the second half of which reads *upon taking them into custody*. This appears to be a restatement of choice **d**, the best answer yet, so put a check mark beside it.

Now your question looks like this:

1. When must police officers read Miranda rights to a suspect?
   X a. while questioning the suspect
   ? b. before taking the suspect to the police station
   X c. before releasing the suspect
   ✓ d. while placing the suspect under arrest

You've got just one check mark, for a good answer. If you're pressed for time, you should simply mark choice **d** on your answer sheet. If you've got the time to be extra careful, you could compare your checkmark answer to your question-mark answers to make sure that it's better.

It's good to have a system for marking good, bad, and maybe answers. We're recommending this one:

X = bad
✓ = good
? = maybe

If you don't like these marks, devise your own system. Just make sure you do it long before test day—while you're working through the practice exams in this book—so you won't have to worry about it during the test.

Even when you think you're absolutely clueless about a question, you can often use process of elimination to get rid of one answer choice. If so, you're better prepared to make an educated guess, as you'll see in Step 6. More often, the process of elimination allows you to get down to only *two* possibly right answers.

Then you're in a strong position to guess. And sometimes, even though you don't know the right answer, you find it simply by getting rid of the wrong ones, as you did in this example.

Try using your powers of elimination for the worksheet called "Using the Process of Elimination." The answer explanations for this worksheet show one possible way you might use the process to arrive at the right answer.

The process of elimination is your tool for the next step, which is knowing when to guess.

Using the Process of Elimination

Use the process of elimination to answer the following questions.

1. Ilsa is as old as Meghan will be in five years. The difference between Ed's age and Meghan's age is twice the difference between Ilsa's age and Meghan's age. Ed is 29. How old is Ilsa?
   a. 4
   b. 10
   c. 19
   d. 24

2. "All drivers of commercial vehicles must carry a valid commercial driver's license whenever operating a commercial vehicle." According to this sentence, which of the following people need NOT carry a commercial driver's license?
   a. a truck driver idling his engine while waiting to be directed to a loading dock
   b. a bus operator backing her bus out of the way of another bus in the bus lot

   c. a taxi driver driving his personal car to the grocery store
   d. a limousine driver taking the limousine to her home after dropping off her last passenger of the evening

3. Smoking tobacco has been linked to
   a. increased risk of stroke and heart attack.
   b. all forms of respiratory disease.
   c. increasing mortality rates over the past ten years.
   d. juvenile delinquency.

4. Which of the following words is spelled correctly?
   a. incorrigible
   b. outragous
   c. domestickated
   d. understandible

Answers

Here are the answers, as well as some suggestions as to how you might have used the process of elimination to find them.

1. d. You should have eliminated answer **a** immediately. Ilsa can't be four years old if Meghan is going to be Ilsa's age in five years. The best way to eliminate other answer choices is to try plugging them in to the information given in the problem. For instance, for answer **b**, if Ilsa is 10, then Meghan must be 5. The difference in their ages is 5. The difference between Ed's age, 29, and Meghan's age, 5, is 24. Is 24 two times 5? No. Then answer **b** is wrong. You could eliminate answer **c** in the same way and be left with answer **d**.

2. c. Note the word *not* in the question, and go through the answers one by one. Is the truck driver in choice **a** "operating a commercial vehicle"? Yes, idling counts as "operating," so he needs to have a commercial driver's license. Likewise, the bus operator in answer **b** is operating a commercial vehicle; the question doesn't say the operator has to be on the street. The limo driver in **d** is operating a commercial vehicle, even if it doesn't have a passenger in it. However, the cabbie in answer **c** is *not* operating a commercial vehicle, but his own private car.

3. a. You could eliminate answer **b** simply because of the presence of the word *all*. Such absolutes hardly ever appear in correct answer choices. Choice **c** looks attractive until you think a little about what you know—aren't *fewer* people smoking these days, rather than more? So how could smoking be responsible for a higher mortality rate? (If you didn't know that *mortality rate* means the rate at which people die, you might keep this choice as a possibility, but you'd still be able to eliminate two answers and have only two to choose from.) And choice **d** seems like a stretch, so you could eliminate that one, too. And you're left with the correct choice, **a**.

4. b. How you used the process of elimination here depends on which words you recognized as being spelled incorrectly. If you knew that the correct spellings were *outrageous*, *domesticated*, and *understandable*, then you were home free.

▶ Step 6: Know When to Guess

Time to complete: 20 minutes
Activity: Complete worksheet on "Your Guessing Ability."

Armed with the process of elimination, you're ready to take control of one of the big questions in test-taking: Should I guess? In general, the answer is a resounding yes!

Some exams have what's called a "guessing penalty," in which a fraction of your wrong answers is subtracted from your right answers—but the Border Patrol isn't one of them. The number of questions you answer correctly yields your raw score. So you have nothing to lose and everything to gain by guessing.

The more complicated answer to the question "Should I guess?" depends on you—your personality and your guessing intuition. There are two things you need to know about yourself before you go into the exam:

- Are you a risk-taker?
- Are you a good guesser?

You'll have to decide about your risk-taking quotient on your own. To find out if you're a good guesser, complete the worksheet, "Your Guessing Ability," which begins on this page. Even if you're a play-it-safe person with lousy intuition, you're still safe in guessing every time since there is no penalty. The best thing would be if you could overcome your anxieties and go ahead and mark an answer. But you may want to have a sense of how good your intuition is before you go into the exam.

Your Guessing Ability

The following are ten really hard questions. You're not supposed to know the answers. Rather, this is an assessment of your ability to guess when you don't have a clue. Read each question carefully, just as if you did expect to answer it. If you have any knowledge at all of the subject of the question, use that knowledge to help you eliminate wrong answer choices. Use this answer grid to fill in your answers to the questions.

ANSWER GRID

1. (a) (b) (c) (d)
2. (a) (b) (c) (d)
3. (a) (b) (c) (d)
4. (a) (b) (c) (d)
5. (a) (b) (c) (d)
6. (a) (b) (c) (d)
7. (a) (b) (c) (d)
8. (a) (b) (c) (d)
9. (a) (b) (c) (d)
10. (a) (b) (c) (d)

1. September 7 is Independence Day in
   a. India.
   b. Costa Rica.
   c. Brazil.
   d. Australia.

2. Which of the following is the formula for determining the momentum of an object?
   a. $p = mv$
   b. $F = ma$
   c. $P = IV$
   d. $E = mc^2$

3. Because of the expansion of the universe, the stars and other celestial bodies are all moving away from each other. This phenomenon is known as
   a. Newton's first law.
   b. the big bang.
   c. gravitational collapse.
   d. Hubble flow.

4. In what year was American author Gertrude Stein born?
   a. 1713
   b. 1830
   c. 1874
   d. 1901

5. Which of the following is NOT one of the Five Classics attributed to Confucius?
   a. *I Ching*
   b. *Book of Holiness*
   c. *Spring and Autumn Annals*
   d. *Book of History*

6. The religious and philosophical doctrine that holds that the universe is constantly in a struggle between good and evil is known as
   a. Pelagianism.
   b. Manichaeanism.
   c. neo-Hegelianism.
   d. Epicureanism.

7. The third Chief Justice of the U.S. Supreme
Court was
a. John Blair.
b. William Cushing.
c. James Wilson.
d. John Jay.

8. Which of the following is the poisonous portion
of a daffodil?
a. the bulb
b. the leaves
c. the stem
d. the flowers

9. The winner of the Masters golf tournament in
1953 was
a. Sam Snead.
b. Cary Middlecoff.
c. Arnold Palmer.
d. Ben Hogan.

10. The state with the highest per capita personal
income in 1980 was
a. Alaska.
b. Connecticut.
c. New York.
d. Texas.

Answers

Check your answers against the correct answers
below.
1. c.
2. a.
3. d.
4. c.
5. b.
6. b.
7. b.
8. a.
9. d.
10. a.

How Did You Do?

You may have simply gotten lucky and actually known the answers to one or two questions. In addition,
your guessing was more successful if you were able to use the process of elimination on any of the questions. Maybe you didn't know who the third Chief Justice was (question 7), but you knew that John Jay
was the first. In that case, you would have eliminated answer **d** and therefore improved your odds of
guessing right from one in four to one in three.

According to probability, you should get $2\frac{1}{2}$ answers correct, so getting either two or three right would
be average. If you got four or more right, you may be a really terrific guesser. If you got one or none right,
you may be a really bad guesser.

Keep in mind, though, that this is only a small sample. You should continue to keep track of your guessing ability as you work through the sample questions in this book. Circle the numbers of questions you
guess on when you make a guess; or, if you don't have time during the practice tests, go back afterward
and try to identify the questions you guessed. Remember, on a test with four answer choices, your
chances of getting a right answer is one in four. So keep a separate "guessing" score for each exam. How
many questions did you guess? How many did you get right? If the number you got right is at least one-
fourth of the number of questions you guessed, you are at least an average guesser, maybe better—and
you should always go ahead and guess on the real exam. If the number you got right is significantly lower
than one-fourth of the number you guessed, you would be safe in guessing anyway, but maybe you'd feel
more comfortable if you guessed only selectively. Then you can eliminate a wrong answer or at least have
a good feeling about one of the answer choices.

▶ Step 7: Reach Your Peak Performance Zone

Time to complete: 10 minutes to read; weeks to complete!
Activity: Complete the "Physical Preparation Checklist."

To get ready for a challenge like a big exam, you have to take control of your physical, as well as your mental, state. Exercise, proper diet, and rest will ensure that your body works with, rather than against, your mind during your test preparation and on exam day.

Exercise

If you don't already have a regular exercise program going, the time during which you're preparing for an exam is actually an excellent time to start one. And if you're already keeping fit—or trying to get that way—don't let the pressure of preparing for an exam force you to quit. Exercise helps reduce stress by pumping wonderful good-feeling hormones called *endorphins* into your system. It also increases the oxygen supply throughout your body and your brain, so you'll be at peak performance on test day.

A half hour of vigorous activity—enough to raise a sweat—every day should be your aim. If you're really pressed for time, every other day is OK. Choose an activity you like and get out there and do it. Jogging with a friend always makes the time go faster, or take a radio.

But don't overdo it. You don't want to exhaust yourself. Moderation is the key.

Diet

First of all, cut out the junk. Go easy on caffeine and nicotine, and eliminate alcohol and any other drugs from your system at least two weeks before the exam.

What your body needs for peak performance is simply a balanced diet. Eat plenty of fruits and vegetables, along with protein and carbohydrates. Foods high in lecithin (an amino acid), such as fish and beans, are especially good for your brain.

The night before the exam, you might carbo-load the way athletes do before a contest. Eat a big plate of spaghetti, rice and beans, or whatever your favorite carbohydrate is.

Rest

You probably know how much sleep you need every night to be at your best, even if you don't always get it. Make sure you do get that much sleep, though, for at least a week before the exam. Moderation is important here, too. Extra sleep will just make you groggy.

If you're not a morning person and your exam will be given in the morning, you should reset your internal clock so that your body doesn't think you're taking an exam at 3 A.M. You have to start this process well before the exam. The way it works is to get up half an hour earlier each morning, and then go to bed half an hour earlier that night. Don't try it the other way around; you'll just toss and turn if you go to bed early without having gotten up early. The next morning, get up another half an hour earlier, and so on. How long you will have to do this depends on how late you're used to getting up. Use the Physical Preparation Checklist on page 35 to make sure you're in tip-top form.

▶ Step 8: Get Your Act Together

Time to complete: 10 minutes to read; time to complete will vary
Activity: Complete the "Final Preparations" worksheet.

You're in control of your mind and body; you're in charge of test anxiety, your preparation, and your test-taking strategies. Now it's time to take charge of external factors, like the testing site and the materials you need to take the exam.

Find Out Where the Test Is and Make a Trial Run

The testing agency or OPM will notify you when and where your exam is being held. Do you know how to get to the testing site? Do you know how long it will take to get there? If not, make a trial run, preferably on the same day of the week at the same time of day. Make note, on the "Final Preparations" worksheet on page 36, of the amount of time it will take you to get to the exam site. Plan on arriving 10–15 minutes early so you can get the lay of the land, use the bathroom, and calm down. Then figure out how early you will have to get up that morning, and make sure you get up that early every day for a week before the exam.

Gather Your Materials

The night before the exam, lay out the clothes you will wear and the materials you have to bring with you to the exam. Plan on dressing in layers; you won't have any control over the temperature of the examination room. Have a sweater or jacket you can take off if it's warm. Use the checklist on the "Final Preparations" worksheet on page 36 to help you pull together what you'll need.

Don't Skip Breakfast

Even if you don't usually eat breakfast, do so on exam morning. A cup of coffee doesn't count. Don't have doughnuts or other sweet foods, either. A sugar high will leave you with a sugar low in the middle of the exam. A mix of protein and carbohydrates is best: Cereal with milk, or eggs with toast, will do your body a world of good.

Physical Preparation Checklist

For the week before the test, write down 1) what physical exercise you engaged in and for how long, and 2) what you ate for each meal. Remember, you're trying for at least half an hour of exercise every other day (preferably every day) and a balanced diet that's light on junk food.

Exam minus 7 days

Exercise: _____ for _____ minutes

Breakfast: _____

Lunch: _____

Dinner: _____

Snacks: _____

Exam minus 6 days

Exercise: _____ for _____ minutes

Breakfast: _____

Lunch: _____

Dinner: _____

Snacks: _____

Exam minus 5 days

Exercise: _____ for _____ minutes

Breakfast: _____

Lunch: _____

Dinner: _____

Snacks: _____

Exam minus 4 days

Exercise: _____ for _____ minutes

Breakfast: _____

Lunch: _____

Dinner: _____

Snacks: _____

Exam minus 3 days

Exercise: _____ for _____ minutes

Breakfast: _____

Lunch: _____

Dinner: _____

Snacks: _____

Exam minus 1 day

Exercise: _____ for _____ minutes

Breakfast: _____

Lunch: _____

Dinner: _____

Snacks: _____

Exam minus 2 days

Exercise: _____ for _____ minutes

Breakfast: _____

Lunch: _____

Dinner: _____

Snacks: _____

Final Preparations

Getting to the Exam Site

Location of exam site: _____

Date of exam: _____

Time of exam: _____

Do I know how to get to the exam site?   Yes ____   No ____

(If no, make a trial run.)

Time it will take to get to exam site: _____

Things to Lay Out the Night Before

Clothes I will wear   ____

Sweater/jacket   ____

Watch   ____

Photo ID   ____

Proof of citizenship, etc.   ____

Four #2 pencils   ____

_____   ____

_____   ____

► Step 9: Do It!

Time to complete: 10 minutes, plus test-taking time
Activity: Ace the Border Patrol Exam!

Fast forward to exam day. You're ready. You made a study plan and followed through. You practiced your test-taking strategies while working through this book. You're in control of your physical, mental, and emotional state. You know when and where to show up and what to bring with you. In other words, you're better prepared than most of the other people taking the Border Patrol Exam with you.

Just one more thing. When you're done with the exam, you will have earned a reward. Plan a celebration. Call up your friends and plan a party, or have a nice dinner for two—whatever your heart desires. Give yourself something to look forward to.

And then do it. Go into the exam, full of confidence and armed with test-taking strategies you've practiced till they're second nature. You're in control of yourself, your environment, and your performance on the exam. You're ready to succeed. So do it. Go in there and ace the exam. And look forward to your future career as a Border Patrol Agent!

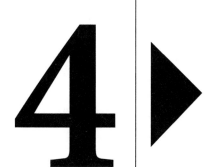

Logical Reasoning

CHAPTER SUMMARY

The Border Patrol Exam includes a Logical Reasoning section that tests your ability to read, understand, and apply critical thinking skills presented in real-life situations. While on the job, Border Patrol Agents make many decisions using logical reasoning skills. It is important to understand how logical reasoning is used in legal situations, because as a Border Patrol Agent, you may be called on to testify in court. This section of the test is very important and will determine whether you'll secure a job as a Border Patrol Agent. The tips and examples in this chapter are designed to help you develop your ability to reason logically and then boost your scores on the exam.

The Logical Reasoning section of the exam is a series of scenarios followed by multiple-choice questions. The questions will test your ability to understand complex written information and draw some type of conclusion. You will be asked to make your conclusion based on only the facts, so you will need to read carefully and concentrate on what is being asked. You will not need to know any extra information other than what is in the paragraph.

The examples in this chapter are similar to the ones that will be asked on the exam. This chapter will allow you to become comfortable with the format and familiar with the different logical reasoning question types. Additionally, it will explain why each example is correct and how the conclusion has been drawn.

►Logical Reasoning Skills

The most important part of being a successful Border Patrol Agent is your ability to reason competently. Logical reasoning is used in decision making and problem solving, both on the job and in everyday life.

The questions in this test are different from regular reading comprehension questions that ask you to understand the meaning of a passage. Specifically, this is the kind of reading that will test your ability to draw conclusions and take action. Often, the situations presented in the questions can be quite complex. Careful reading and focused thinking are required to determine what *is* being asked and what *is not* being asked. The logical reading questions vary in level of difficulty from average to difficult.

►Read Carefully

The paragraphs are related to some aspect of Border Patrol or government work. It is important to read very carefully. You are being tested on your ability to read and draw conclusions based only on the facts given, so assume that the facts are correct as given even if they differ from information you know to be true. Remember, you are not being tested on your own knowledge of facts.

There may be different types of information in the paragraph. Take the time to study carefully what information is being given. Sometimes, there may be facts about two or more situations or subjects that can be linked. Some of the information may be positive or negative.

►Identify the Key Lead-In Question

The paragraphs in this test will be followed by a key lead-in phrase that asks you to complete a sentence by selecting choice **a**, **b**, **c**, **d**, or **e**. The lead-in phrase will be either positive or negative: *From the information given above, it **can** be validly concluded that* or *From the information given above, it **CANNOT** be validly concluded that*. Take time to carefully consider what is being asked by the lead-in question and whether it is positive or negative. This is the key to answering the question correctly.

For the positive lead-in phrases, you are given a choice of four incorrect conclusions and one correct conclusion. Negative lead-in phrases, on the other hand, have four correct conclusions and one incorrect conclusion; the trick is to identify what **CANNOT** be concluded from the facts given in the paragraph.

In some of the paragraphs, the lead-in phrase may be limiting in some way. An example of this is the lead-in phrase, "From the information given above, it can be validly concluded that *in 2006 in the state of Arizona . . .*". There may be answers that concern other states in other years. However, for the test question, only information from the paragraph dealing with the state of Arizona in 2006 would be valid.

►Avoid Hasty Conclusions

Everyday speech habits can encourage us to make hasty, and often faulty, conclusions. Ordinarily, you wouldn't hear someone say, "Some of the sandwich has no mustard," unless they are also suggesting that some of the sandwich has mustard. This is not the case when reasoning logically, however, so beware of this type of hasty conclusion. For instance, if a law enforcement officer says, "Some of the tracks were not made by animals," it would be incorrect to conclude that "Some of the tracks were made by animals." That may be the case, but you have not been given enough information to reach this conclusion.

Be careful not to reach conclusions too quickly in the practice tests. Think each question through and remember to base your answer on the information given in the statement. You are only interested in the facts.

The following sections will familiarize you with the different types of questions on the exam and hone your reasoning skills.

► Reasoning about Groups or Categories

Some of the information in the Logical Reasoning test is about events or situations, and some information is about individuals or groups (categories). We'll be talking about groups or categories in this section.

All Statements

When a test question about two different groups begins with the word *all* or *every*, you are being given an important clue to help draw the right conclusion. When the word *all* or *every* begins a phrase, you now know that the two groups are connected in some way: Everything that is true about one group is also true about the other group. For example, the statement "All the agents at the station are Border Patrol Agents" means that the first group, the agents at the station, are included in the second group, Border Patrol Agents. The *all* statement does not provide enough information to determine whether all members of the second group, Border Patrol Agents, are included in the first group, agents at the station.

This may sound complicated, but it is actually an easy concept once you get the hang of it. Here's another example: A teacher at the academy tells you that all of the Border Patrol uniforms are at the supply office. You might conclude from this information that all of the uniforms at the supply office are Border Patrol uniforms. This is incorrect, however, because the supply office (the second group) may also have uniforms other than Border Patrol uniforms (the first group). The statement does not let you know whether or not there are other uniforms at the supply office.

Here are some other examples of *all* statements (all of Group A are Group B) followed by an invalid *all* statement (all of Group B are Group A).

True:	All Border Patrol Agents are law enforcement officers.
Therefore, Invalid:	All law enforcement officers are Border Patrol Agents.
True:	Every Border Patrol Agent is a graduate of the Academy.
Therefore, Invalid:	Every graduate of the Academy is a Border Patrol Agent.
True:	All U.S. senators are elected.
Therefore, Invalid:	All elected officials are U.S. senators.
True:	Every Border Patrol Agent knows Spanish.
Therefore, Invalid:	Everyone who knows Spanish is a Border Patrol Agent.

To help reinforce this concept, try creating some statements yourself. Remember, you don't have to know about the subject of the sentence. You are only concerned about the logical order of the facts given in the sentence.

Some Statements

All statements give enough information to conclude that at least *some* of the second group are contained in the first group. Following are more examples of true *all* statements (all of Group A are group B) and a *some* statement (some of Group B are Group A).

True:	All Border Patrol Agents are law enforcement officers.
Therefore, Valid:	Some law enforcement officers are Border Patrol Agents.

True:	Every Border Patrol Agent is a graduate of the academy.
Therefore, Valid:	Some graduates of the academy are Border Patrol Agents.
True:	All U.S. senators are elected.
Therefore, Valid:	Some elected officials are U.S. senators.
True:	Every Border Patrol Agent knows Spanish.
Therefore, Valid:	Some individuals who know Spanish are Border Patrol Agents.

Practice creating statements on your own to gain proficiency with questions that involve reasoning about groups or categories.

None and *Not* Statements

When something is NOT true, this is your key to another type of statement where two groups of things are not related. In this type of statement, you can be sure that the two groups have nothing in common. If you can say that no vegetables are sweet, then you also can say that no sweet-tasting food is a vegetable because the two groups do not overlap. A phrase on the test that begins with the prefix *not* or with the phrase *not all of* or *It is not the case that* establishes a negative fact.

Reasoning about Parts of a Group

When you see the term *some* on the exam, this refers to a part of a larger group. In the example *Some trainees are learning Spanish*, the term *some trainees* means a part of a larger group of trainees. Remember, because you know that *some trainees are learning Spanish* does not mean that all trainees are learning Spanish and does not suggest this. A good rule of thumb is that unless information is provided to the contrary, *some* means *at least some*.

Sometimes, statements will use phrases that refer to part of a set. Some of these key phrases are *most*, *a few*, and *almost all*. Some of these statements may also be negative, such as *most trainees do not know Spanish*. While you may be tempted to conclude that there are some trainees who do know Spanish, this would be an incorrect conclusion because you do not have enough information to know if anyone in the entire group of trainees knows Spanish.

Read very carefully when you see a statement about part of a group. Ask yourself if the statement is talking about part of a group or about the entire group This will help you reason soundly and avoid errors on the exam.

▶ Reasoning about Events or Situations

Up to this point, we have discussed statements that deal with information about groups or categories. Now let's discuss relationships between events or situations.

The idea of a *chain of events* is important when reasoning about events or situations. This is a line of logical reasoning where one thing leads to another, which in turn leads to another, and so on. An example of chain of events is *If a driver is convicted of speeding in Orleans County, the driver is guilty of a traffic violation, and drivers found guilty of a traffic violation in Orleans County have points deducted from their driver's license.* With this line of reasoning, you can go backward or forward along the chain of events.

You can think forward, meaning that when the first thing happens, then the other events follow. Suppose a friend tells you she has just been convicted of speeding in Orleans County. From the chain of events just described, you also know that your friend is guilty of a traffic violation and that she has had points deducted from her driver's license.

You can also think backward, meaning that if the later events don't happen, then the earlier events can't have happened either. If your friend mentions to you, instead, that she has not had any points deducted from her driver's license, you will know that she has not been found guilty of a traffic violation in Orleans County and that she has not been convicted of speeding in Orleans County.

If-Then Statements

The phrase typically used to connect a chain of events is *if-then*. The first event is marked by the word *if* and the second event is marked by the work *then*. An example of this is *If Dick is sent to linewatch duty tonight, then the linewatch duty unit will need an extra vehicle*. *If-then* can also be used to connect two events that have already happened. *If there are leaves on the ground, then it is fall*.

Another way to express the same connection is to use the words *whenever*, *each time*, or *every time*. When you see a sentence that begins with one of these words, two events are being connected: *Whenever I go home, I feel happy*, or *Each time I go home, there is a storm*.

An important point to remember is that the order of the two statements cannot be validly switched. In other words, if you switch the order of the two statements, the wrong conclusion may be reached. Consider the statement *If the tire goes flat, the car will come to a stop*. It cannot be validly concluded that *If the car comes to a stop, the tire has gone flat*.

Here are more examples of this line of reasoning. The first example is a true *if-then* statement and is followed by an invalid *if-then* statement with the statements reversed.

True:	If an individual is a Border Patrol Agent, the individual works for the DHS.
Therefore, Invalid:	If an individual works for the DHS, then the individual is a Border Patrol Agent.

True:	If a person resides in Canada, then the person resides in North America.
Therefore, Invalid:	If a person resides in North America, then the person resides in Canada.
True:	If a car crosses the border into California, then the car is in the United States.
Therefore, Invalid:	If a car is in the United States, then the car has crossed the border into California.
True:	If a criminal receives the death sentence, then the criminal has been found guilty.
Therefore, Invalid:	If a criminal has been found guilty, then the criminal receives the death sentence.
True:	If a plane has no fuel, the plane will not fly.
Therefore, Invalid:	If the plane will not fly, the plane has no fuel.

However, the order of these statements can be validly reversed if the statements are negated, or made opposite. Use our example, *If the tire goes flat* (the first statement), *the car will come to a stop* (the second statement). Based on this information, you can validly conclude that *If the car does not stop* (the second statement), *then the tire has not gone flat* (the first statement).

Here are some examples of a true *if-then* statement with a true (or valid) *if-then* statement following where the first and second statements have been reversed and made opposite.

True:	If an individual is a Border Patrol Agent, the individual works for the DHS.
Therefore, True:	If an individual does not work for the DHS, then the individual is not a Border Patrol Agent.
True:	If a person resides in Canada, then the person resides in North America.
Therefore, True:	If a person does not reside in North America, then the person does not reside in Canada.
True:	If a car crosses the border into California, then the car is in the United States.
Therefore, True:	If a car is not in the United States, then the car has not crossed the border into California.
True:	If a criminal receives the death sentence, then the criminal has been found guilty.
Therefore, True:	If a criminal has not been found guilty, then the criminal has not received the death sentence.
True:	If a plane has no fuel, the plane will not fly.
Therefore, True:	If the plane is flying, the plane has fuel.

It is important to note that the opposite of the second statement cannot be validly concluded from the opposite of the first statement. Let's use our earlier example: *If the tire goes flat, the car will stop*. It cannot be concluded that *If the tire does not go flat* (the opposite of the first statement), *then the car will not stop* (the opposite of the second statement).

Here are more examples of a true *if-then* statement followed by an invalid conclusion statement.

True:	If an individual is a Border Patrol Agent, the individual works for the DHS.
Therefore, Invalid:	If an individual is not a Border Patrol Agent, the individual does not work for the DHS.
True:	If a person resides in Canada, then the person resides in North America.
Therefore, Invalid:	If a person does not reside in Canada, then the person does not reside in North America.
True:	If a car crosses the border into California, the car is in the United States.
Therefore, Invalid:	If a car does not cross the border into California, the car is not in the United States.
True:	If a criminal receives the death sentence, then the criminal has been found guilty.
Therefore, Invalid:	If a criminal does not receive the death sentence, then the criminal has not been found guilty.
True:	If a plane has no fuel, the plane will not fly.
Therefore, Invalid:	If the plane has fuel, the plane will fly.

►Warnings about Words

All and None

If you have ever had test-preparation training, you may have been advised to avoid answers in reasoning tests that start with the words *all* or *none*. This is not true for the Logical Reasoning Exam. There is a common belief that these two words represent extremes and that correct answers fall somewhere in the mid-range between *all* or *none*. This is absolutely untrue for this exam. In both the reading paragraphs as well as the correct and incorrect responses, there will be *all* statements and *none* statements that are correct. This is an exam that will test you with real-life scenarios where *all* and *none* situations do actually exist.

Positive and Negative Words, Prefixes, and Connectors

As a rule, pay careful attention to words that give you clues about information on groups or linked events. These include positive words such as

> *all*
> *some*
> *most*

Negative words and prefixes that should throw up a red flag are

> *seldom*
> *never*
> *illegal*
> *prohibited*
> *non-*
> *un-*
> *dis-*

Carefully read for connectors that have the key information about the relationship among the facts given in the paragraph. Some common connectors are

> *whenever*
> *unless*
> *except*

Double Negatives

Single negatives are used commonly in the English language. When the word *not* is used in a sentence, it makes the sentence negative, as in the sentence *That flower is not a sunflower.* On the test, there may be sentences such as *The door is not unlocked,* which means the door IS locked. Double negatives in English make a statement positive. The statement *This question is not unfair* means that the question IS fair. *The gun was fired* might be stated on the test as *It is NOT the case that the gun was not fired.*

The Use of the Word *Only*

It is very important to pay careful attention to the word *only* in a statement. Use of the word *only* restricts the meaning of a sentence. For example, *The computer is on only when both buttons are pushed* means very clearly that it is necessary to push both buttons to turn on the computer. Now consider the sentence *The computer is on when both buttons are pushed.* This sentence is less restrictive because, although the computer can be turned on by pushing both buttons, it is possible there are other, unstated, ways to turn it on as well.

The phrase *if and only if* restricts the meaning even further. *The computer is on if and only if both buttons are pushed* means it MUST be the case that both buttons were pushed if the computer is on.

► Summary of Logical Reasoning Test Tips

1. When choosing a conclusion, always look for one that can be made based only on the information in the paragraph.

2. Assume all information in the paragraph is true. Do not use other factual information you may already know to reach your conclusion.

3. Focus on the key lead-in sentence and read the paragraph carefully. Consider all of the answer choices carefully before making your final answer selection.

4. Pay special attention to words such as *all, some, none, unless, except*, and *only*. These qualifying words help define the facts in the statement.

5. Keep in mind that negative prefixes such as *non-* or negative words such as *disorganized* or *unfasten* can be critical to an understanding of the information in the statement.

6. If you have been told to avoid answers that contain the word *all* or *none*, disregard this advice. These words do not indicate an incorrect answer in this test. *All* and *none* can be in both the incorrect and the correct answers.

7. Answer every question on the test. Guess at an answer only after eliminating answers that you know to be false. While you are not penalized for guessing, your chances of picking a correct answer are greatly improved by using the process of elimination. You have a one in five chance of picking a right answer by blindly guessing. Your chances improve with every choice that is eliminated.

8. Do not pay attention to patterns made by **a**, **b**, **c**, **d**, or **e** on the answer sheet. Correct answer positions are selected randomly. You cannot improve your chances of guessing based on a pattern on the answer sheet. Trying to figure out a pattern is a poor test strategy.

9. The best way to improve your chances on the exam is through practice. Take the tests found in this book and study their answer explanations. This will hone your logical reasoning ability. Remember that the time you put into preparing for the Logical Reasoning test is time well spent and will increase your chances of doing well on the exam.

CHAPTER

5▶

Official Sample Questions for Logical Reasoning

CHAPTER SUMMARY

This chapter consists of the official Logical Reasoning explanations and sample questions, provided by the U.S. Department of Homeland Security Bureau of Customs and Border Protection and the U.S. Border Patrol. These sample questions are similar to the questions you will find in the actual test in terms of difficulty and form. In general, the test questions deal with situations that you might encounter in law enforcement positions. Remember, knowledge of any job-specific subject matter is not required to answer the questions correctly.

▶Logical Reasoning Practice Test

In questions 1 through 8, some questions will ask you to select the only answer that can be validly concluded from the paragraph. These questions include a paragraph followed by five response options. Preceding the five response options will be the phrase *From the information given above, it can be validly concluded that.* In other questions, you may be asked to select the only answer that cannot be validly concluded from the paragraph. These questions include a paragraph followed by five response options. Preceding the five response options will be the phrase *From the information given above, it **CANNOT** be validly concluded that.*

You must use only the information provided in the paragraph, without using any outside information whatsoever.

It is suggested that you take no more than 20 minutes to complete questions 1 through 8. The questions on this practice test will not be on the real test, but the real questions will be similar in form and difficulty. The explanations for the correct and incorrect responses are found after the sample questions.

1. Often, crimes are characterized as either *malum in se*—inherently evil—or *malum prohibitum*—criminal because they are declared as offenses by the legislature. Murder is an example of the former. Failing to file a tax return illustrates the latter. Some jurisdictions no longer distinguish between crimes *malum in se* and *malum prohibitum*, although many still do.

   From the information given above, it can be validly concluded that
   a. many jurisdictions no longer distinguish between crimes *malum in se* and *malum prohibitum*.
   b. some jurisdictions still distinguish between crimes *malum in se* and *malum prohibitum*.
   c. some crimes characterized as *malum in se* are not inherently evil.
   d. some crimes characterized as *malum prohibitum* are not declared by a legislature to be an offense.
   e. sometimes failing to file a tax return is characterized as *malum in se*.

2. A trucking company can act as a *common carrier*—for hire to the general public at published rates. As a common carrier, it is liable for any cargo damage, unless the company can show that it was not negligent. If the company can demonstrate that it was not negligent, then it is not liable for cargo damage. In contrast, a *contract carrier* (a trucking company hired by a shipper under a specific contract) is only responsible for cargo damage as spelled out in the contract. A Claus Inc. tractor-trailer, acting under common carrier authority, was in a 5-vehicle accident that damaged its cargo. A Nichols Inc. tractor-trailer, acting under contract carrier authority, was involved in the same accident, and its cargo was also damaged.

   From the information given above, it can be validly concluded that, in reference to the accident,

   a. if Claus Inc. is liable, then it can show that it was not negligent.
   b. if Claus Inc. cannot show that it was not negligent, then it is not liable.
   c. if Claus Inc. can show that it was not negligent, then it is not liable.
   d. if Nichols Inc. is liable, then it cannot show that it is negligent.
   e. if Nichols Inc. can show that it is not negligent, then it is not liable.

3. A rapidly changing technical environment in government is promoting greater reliance on electronic mail (e-mail) systems. As this usage grows, there are increasing chances of conflict between the users' expectations of privacy and public access rights. In some investigations, access to *all* e-mail, including those messages stored in archival files and messages outside the scope of the investigation, has been sought and granted. In spite of this, some people send messages through e-mail that would never be said face to face or written formally.

   From the information given above, it CANNOT be validly concluded that
   a. some e-mail messages that have been requested as part of investigations have contained messages that would never be said face to face.
   b. some messages that people would never say face to face are sent in e-mail messages.
   c. some e-mail messages have been requested as part of investigations.
   d. e-mail messages have not been exempted from investigations.
   e. some e-mail messages contain information that would be omitted from formal writing.

4. Phyllis T. is a former federal employee who was entitled to benefits under the Federal Employee Compensation Act because of a job-related, disabling injury. When an eligible federal employee has such an injury, the benefit is determined by this rule: If the beneficiary is married or has dependents, benefits are $\frac{3}{4}$ of the person's salary at the time of the injury; otherwise, benefits are set at $\frac{2}{3}$ of the salary. Phyllis T.'s benefits were $\frac{2}{3}$ her salary when she was injured.

From the information given above, it can be validly concluded that, when Phyllis T. was injured, she

a. was married but without dependents.

b. was not married and had no dependents.

c. was not married but had dependents.

d. was married and had dependents.

e. had never been married.

5. Some 480,000 immigrants were living in a certain country in 1999. Although most of these immigrants were not employed in professional occupations, many of them were. For instance, many of them were engineers and many of them were nurses. Very few of these immigrants were librarians, another professional occupation.

From the information given above, it can be validly concluded that in 1999, in the country described above,

a. most immigrants were either engineers or nurses.

b. it is not the case that some of the nurses were immigrants.

c. none of the engineers were immigrants.

d. most of those not employed in professional occupations were immigrants.

e. some of the engineers were immigrants.

6. Police officers were led to believe that many weapons sold at a certain gun store were sold illegally. Upon investigating the lead, the officers learned that all of the weapons sold by the store that were made by Precision Arms were sold legally. Also, none of the illegally sold weapons were .45 caliber.

From the information given above, it can be validly concluded that, concerning the weapons sold at the store,

a. all of the .45 caliber weapons were made by Precision Arms.

b. none of the .45 caliber weapons were made by Precision Arms.

c. some of the weapons made by Precision Arms were .45 caliber weapons.

d. all of the .45 caliber weapons were sold legally.

e. some of the weapons made by Precision Arms were sold illegally.

7. Impressions made by the ridges on the ends of the fingers and thumbs are useful means of identification, since no two persons have the same pattern of ridges. If finger patterns from fingerprints are not decipherable, then they cannot be classified by general shape and contour or by pattern type. If they cannot be classified by these characteristics, then it is impossible to identify the person to whom the fingerprints belong.

From the information given above, it CANNOT be validly concluded that

a. if it is possible to identify the person to whom fingerprints belong, then the fingerprints are decipherable.

b. if finger patterns from fingerprints are not decipherable, then it is impossible to identify to whom they belong.

c. if fingerprints are decipherable, then it is impossible to identify the person to whom they belong.

d. if fingerprints can be classified by general shape and contour or by pattern type, then they are decipherable.

e. if it is possible to identify the person to whom fingerprints belong, then the fingerprints can be classified by general shape and contour or pattern type.

8. Explosives are substances or devices capable of producing a volume of rapidly expanding gases that exert a sudden pressure on their surroundings. Chemical explosives are the most commonly used, although there are mechanical and nuclear explosives. All mechanical explosives are devices in which a physical reaction is produced, such as that caused by overloading a container with compressed air. While nuclear explosives are by far the most powerful, all nuclear explosives have been restricted to military weapons.

From the information given above, it can be validly concluded that

a. all explosives that have been restricted to military weapons are nuclear explosives.

b. no mechanical explosives are devices in which a physical reaction is produced, such as that caused by overloading a container with compressed air.

c. some nuclear explosives have not been restricted to military weapons.

d. all mechanical explosives have been restricted to military weapons.

e. some devices in which a physical reaction is produced, such as that caused by overloading a container with compressed air, are mechanical explosives.

► Analysis of Logical Reasoning Practice Questions

1. b. Some jurisdictions still distinguish between crimes *malum in se* and *malum prohibitum*.

This question is concerned with classification of crimes into sets—that is, with the classification of crimes as either *malum in se* or *malum prohibitum*. The last phrase in the last sentence tells us that many jurisdictions make the distinction between these two categories of crimes. Choice **b** follows from that sentence, because if many jurisdictions make the distinction, some jurisdictions make the distinction. From the fact that many jurisdictions make the distinction, it cannot be inferred that many do *not* make the distinction. Therefore, Choice **a** is incorrect.

Choices **c**, **d**, and **e** are based on erroneous definitions of the two classes of crimes. The paragraph tells us that all crimes characterized as *malum in se* are inherently evil. Choice **c** is false because it cannot be the case that some crimes characterized as *malum in se* are not inherently evil. The paragraph also tells us that all crimes characterized as *malum prohibitum* are declared as offenses by a legislature. Choice **d** is false because it cannot be the case that SOME crimes characterized as *malum prohibitum* are NOT declared by a legislature to be an offense. In the paragraph, we are told that filing a tax return late is *malum prohibitum*, rather than *malum in se*. Choice **e** is incorrect because it cannot be the case that failing to file a tax return is *malum in se*.

2. c. If Claus Inc. can show that it was not negligent, then it is not liable.

The second sentence states the liability rule for common carriers: All common carriers are liable for cargo damage unless they can show that they are not negligent; if they can show that they are not negligent, then they are not liable for cargo damage. Claus Inc. is a common carrier, and accordingly, this rule applies to it. From this rule, it follows that if Claus Inc. can show it was not negligent, then it is not liable, Choice **c**. Choice **a** contradicts this rule by claiming that when Claus Inc. is liable, it can show that it was not negligent. Choice **b** contradicts this rule by claiming that Claus Inc. is not liable even when it cannot show that it is not negligent. Choices **d** and **e** concern Nichols Inc., a contract carrier. However, the terms of the Nichols Inc. contract were not disclosed in the paragraph, so neither choice is supported.

3. a. Some e-mail messages that have been requested as part of investigations have contained messages that would never be said face to face.

This is an example of a test question with a negative lead-in statement. It asks for the conclusion that is **not** supported by the paragraph. That means that four of the statements are valid conclusions from the paragraph while one is not. Choice **b** (some messages that people would never say face to face are sent in e-mail messages) is a valid conclusion because it restates a fact given in the last sentence of the paragraph. Choice **e** (some e-mail messages contain information that would be omitted from formal writing) is valid because it restates the other fact in the last sentence of the paragraph.

The next-to-last sentence in the paragraph is the source of both choice **c** (some e-mail messages have been requested as part of investigations) and choice **d** (e-mail messages have not been exempted from investigations). Both of these choices restate information in that sentence, based on the fact that access to e-mail messages was sought and granted. This leaves only the first option, choice **a** (some e-mail messages that have been requested as part of investigations have contained messages that would never be said face to face). This is the only choice that does **NOT** represent a valid conclusion, because even though we know from the paragraph that there is a group of e-mail messages that are requested in investigations and also that there is a group of messages that contain information that people would not say face to face, there is nothing that says that these groups overlap. We simply do not know.

4. b. Phyllis T. was not married and had no dependents.

This question concerns an either/or situation. The paragraph states that benefits under the Federal Employees Compensation Act are awarded at one level ($\frac{3}{4}$ of salary) if a beneficiary is married or has dependents when injured, and at another level ($\frac{2}{3}$ of salary) if this is not true.

Phyllis T. is eligible for benefits under the Act. The paragraph states that Phyllis T.'s benefit level was $\frac{2}{3}$ of her salary. Given this benefit level, it is clear that Phyllis T. did not meet either of the conditions for the $\frac{3}{4}$ level. Therefore, choices **a**, **c**, and **d** cannot be correct (**a** states that she was married, **c** states that she had dependents, and **d** states that she was both married and had dependents). Choice **e** goes beyond the facts given because prior marriages are not listed as a factor relating to this benefit. The one correct conclusion is that Phyllis T. did not meet either requirement to qualify for the higher benefit level ($\frac{3}{4}$ of salary), so choice **b** is the correct answer to the question.

5. e. Some of the engineers were immigrants.

Choice **e** is correct because it restates the third sentence in terms of the overlap between immigrants and engineers in the country described in the paragraph. Choice **a** says that most immigrants are engineers or nurses, which are professional occupations. However, the second sentence says that most immigrants are not employed in professional occupations, so Choice **a** is false. Choice **b** is false because it denies that there is any overlap between immigrants and nurses, even though this overlap is clear from the third sentence of the paragraph. Choice **c** is false because it denies the overlap between immigrants and engineers. Because the paragraph does not give complete information about the nonprofessionals (immigrant and nonimmigrant) in the country described in the paragraph, Choice **d** is invalid.

6. d. All of the .45 caliber weapons were sold legally.

The second and last sentences are the two main premises in the paragraph. These two sentences give information about three categories of weapons: weapons made by Precision Arms, weapons sold legally, and .45 caliber weapons.

The last sentence states that none of the illegally sold weapons were .45 caliber. This means that none of the .45 caliber weapons were sold illegally. Notice that this new statement is a double negative. In affirmative form, the statement means that all of the .45 caliber weapons were sold legally, choice **d**.

The information that all of the .45 caliber weapons were sold legally (last sentences), combined with the information that all of the weapons made by Precision Arms were sold legally (second sentence), allows us to draw no valid conclusions about the relationship between the .45 caliber weapons and the weapons made by Precision Arms. There is insufficient information about the entire group of weapons sold legally to know whether the group of .45 caliber weapons and the group of weapons made by Precision Arms overlapped entirely (**a**), partially (**c**), or not at all (**b**).

Choice **e** contradicts the second sentence and is therefore invalid.

7. c. If fingerprints are decipherable, then it is impossible to identify the person to whom they belong.

This question asks for the answer choice that **cannot** be validly concluded from the information in the paragraph. The only choice that cannot be validly concluded is choice **c**, so the correct answer is choice **c**. Choice **c** is invalid because the paragraph does not provide enough information to conclude whether or not it would be possible to identify the person to whom the fingerprints belong from the mere fact that the fingerprints are decipherable.

Choice **a** refers to a condition where it is possible to identify the person to whom fingerprints belong. Based on the final sentence in the paragraph, this condition of fingerprints means that the fingerprints could be classified by general shape and contour or by pattern type. Based on the second sentence, the ability to classify the fingerprints means that the fingerprints are decipherable.

Since choice **b** refers to a condition in which finger patterns from fingerprints are not decipherable, we know from the second sentence that, in that circumstance, they cannot be classified by general shape and contour or by pattern type. From the final sentence in the paragraph, we can infer that since they cannot be classified by these char-

acteristics, it is impossible to identify the person to whom the fingerprints belong.

According to the second sentence, fingerprints cannot be classified by general shape and contour or by pattern type when they are not decipherable. Therefore, if fingerprints can be classified by general shape and contour or by pattern type, then the fingerprints must be decipherable, choice **d**. According to the third sentence, it is impossible to identify the owner of a set of fingerprints when the fingerprints cannot be classified by general shape and contour or by pattern type. Therefore, if it is possible to identify the person to whom fingerprints belong, then the fingerprints must be able to be classified by general shape and contour and pattern type, choice **e**. Notice that choices **d** and **e** are valid based on the same type of reasoning. The first and second statements of the second sentence were made opposite and reversed in choice **d**, and the first and second statements of the final sentence were made opposite and reversed in choice **e**.

8. e. Some devices in which a physical reaction is produced, such as that caused by overloading a container with compressed air, are mechanical explosives.

The correct answer is **e**. The third sentence states that overlap between all mechanical explosives and devices in which a physical reaction is produced, such as that caused by overloading a container with compressed air. From this, we can safely conclude that some devices in which a physical reaction is produced, such as that caused by overloading a container with compressed air, are mechanical explosives.

Choice **a** is incorrect because the paragraph does not provide sufficient information to validly conclude that all explosives that have been restricted to military weapons are nuclear weapons. It may be that some types of explosives other than nuclear weapons also have been restricted to military weapons.

Choices **b** and **c** are incorrect because they contradict the paragraph. Choice **b** contradicts the third sentence, and choice **c** contradicts the last sentence.

Choice **d** is incorrect because the paragraph provides no information about whether or not mechanical explosives are restricted to military weapons.

6 ▶ Official Sample Questions for Language

CHAPTER SUMMARY

This chapter consists of the official explanations and sample questions, provided by the Border Patrol, for the Spanish Language and Artificial Language tests. The official explanation for the Spanish Language test begins below. The Artificial Language test begins on page 57.

Y ou will soon take the Spanish Language Proficiency Test. This chapter provides samples of the types of questions found in that test. The test is divided into two parts. Part A consists entirely of vocabulary items; Part B is divided into three sections, each section dealing with a different type of grammar item. These sample questions are similar to the questions you will find in the actual test in terms of difficulty and form.

▶ Part A

Find the suggested answer that is closest in meaning to the key word.

1. Es muy *complicado* pilotar mi avión.
  a. fácil
  b. difícil
  c. divertido
  d. compilado
  e. comparado

The word *complicado* means *complicated*. In the context of the sentence, it refers to something that is hard to do. Hence, choice **b**, *difícil* ("difficult"), is the best synonym. Choice **a**, *fácil* ("easy"), is opposite to the meaning of *complicado*. Choice **c**, *divertido*, has the same beginning syllable (*di-*) as the correct answer, but its meaning ("amusing") is completely different. The basic meanings of choices **d** and **e** ("compiled" and "compared," respectively) are completely different from the meaning of *complicado*, although both *compilado* and *comparado* are phonetically similar to it.

2. Es fácil *comprender* lo que el agente está diciendo.
  a. responder
  b. comprobar
  c. entender
  d. pretender
  e. desentender

The word *comprender* means to understand something after watching, listening to, or reading it. Hence, choice **c**, *entender* ("to understand"), is the best synonym. Choice **e**, *desentender*, is the exact opposite of the correct answer; in fact, it is *entender*, but with a negative prefix added to it, thus giving it the meaning of "to misunderstand." Choices **a**, **b**, and **d** ("to respond," "to verify," and "to pretend") are completely unrelated to the meaning of *comprender*.

▶ Part B

Section I
Supply the correct words that should be used in place of the blanks.

1. Me gusta entrar _____ la puerta que está _____ de la oficina.
  a. a, sobre
  b. en, desde
  c. con, bajo
  d. en, al lado
  e. por, detrás

The correct answer is choice **e**, *por, detrás*. Choices **a**, **b**, **c**, and **d** all use incorrect prepositions.

2. La agente me ____ la correspondencia cuando yo no _____en casa.
  a. traido, estoy
  b. traer, estuviera
  c. trajo, estaba
  d. traerá, habré estado
  e. habrá traido, estar

The correct answer is choice **c**, *trajo, estaba*, since both verbs represent the correct past tense in the indicative mood (preterit indefinite *trajo* and preterit imperfect *estaba*). In choices **a**, **b**, **d**, and **e**, the wrong forms of the verb have been used.

Section II
Read each sentence carefully, and select the only one that is correct.

1. a. Todos los agentes coincidieron del sospechoso cuando entrarían por la puerta.
  b. El sospechoso que entró fue señalado en la puerta con los agentes coincidiendo.

c. Todos los agentes señalaron al mismo sospechoso cuando entró por la puerta.

d. Todos los agentes coincidió en señalar al sospechoso cuando entrarán por la puerta.

The correct answer to this item is choice **c** because it has the proper sentence structure (subject, verb, direct object) and contains no errors. Choices **a**, **b**, and **d** contain various errors, including incorrect prepositions, illogical structures, or incorrect verb forms; hence, none of them can be the correct answer.

2. a. La inmigración ilegal y el contrabando suponen un gran problema para muchos paises.

b. La inmigración ilegal y el contrabando supongo un problema grande para muchos paises.

c. Muchos paises con gran problemas suponían la inmigración ilegal y el contrabando.

d. La inmigración ilegales y el contrabando suponen un gran problema para muchos paises.

The correct answer is choice **a** because it has the proper sentence structure (subject, verb, direct object, indirect object) and contains no errors. Choices **b**, **c**, and **d** contain various errors, including incorrect subjects, illogical structures, incorrect verb forms; hence, none of these choices can be the correct answer.

Section III

Supply the correct word that should be used in place of the word in italics. If the word in italics is correct, choice **e** is the correct response.

1. Los agentes detectaron el contrabando antes de *abrir* la maleta.
   a. abriendo
   b. abrirá
   c. abriremos
   d. abrió
   e. No es necesario hacer ninguna corrección.

The correct answer to this item is choice **e** because after the preposition, *de*, the infinitive form of the verb, *abrir*, must be used. Incorrect forms of the verb have been used in choice **a** (gerund), choice **b** (future imperfect), choice **c** (future imperfect), and choice **d** (preterite indefinite).

2. Es necesario tener *todo las* documentos de identificación en regla.
   a. todos las
   b. todo el
   c. todas las
   d. todos los
   e. No es necessario hacer ninguna corrección.

The correct answer is choice **d** because *todos los* is plural in number and masculine in gender, and thus in agreement with *documentos*. Choices **a**, **b**, and **c** have either the wrong gender or the wrong number.

▶ Sample Questions for the Artificial Language Test

The questions selected as sample questions for the written test are similar to the questions you will find in the actual test in terms of difficulty and form. In general, the test questions deal with an artificial language created to measure your ability to learn a language. Remember that *knowledge of a specific language other than English is not required to answer the questions correctly.*

In the actual test, you will be given a Supplemental Booklet containing the vocabulary for this language, the rules of the language, and a glossary of grammatical terms. It is in this Supplemental Booklet that you will find information necessary to answer the questions in the test.

The following sample questions give examples of test questions and provide the information needed to answer the sample questions. This information is in the same form as the information provided in the Supplemental Booklet.

Grammar Rules

1. To form the feminine singular of a noun, a pronoun, or an adjective, add the suffix *-exc* to the masculine singular form. In the artificial language, there are only masculine and feminine forms for words. There are no neuter forms.

    Example: If a male baby is a *belkoy*, then a female baby is a *belkoyexc*.

2. To form the plural of nouns, pronouns, or adjectives, add the suffix *-am* to the correct singular form.

    Example: If one male baby is a *belkoy*, then two or more male babies are *belkoyam*.

    If an ambitious woman is a *tosleexc* woman, several ambitious women are *tosleexcam* women.

3. Adjectives modifying nouns and pronouns with feminine and/or plural endings must have endings that agree with the words they modify.

    Example: If an active male baby is a *sojle belkoy*, an active female baby is a *sojleexc belkoyexc*, and

several active female babies are *sojleexcam belkoyexcam*.

4. The stem of a verb is obtained by omitting the suffix *-gar* from the infinitive form of the verb.

    Example: The stem of the verb *tilgar* is *til-*.

5. All subjects and their verbs must agree in number; that is, singular subjects require singular verbs and plural subjects require plural verbs. (See Rules 6 and 7.)

6. To form the present tense of a verb, add the suffix *-il* to the stem for the singular or the suffix *-al* to the stem for the plural.

    Example: If *nalgar* means to bark, then *nalil* is the present tense for the singular (the dog barks), and *nalal* is the present tense for the plural (the dogs bark).

7. To form the past tense of a verb, first add the suffix *-con* to the stem; then add either the suffix *-il* if the verb is singular or *-al* if it is plural.

    Example: If *nalgar* means to bark, then *nalconil* is the past tense of the singular (the dog barked). *Nalconal* is the past tense of the plural (the dogs barked).

Word List

yev	he, him
bex	a, an (all genders)
avekoy	enemy (masculine form)
syngar	to be
wir	the (all genders and numbers)
deggar	to fire
fo	at
daqkoy	jeep

Sample Questions

Translate the following sentences:

1. She was an enemy.

Yevexc synconil bex avekoyexc.

In the first word *Yevexc*, the suffix *-exc* was added to the masculine singular form of the pronoun *he*, making it the feminine singular form.

Two suffixes were added to the stem of the verb *synconil*: *con* because the verb is in the past tense, and *il* because it is the singular form.

In the word *avekoyexc*, the suffix *-exc* was added to the masculine singular form, making it the feminine singular form.

2. The enemies fired at the jeep.

Wir avekoyam degconal fo wir daqkoy.

In the word *avekoyam*, the suffix *-am* was added to the masculine singular form to make it the plural form.

Two suffixes were added to the stem of the verb *degconal*: *con* because the verb is in the past tense, and *al* because it is the plural form.

CHAPTER

7

Artificial Language Manual

CHAPTER SUMMARY

This chapter presents the complete official Preparation Manual for the Border Patrol Artificial Language test, as provided by the Department of Homeland Security. This manual will help you prepare for the test you have to take if you don't speak Spanish. Luckily, you don't have to memorize the information here; most of it will be available to you as you take the test. See Chapter 8 for tips on using this manual to your best advantage.

The purpose of this manual is to prepare you to take the U.S. Border Patrol test of ability to learn a foreign language. This test is part of the examination battery used in the selection of Border Patrol Agent trainees.

The test of ability to learn a foreign language is intended to assess an applicant's ability to learn neo-Latin languages such as Spanish or French. Therefore, the test is based on an Artificial Language, the rules of which are based on some of the grammatical structures of neo-Latin languages. (The term *neo-Latin languages*, which is a synonym of the expression *Romance languages*, is used to refer to languages that are derived directly from Latin.)

Since all Border Patrol Agents are required to know the Spanish language, it is important to assess language-learning abilities in all applicants to the Border Patrol Agency. All applicants who successfully pass the entry-level examination battery for Border Patrol Agent are eligible to become Agent Trainees at the U.S Border Patrol Academy in Glynco, GA. Applicants selected to become Agent Trainees will receive extensive training in many areas, including the Spanish language.

A validation study conducted by the U.S. Office of Personnel Management in 1991, and an attrition study conducted at the Border Patrol Academy in 1993, demonstrate that the Artificial Language Test (ALT) is an extremely effective predictor of success in learning Spanish at the academy. Accordingly, you are encouraged to study this manual with special care and attention.

As you progress through the Artificial Language Manual practice questions and exams, you will see variations in suffixes, vocabulary, and rules, as well as how these three critical components interact with one another. Please note slight variations for sets of rules and practice questions in Chapters 10 and 11, for instance. However, you will always be provided the relevant information you need to arrive at the correct answer. These deviations—some minor and some major—are intentional and, when combined, provide multiple variations of the ALT. You must not depend on memorization, but instead rely on your understanding of the rules, suffixes, and vocabulary words that are provided at the time you take the test.

▶ The Preparation Manual

Purpose of the Manual

The purpose of the manual is to help you prepare well for the ALT. The ALT can be a challenging test, especially for applicants who have never studied a foreign language.

The present manual was designed to allow you every opportunity to study the grammatical rules of the Artificial Language prior to taking the ALT. In this way, you can spend concentrated time in learning to use grammatical rules that you will need to apply not only in the test, but also in the process of learning Spanish if you are selected for a Border Patrol Agent trainee position.

Organization of the Manual

The manual contains several parts: vocabulary lists (or dictionary) for the Artificial Language; a set of grammatical rules; a glossary of grammatical terms (for applicants who do not remember the meaning of some of these terms); a practice test (which is exactly the same in format and length as the actual test); and, finally, a clear and concise explanation of why each response in the test is right or wrong. This last part should greatly assist you in learning how to apply each of the rules.

The parts of the manual are organized in the following sequence.

First: The Vocabulary Lists

The lists of words need not be memorized because during the actual test, they will be available to you for consultation.

Second: The Set of Grammatical Rules for the Artificial Language

These rules are the backbone of the Artificial Language because they are its connection to the structures of the Spanish language. There is no need to memorize the rules because they will be available to you during the test. Also, you should note that some details of the rules will be different in the actual test. For example, if the feminine form of a noun takes the suffix -*nef* in the rules presented in this manual, in the actual test the feminine form of a noun may take a different ending. Other than these minor variations, the rules are identical in the sense that they deal with the same grammatical structures as the actual test.

Third: Glossary of Grammatical Terms

This glossary will provide a refresher mini-course in grammatical terms (such as *verb*, *noun*, *adjective*, and *adverb*) for applicants who have forgotten the meanings of these terms. The glossary will also be available for consultation during the actual test. In this manual, however, the meaning of the terms will be discussed in greater depth, and it is therefore advisable for you to study the discussion in this manual with special attention and concentration.

Fourth: The Practice Test

The practice test is identical in length and format, as well as in its application of the same grammatical rules, to the actual test that you will take.

The test contains questions which are subdivided into tasks that require a correct translation from English into the Artificial Language and the application of grammatical rules to Artificial Language sentences. In some cases, these tasks involve an entire sentence, while in others, they involve only part of a sentence.

While taking the practice test, you should refer to the vocabulary lists, the grammatical rules for the Artificial Language, and the glossary of grammatical terms. During the actual test, you will be able to refer to these sources at all times. When taking the actual test, you will be given two booklets. The Supplemental Booklet will contain the reference materials (the vocabulary lists, the grammatical rules, and the glossary of grammatical terms), while the other booklet will contain the test questions. You will have access to the Supplemental Booklet at all times while taking the test, and you will be able to consult the reference materials in the Supplemental Booklet while answering the test questions. Therefore, it would be advisable for you to practice using the reference materials while taking the practice test included in this manual.

Fifth: The Rationale for Each Response

The last part of this manual contains a clear and concise explanation of why each response choice in the test is right or wrong. Since the test is a multiple-choice test, each response choice must be evaluated by the applicants. Consequently, it is important for you to know which rule is pertinent to each response choice. As will be clear from the study of this part of the manual, some response choices (those that are correct) conform to the appropriate rules, while the majority of response choices (those that are incorrect) violate one or more of the rules.

It is advisable for you to analyze each and every one of the explanations in this part of the manual after taking the practice test. If you find that many of your answers to the test questions are incorrect, it would be a good idea for you to retake the practice test after (1) studying the rationale for each response choice provided in this part of the manual, and (2) studying the grammatical rules once again, with more attention to detail.

▶ Part One: The Vocabulary Lists

The words on the following lists are the same; they are merely arranged differently, as they would be in a bilingual dictionary. In the first list, you can look up words in English to find their equivalent words in the Artificial Language. In the second list, you can look up words in the Artificial Language to find their equivalents in English. During the test, you will have the vocabulary lists with you for consultation at all times. You should note that the following words are not exactly the same as those given in the actual test (some are and some are not). Therefore, it is best not to try to memorize them before taking the actual test.

▶ Word List

ARRANGED ALPHABETICALLY BY THE ENGLISH WORD			
English	**Artificial Language**	**English**	**Artificial Language**
a, an	bex*	skillful	janle
alien	huslek	that	velle
and	loa	the	wir**
boy	ekaplek	this	volle
country	failek	to be	synker
difficult	glasle	to border	regker
enemy	avelek	to cross	chonker
friend	kometlek	to drive	arker
from	mor	to escape	pirker
government	almanlek	to guard	bonker
he, him	yev	to have	tulker
jeep	daqlek	to identify	kalenker
legal	colle	to injure	liaker
loyal	inle	to inspect	zelker
man	kaplek	to shoot	degker
of	quea	to spy	tatker
paper	trenedlek	to station	lexker
river	browlek	to work	frigker

 * *Applies to all genders*
** *Applies to all genders and numbers*

► Word List

ARRANGED ALPHABETICALLY BY THE ARTIFICIAL LANGUAGE WORD			
Artificial Language	**English**	**Artificial Language**	**English**
almanlek	government	kaplek	man
arker	to drive	kometlek	friend
avelek	enemy	lexker	to injure
bex*	a, an	liaker	to injure
bonker	to guard	loa	and
browlek	river	mor	from
chonker	to cross	pirker	to escape
colle	legal	quea	of
daqlek	jeep	regker	to border
degker	to shoot	synker	to be
ekaplek	boy	tatker	to spy
failek	country	trenedlek	paper
frigker	to work	tulker	to have
glasle	difficult	velle	that
huslek	alien	volle	this
inle	loyal	wir	the**
janle	skillfull	yev	he him
kalenker	to identify	zelker	to inspect

  * *Applies to all genders*
** *Applies to all genders and numbers*

▶ Part Two: Grammatical Rules for the Artificial Language

The grammatical rules given in this part of the manual are exactly the same as those used in the ALT, with the only exception being that some of the suffixes (word endings) used in the test differ from those used in this manual.

During the test, you will have access to the rules at all times. Consequently, it is important that you understand these rules, but it is not necessary that you memorize them. In fact, memorizing them will hinder rather than help you, since the endings of words are different in the version of the Artificial Language that appears in the actual test.

You should note that Part Three of this manual contains a glossary of grammatical terms to assist you if you are not thoroughly familiar with their meanings.

Rule 1

To form the feminine singular of a noun, a pronoun, or an adjective, add the suffix *-nef* to the masculine singular form. In the Artificial Language, there are only masculine and feminine forms for these words. There are no neuter forms.

> Example: If a male eagle is a *verlek* then a female eagle is a *verleknef.*

> If an ambitious man is a *tosle* man, an ambitious woman is a *toslenef* woman.

Rule 2

To form the plural of nouns, pronouns, and adjectives, add the suffix *-oz* to the correct singular form.

> Example: If one male eagle is a *verlek*, several male eagles are *verlekoz.*

If an ambitious woman is a *toslenef* woman, several ambitious women are *toslenefoz* women.

Rule 3

Adjectives modifying nouns and pronouns with feminine and/or plural endings must have endings that agree with the words they modify.

> Example: If an active male eagle is a *sojle verlek,* an active female eagle is a *sojlenef verleknef,* and several active female eagles are *sojlenefoz verleknefoz.*

Rule 4

The stem of a verb is obtained by omitting the suffix *-ker* from the infinitive form of the verb.

> Example: The stem of the verb *tirker* is *tir.*

Rule 5

All subjects and their verbs must agree in number; that is, singular subjects require singular verbs and plural subjects require plural verbs. (See Rules 6 and 7.)

Rule 6

To form the present tense of a verb, add the suffix *-em* to the stem for the singular or the suffix *-im* to the stem for the plural.

> Example: If to bark is *nalker*, then *nalem* is the present tense for the singular (the dog barks) and *nalim* is the present tense for the plural (the dogs bark).

Rule 7

To form the past tense of a verb, first add the suffix *-zot* to the stem, and then add the suffix *-em* if the verb is singular or the suffix *-im* if it is plural.

> Example: If to bark is *nalker*, then *nalzotem* is the past tense for the singular (the dog barked)

and *nalzotim* is the past tense for the plural (the dogs barked).

Rule 8

To form a noun from a verb, add the suffix *-lek* to the stem of the verb.

Example: If *longker* is *to write*, then a *writer* is a *longlek*.

Rule 9

To form an adjective from a noun, substitute the suffix *-le* for the suffix *-lek*.

Example: If *pellek* is beauty, then a beautiful male eagle is a *pelle verlek* and a beautiful female eagle is a *pellenef verleknef*. (Note the feminine ending *nef*.)

Rule 10

To form an adverb from an adjective, add the suffix *-ki* to the masculine form of the adjective. (Note that adverbs do not change their form to agree in gender or number with the words they modify.)

Example: If *pelle* is beautiful, then beautifully is *pelleki*.

Rule 11

To form the possessive of a noun or pronoun, add the suffix *-ae* to the noun or pronoun.

Example: If a *boglek* is a dog, then a dog's collar is a *boglekae* collar. If he is *yev*, then his book is *yevae* book.

Rule 12

To make a word negative, add the prefix *fer-* to the correct affirmative form.

Example: An inactive male eagle is a *fersojle verlek*. If the dog barks is *boglek nalem*, then the dog does not bark is *boglek fernalem*.

▶ Part Three: Glossary of Grammatical Terms

Adverb

An adverb is a word used to modify a verb. For example, the sentence "It was produced" could be modified to express *where* it was produced by saying "It was produced *locally*."

Generally, an adverb is used to answer the questions *where* (as in the example above), *when* (for example, "he comes *frequently*"), or *how* (for example, "she thinks *logically*").

Adverbs sometimes are used to modify an adjective or another adverb. An example of an adverb modifying an adjective is the sentence "She has a *really* beautiful mind," in which the adverb *really* modifies the adjective *beautiful* to intensify its meaning. An example of an adverb modifying another adverb is the sentence "She thinks *very* logically," in which the adverb *very* modifies the adverb *logically*, again to intensify its meaning.

In the Artificial Language (and hence in the ALT), the only adverbs used are those that modify verbs. In the Spanish language, as well as in the English language, adverbs are used to modify verbs, adjectives, and other adverbs.

Gender

As a grammatical concept, gender refers to the classification of words according to whether they are masculine, feminine, or neuter.

Neo-Latin languages take masculine or feminine endings for nouns, adjectives, and articles. The neuter form is used sometimes to express abstraction in a more emphatic manner. For example, the noun *wisdom*, which is an abstract noun, takes a feminine ending in

Spanish (*la sabiduría*), but its abstract nature can be conveyed more emphatically by changing the nominal form (i.e., the noun) to the adjectival form *sabio* and using this form preceded by the neuter article *lo*. Accordingly, *lo sabio* acts as a clearly abstract neuter noun. The neuter form is not used in the Artificial Language. Consequently, it is very important for you to remember that in the Artificial Language, *all* nouns and adjectives take either a masculine or a feminine ending according to whether the sentence refers to a man or a woman (or a girl or a boy). Also, all nouns and adjectives in the Artificial Language were conceived (for the sake of simplicity) to be masculine. Thus, unless the feminine gender is specified in the sentence, the masculine gender is always used.

Similarly, contrary to neo-Latin language structures, the Artificial Language does not change its ending according to gender for the articles *the* and *a/an*.

Infinitive

Infinitive is the name given to the general, abstract form of a verb: i.e., *to look, to think, to remember, to walk.* Once the action expressed by a verb is attached to a specific subject (a person, animal, or thing), then we say the verb is *conjugated,* or linked to that subject: *she thinks, the dog runs,* or *the table broke.*

In contrast to the way that an infinitive in English is preceded by the word *to* (as in *to think*), in the Artificial Language, all infinitives have the same ending. In the version of the Artificial Language used in this manual, this ending (or suffix) is -*ker* (in the actual test, the ending will be different).

The fact that in the Artificial Language the infinitive is defined by an ending makes the Artificial Language similar to Spanish and other neo-Latin languages. However, you should be aware of the fact that Spanish has three different suffixes that distinguish three separate infinitives and three different conjugations. Although you will study these three conjugations when learning Spanish, the Artificial Language has only one conjugation, which will considerably simplify your work in the actual test.

Noun

A noun is a word that names a person, place, thing, or abstraction: *Lindsay, Chicago, tree, wisdom.* A noun can refer to an individual (as in *Lindsay,* an individual person, or *Chicago,* an individual place) or to a set (as in "all *stones,*" "all *trees,*" "all *cities*").

A noun can also refer to an abstraction that cannot be touched or seen, like *wisdom* or *electromagnetism.*

The vocabulary of the Artificial Language, as can be appreciated from reading the vocabulary lists, contains strictly concrete nouns. Consequently, your work in the actual test will not include any tasks involving abstract nouns.

The design of the test is intended to assess your ability to apply grammatical rules, rather than your ability to deal with abstract theories. Accordingly, every effort has been made to avoid concepts that are not perfectly concrete.

Prefix

A prefix always occurs at the beginning of a word. It can be a single letter or a sequence of letters: *a*moral, *il*legal, *dys*functional.

A prefix is the opposite of a suffix (which always occurs at the end of a word), but both serve to change the basic word in some way. For example, *polite* is the basic word (in this case an adjective) to express the concept of behavior that conforms to accepted social norms, while adding the prefix *im-* and creating the word *impolite* transforms the word *polite* into its contradictory concept.

You should note that in the Artificial Language, a prefix is used to create a negative concept (see Rule 12 on page 67). This rule mimics both neo-Latin languages and English, in which negation is usually expressed by using a negative prefix.

Pronoun

A pronoun is a word used in place of a noun: *she* instead of *Lindsay, they* instead of *the guards, it* instead of *the stone, herself* instead of *the judge.*

In English, as well as in other languages, including neo-Latin languages, there is a difference between a pronoun that stands for the subject of an action (as in "*He* threw the stone," meaning that *Lindsay* threw the stone), and a pronoun that stands for the object of an action (as in "The stone was thrown at *him,*" meaning that the stone was thrown at *Lindsay*).

By contrast, in the Artificial Language, there is no grammatical difference between *he* and *him,* both being *yev.* You should remember, however, that in the Artificial Language, pronouns take feminine endings when the subject or object of the action is feminine. Accordingly, in the version of the Artificial Language given in this manual, both *she* (subject) and *her* (object) would be *yevnef* (i.e., *yev* plus the feminine suffix *-nef*).

Suffix

A suffix always occurs at the end of a word. It can be a single letter or a sequence of letters: i.e., cream*y*, read*able*, nice*ly*. It should be noted that, unlike prefixes, suffixes often change the figure of speech (the type of word). For example, in the case of cream*y*, the suffix *-y* changes the noun *cream* into the adjective *creamy*, and in the case of *nicely*, the suffix *-ly* changes the adjective *nice* into the adverb *nicely.*

In addition, suffixes are used to conjugate verbs (for example, to change the present tense into the past tense: you walk, you walk*ed*) and to create the plural form of nouns (for example, boy, boy*s*).

In neo-Latin languages, suffixes are used for the same purposes, but they are used for other purposes too, such as creating plural forms for adjectives and changing the gender of a word.

In the Artificial Language, suffixes are used extensively for all these purposes. Specifically, suffixes are used (1) to change the figure of speech (for example,

Rule 10 uses a suffix to change an adjective into an adverb); (2) to conjugate verbs (for example, Rules 6 and 7 use suffixes to express the present and past tenses); and (3) to create the plural form of nouns, pronouns, and adjectives (Rule 2). In addition, the Artificial Language conforms to the structure of neo-Latin languages in using a suffix to express gender. However, the Artificial Language differs from neo-Latin languages in that it uses a suffix to form the possessive (Rule 11); in this instance, the Artificial Language is more similar to English than to the structure of neo-Latin languages.

You should study all the rules on suffixes in the Artificial Language, and you should practice using these rules, but you should not memorize them because (1) you will have them available to you at all times during the actual test, and (2) in the actual test, some of the suffixes will be different from the ones used in this manual.

Verb

A verb is used to express either an action or a state of being. For example, "he *prepared* dinner" expresses the action of making all the preparations for dinner, while "he *is* a citizen" expresses the state or condition of being a citizen.

You should note that a "state of being" can be permanent or transitory. For example, *the agent's horse is a bay mare* expresses a permanent condition for the horse (its being a bay mare), while *George is at lunch* expresses a transitory condition for George (that of being at lunch at the present moment).

The Spanish language, unlike English, has two different verbs to express permanent and transitory conditions. The Artificial Language is akin to English, rather than to Spanish, in its use of a single verb to express any state of being.

Lastly, you should note that a verb is the central component of a sentence. In fact, by definition, a sentence exists only when it has a verb (implicitly or explicitly), and a verb is sufficient by itself to form a sentence about something or someone: *He escaped* or *Run!* By contrast, adjectives, adverbs, and nouns do not by themselves form sentences, because in and of themselves, they do not say anything about a subject (a person or thing).

You should recall from the discussion of the infinitive that when a verb is linked to a subject (conjugated), it changes from the abstract infinitive form to a specific form such as present or past. You will have noted from a study of the rules of the Artificial Language that it has only two tenses: the simple past tense and the simple present tense in the indicative mood (Rules 6 and 7). (Note: The indicative mood refers to forms of verbs that express a *real* action or condition, as distinguished from the subjunctive mood, which expresses hypothetical actions or conditions. The subjunctive mood does not exist in the Artificial Language, but it is very important in Spanish and will be studied in language training by Border Patrol Trainees.)

Occasionally, you will find a past participle used in the test (for example, "she was *arrested*"), but since the past participle is treated the same as a simple past, you simply have to apply the rule for the simple past to create the participle. Thus, *has inspected* is translated into *tulem zelzotem* (*tulem* applies Rule 6 to form the present tense *has* and *zelzotem* applies Rule 7 to form the past tense *inspected*).

▶ Part Four: Practice Test

> Here, you will find only the directions and sample questions from the official Artificial Language Manual. For more practice, see Chapters 10 and 11.

Directions for Questions 1 through 20

For each sentence, decide which words have been translated correctly. Add a check mark to each *numbered* word that is correctly translated into the Artificial Language. When you have finished checking these words in sentences 1 through 20, for each question, select **a**, **b**, **c**, **d**, or **e** according to the following instructions:

Mark:
a. if *only* the word numbered 1 is checked as correctly translated
b. if *only* the word numbered 2 is checked as correctly translated
c. if *only* the word numbered 3 is checked as correctly translated
d. if *two or more* of the numbered words are checked as correctly translated
e. if *none* of the numbered words is checked as correctly translated

Be sure to check only the *numbered* words that are *correctly* translated.

Study the sample question before going on to the test questions.

Sample Sentence	*Sample Translation*
	✓
He identifies the driver.	Volle kalenim wir arlek.
	1 2 3

The word numbered 1, *volle*, is incorrect since the translation of *volle* is *this*. The word *yev* should have been used.

The word numbered 2, *kalenim*, is also incorrect because the singular form *kalenem* should have been used.

The word numbered 3 is correct and should be checked. *Arlek* has been correctly formed from the infinitive *arker* (to drive) by applying rules 8 and 4. Since the word numbered 3 has been checked, the answer to the sample question is **c**.

Directions for Questions 21 through 30

For each question in this group, select the choice that correctly translates the underlined word or group of words into the Artificial Language. Mark the letter of the correct translation on a separate piece of paper.

Sample question

There is <u>the boy</u>.
a. bex kaplek
b. wir kaplek
c. wir ekaplek
d. velle ekaplek
e. bex ekaplek

Since **c** is the correct translation of the underlined words <u>the boy</u>, the answer to the sample question is **c**.

Directions for Questions 31 through 42

For this group of questions, select the choice that is the correct translation of the English word or words in parentheses. You should translate the entire sentence in order to determine what form should be used.

Sample question

(The man) synem bex avelek.
a. Bex kaplek
b. Bex ekaplek
c. Loa kaplek
d. Wir kaplek
e. Wirlek kaplek

Since *Wir kaplek* is the only one of these expressions that means *the man,* **d** is the correct answer to the sample question.

Directions for Questions 43 through 50

For the last group of questions, select the choice that is the correct form of the underlined expression as it is used in the sentence. At the end of the sentence, you will find instructions in parentheses telling you which form to use. In some sentences, you will be asked to supply the correct forms of two or more expressions. In this case, the instructions for these expressions are presented consecutively in the parentheses and are separated by a dash. Be sure to translate the entire sentence before selecting your answer.

Sample question

Yev *bonker* wir browlek. (present tense)
a. bonzotem
b. bonzotim
c. boneim
d. bonim
e. bonem

Choices **a** and **b** are incorrect because they are in the past tense. Choice **c** is misspelled. Choice **d** is in the present tense, but it too is incorrect because the subject of the sentence is singular and therefore takes a verb with a singular rather than a plural ending. Choice **e** is the correct answer to the sample question.

▶ Part Five: Rationale for Each Response Choice

A rationale, or justification, is provided for each answer choice in the test, including both correct and incorrect choices. The purpose of this part of the manual is to help you understand *why* each choice is right or wrong and, consequently, to help you familiarize yourself with the structures of the Artificial Language.

Using the Artificial Language Manual

CHAPTER SUMMARY

This chapter provides instructions and suggestions on using all sections of the Artificial Language Manual to help you prepare for the Artificial Language Test (ALT). The chapter then provides you with a short practice test.

The Artificial Language, of course, is of no use by itself—you'll never hear anyone speak it. It was devised to test your ability to learn languages, especially Spanish. The Artificial Language Manual may look daunting at first. It's almost 50 pages long and is probably like nothing you've ever encountered before, although later you'll see that the Artificial Language rules are very similar to those of Spanish. With study, and especially with practice using the Manual and taking the practice tests in this book, this pseudo-language will come to make sense, though, and begin to seem familiar. You may even start dreaming in Artificial Language before you're through!

▶ Purposes of the Artificial Language Manual

The Artificial Language Manual has two main purposes:

1. To help you prepare for the ALT by giving you a chance to study the Artificial Language grammatical rules ahead of time—not to memorize them, just to study them—so that you'll have a leg up when you actually start answering the Artificial Language questions during the test-taking process.

2. To give you a start on mastering the Spanish language, which you will have to do if you become a Border Patrol Agent trainee. As mentioned, the grammatical rules of Artificial Language are very similar to those of Spanish.

▶ Tips on Using the Artificial Language Manual

As with most tasks, approaching the Artificial Language Manual in separate small steps, rather than trying to grasp the whole thing at once, will help immensely. First, let's look at the manual's separate parts.

The Vocabulary Lists

Part One of the Manual consists of two word lists. The lists actually contain the same words; they're just arranged differently. One is arranged by the English word and one by the Artificial Language word, just as is the case in most bilingual dictionaries.

It is important to note that, for two reasons, it is not to your advantage to memorize the vocabulary lists in the Manual:

1. The lists for the actual test will not necessarily contain the same words that appear in the Manual.

2. You will have vocabulary lists in front of you during the test, so you can refer to them throughout.

The Grammatical Rules

In Part Two of the Manual, you will find the grammatical rules for the Artificial Language. Again, as with the vocabulary lists, it is not to your advantage to memorize them. They will be provided for you during the test. Also, some or all of the prefixes (beginnings) and suffixes (endings) given in the Manual will be different from those employed on the test. However, since the way the rules work (that is, the way words are formed) will be the same in the Manual as on the test, you should learn how the formation of the various grammatical parts of speech works in the Artificial Language. In other words, you do need to understand how to apply the rules.

You may find it helpful to practice forming words from items on the vocabulary lists. For example, you could form the past and present singular tenses of each verb on the vocabulary list. Examples that conform to each rule are given in the list of rules in Part Two.

The Glossary of Grammatical Terms

Be sure to thoroughly familiarize yourself with the meaning and use of each grammatical term in Part Three. The Manual will be helpful in that it will remind you of definitions of parts of speech in English, in case you have forgotten. Once you feel sure you are familiar with each grammatical term, work on how the parts of speech function together in actual sentences. For example, you might practice by identifying which grammatical terms apply to each of the words in some simple English sentences.

Another helpful way to practice is to identify which grammatical terms apply to each word on the vocabulary lists for the Artificial Language. Note: There may be more than one grammatical term that applies to a single word in both English and the Artificial Language. For example:

- "I will guard the door" uses the word *guard* as a verb.

- "The guard stood by the door" uses the word *guard* as a noun.

Knowing the grammatical terms and their functions will help you learn and understand the grammar of the Artificial Language efficiently; moreover, it will help you apply the grammar of the Artificial Language more quickly to translations in the exam.

▶ The Practice Test

The following is the most important part of this chapter—the practice test items. You can learn much more by doing than by reading about, so these items, as well as those on the tests in Chapters 10 and 11, will help you more than anything else if you apply yourself diligently.

There are four different types of questions on the Artificial Language Exam. This practice test gives you two examples of each type of question. Please refer to the vocabulary lists and grammatical rules for the Artificial Language included in the Artificial Language Manual in Chapter 7 to answer these questions.

Be sure to pay special attention to the answer explanations that follow the questions.

For questions 1 and 2, make a check mark beside each NUMBERED word that is correctly translated into the Artificial Language. When you have finished this process, fill out your answer sheet (which is provided at the end of the test) by marking

a, if ONLY the word numbered 1 is checked as correctly translated.

b, if ONLY the word numbered 2 is checked as correctly translated.

c, if ONLY the word numbered 3 is checked as correctly translated.

d, if TWO or MORE of the numbered words are checked as correctly translated.

e, if NONE of the words is checked as correctly translated.

Be sure to check only the NUMBERED words that are CORRECTLY translated.

Sentence

1. Those women are illegal aliens.

Translation

Velleoz kapleknefoz synzotim pohcollenefoz
    1   2   3
husleknefoz.

Sentence

2. The inspector shot the enemy spy.

Translation

Wir zellek degem wir avele tatlek.
      1   2   3

For questions 3 and 4, select the correct translation of the numbered, italicized word or group of words in the following paragraph. Mark on your answer sheet the letter of the correct translation.

The men and women who *guard the border loyally*
                                    3
have a complex and difficult job. They have to deal with both friendly and unfriendly aliens, as well as with well-trained and skillful spies. *They have to inspect* and
                                                              4
identify complex governmental papers, and they have to make difficult decisions, often alone and away from their stations.

3. a. bonem wir reglek inle
   b. bonim wir reglek inleki
   c. bonim wir regker inleki
   d. bonim wir reglek inle
   e. bonem wir reglek inleki

4. a. Yevoz tulzotim zelker
   b. Yev tulem zelker
   c. Yevoz tulim zelim
   d. Yev tulzotim zelzotim
   e. Yevoz tulim zelker

Of the five suggested answers to questions 5 and 6, select the one that correctly translates the English word or words in parentheses into the Artificial Language. You should translate the entire sentence in order to determine what form should be used.

5. The (papers were skillfully) forged.
   a. trenedlekoz synzotim janleki
   b. trenedleknefoz synzotim janleki
   c. trenedlekoz synim janleki
   d. trenedlekoz synzotem janleki
   e. trenedlekoz synzotim janle

6. An inspector was (injured from the shooting).
   a. liazotem mor bex deglek
   b. liazotem mor wir degker
   c. liazotem mor wir deglek
   d. liazotem quea wir deglek
   e. liazotim mor wir deglek

For questions 7 and 8, select the answer choice that is the correct form of the expression as it is used in the sentence. Mark on your answer sheet the letter of the correct translation.

At the end of the sentence, you will find instructions in parentheses telling you which grammatical form the answer will be. In some sentences, you will be asked to supply the correct forms of two or more expressions. In this case, the instructions for these expressions are presented consecutively in the parentheses and are separated by a dash. Be sure to translate the entire sentence before selecting your answer.

7. Wir ekaplek kometlek synem bex tatlek. (feminine plural possessive noun)
   a. ekapleknefoz
   b. ekaplekozae
   c. ekaplekefozae
   d. ekapleknefozae
   e. ekapleknefae

8. Bex kometlek huslek pirzotem janleki mor reglenef bonker. (negative masculine adjective—feminine singular noun)
   a. kometlek—bonleknef
   b. pohkometle—bonleknefoz
   c. pohkometle—bonleknef
   d. kometle—bonleknef
   e. pohkometle—bonlek

▶ Answers

1. c. The word numbered 1, *velleoz* (*those*), is incorrect. Although this adjective has the plural ending, *oz,* it must have the feminine plural ending, *nefoz,* to agree in number and gender with the feminine plural noun it modifies (see Grammatical Rules 1, 2, and 3). The correct translation would be the feminine plural adjective, *vellenefoz.* The word numbered 2, *synzotim,* is an incorrect translation of the verb *are.* It is incorrect because *synzotim* (*were*) is the past plural conjugation of the verb; the correct translation is *synim* (*are*), which is the present plural conjugation of the verb (Grammatical Rules 4 and 6). The word numbered 3, *pohcollenefoz* (*illegal*), is correctly translated. As an adjective modifying the feminine plural noun *husleknefoz* (*aliens*), it has the correct feminine plural ending (Rules 1, 2, and 3). Furthermore, it has the correct negative prefix, *poh-,* to change the meaning of the adjective *legal* to *illegal* (Rule 12). Because only the word numbered 3 should be checked as correct, **c** is the correct choice.

2. d. The word numbered 1, *zellek,* is correct; it is the noun, *guard,* formed from the infinitive *zelbar* (*to guard*), following Rule 8. The word numbered 2, *degem,* is incorrect because it is the present singular conjugation of *degker* (*to shoot*); the correct translation is the past singular conjugation, *degzotem* (Rules 4, 5, and 7). The word numbered 3, *avele* (*enemy*), is in the correct form. In this sentence, the word *enemy* is an adjective modifying the word *spy*; therefore, it takes the adjectival ending, following Rule 9. Because both the words numbered 1 and 3 should be checked as correct, the correct answer is **d.**

3. b. Choice **a** is incorrect because the verb, *bonem,* is in the present singular conjugation; it should be in the present plural form, *bonim,* to agree in number with the subject of the sentence, *men and women* (Rules 5 and 6). Also, the word *inle* (*loyal*) is lacking the suffix needed to make it into the adverb, *inleki* (*loyally*), following Rule 10. Choice **c** is incorrect because the noun *reglek* (*border*), formed according to Rule 9, is incorrectly translated as the infinitive *regker* (*to border*). Choice **d** is incorrect because the word *inle* (*loyal*) is lacking the suffix needed to make it into the adverb *inleki* (*loyally*), following Rule 10. Choice **e** is incorrect because the verb, *bonem,* is in the present singular conjugation; it should be in the present plural form, *bonim,* to agree in number with the subject of the sentence, *men and women* (Rules 5 and 6). Choice **b** is correct because the verb is in the correct present plural conjugation (Rules 4, 5, and 6); the noun, *reglek,* is correctly formed according to Rule 8; and the adverb, *inleki,* is correctly formed according to Rule 10.

4. e. Choice **a** is incorrect because the verb, *tulzotim,* is in the past plural conjugation; it should be the present plural, *tulim* (Rules 4, 5, and 6). Choice **b** is incorrect because the pronoun, *yev* (*he*), is in the masculine singular form; it should have the masculine plural ending to form the plural pronoun, *yevoz* (*they*), according to Rule 2. The verb, *tulem,* is in the present singular form; it should be present plural to agree with the subject, *they* (Rules 5 and 6). Choice **c** is incorrect because the verb, *zelim,* is in the present plural conjugation; it should be in the infinitive form, *zelker,* to correctly translate as *to inspect.* Choice **d** is incorrect because the pronoun, *yev,* should be in the masculine plural form, *yevoz* (*they*) according to Rule 2. Also, the verb, *tulzotim*, is in the past plural form; it should be the present plural (*tulim*), according to Rules 4, 5, and 6, and the infinitive, *to inspect* (*zelker*), is incorrectly translated as the past plural conjugation, *zelzotim*, of the verb. Choice **e** is correct because the pronoun is in the correct masculine plural form, *yevoz* (Rule 2); the verb, *tulim*, is in the correct present plural conjugation (Rules 4, 5, and 6); and the infinitive, *to inspect*, is correctly translated as *zelker*.

5. a. Choice **b** is incorrect because the noun, *trenedleknefoz*, is in the feminine plural form; it should be the masculine plural, *trenedlekoz* (Rules 2 and 3). Choice **c** is incorrect because the verb, *synim*, is in the present plural form; it should be the past plural form, *synzotim* (Rules 4, 5, and 7). Choice **d** is incorrect because the verb, *synzotem*, is in the past singular conjugation; it should be the past plural, *synzotim* (Rules 4, 5, and 7). Choice **e** is incorrect because the word *janle* is in its adjectival form; it should be in the adverbial form, *janleki* (*skillfully*), formed according to Rule 10. Choice **a** is correct because the noun, *trenedlekoz*, is in the proper masculine plural form (Rule 2); the verb, *synzotim*, is in the correct past plural conjugation (Rules 4, 5, and 7); and the adverb, *janleki*, has the correct adverbial suffix (Rule 10).

6. c. Choice **a** is incorrect because the word *the* (*wir*) is mistranslated as *bex*. Choice **b** is incorrect because the noun, *shooting* (*deglek*) formed according to Rule 8, is mistranslated as the infinitive, *degker* (*to shoot*). Choice **d** is incorrect because the word *from* (*mor*) is mistranslated as *quea* (*of*). Choice **e** is incorrect because the verb, *liazotim*, is in the past plural form; it should be in the past singular form, *liazotem*, to agree with the singular subject, *inspector* (Rules 4, 5, and 7). Choice **c** is correct because the verb is in the correct past singular conjugation, *liazotem* (Rules 4, 5, and 7); the words *from* (*mor*) and *the* (*wir*) are correctly translated; and the noun, *shooting* (*deglek*) is correctly formed from the infinitive, *degker*, following Rule 8.

7. d. Choice **a** is incorrect because it is the feminine plural noun; it lacks the possessive ending. Choice **b** is incorrect because it is the masculine plural possessive form; it should be feminine plural possessive. Choice **c** is incorrect because it is misspelled. Choice **e** is incorrect because it is the feminine singular possessive. Choice **d** is correct because it is the feminine plural possessive noun, formed according to Rules 2 and 11.

8. c. Choice **a** is incorrect because *kometlek* is the masculine singular noun, not the negative adjective. Choice **b** is incorrect because *bonleknefoz* is the feminine plural noun, not the feminine singular. Choice **d** is incorrect because *kometle* is lacking the negative prefix, *poh-*. Choice **e** is incorrect because *bonlek* is the masculine singular noun, not the feminine singular. Choice **c** is correct because *pohkometle* is the negative masculine adjective, formed according to Rule 9, and *bonleknef* is the feminine singular noun, formed according to Rules 2 and 8.

▶ Summary

Focus your study time on learning and recognizing the meanings and the relationships of the various grammatical parts of language as detailed in the glossary of grammatical terms. Understanding the parts of speech and their relationships in sentences will help you understand and use the grammatical rules of the Artificial Language to form various parts of speech. Be careful to learn and understand relationships between words, such as agreement in gender between nouns and their adjectives, that are not used in English but are important features of the Artificial Language.

Remember also that the Artificial Language questions will become clearer and easier as you progress through the practice tests in this book, so approach them with confidence.

Tips for Using the Artificial Language Manual

- **Do not** memorize the vocabulary lists.
- **Do not** memorize the grammatical terms in the glossary.
- **Do** study and familiarize yourself with the grammatical terms in the glossary.
- **Do** learn thoroughly how to apply the grammatical rules, but do not memorize the prefixes and suffixes.
- **Do** practice applying the rules as often as you can before the exam—that is, you should do not only the practice exam questions in this chapter, but the two full-length practice exams in this book, as well.

CHAPTER

9 ▶ Checking Your Spanish Proficiency

CHAPTER SUMMARY

This chapter will give you hints and suggestions on how to score well on the Spanish Language portion of the Border Patrol Exam, along with a list of resources to help you study more effectively. Use this chapter only if you speak Spanish. If you don't, you'll be taking the Artificial Language Test in Chapter 8 instead of the Spanish test.

Today, more than ever before, the ability to speak a second language is in demand. Modern technology has enabled people anywhere on Earth to communicate with each other quickly and easily. For many millions of people, this communication takes place in the Spanish language. Someone who speaks Spanish can function more productively in the modern workplace both at home and abroad. Also, if you know the language, you will have a much richer experience when traveling to Spanish-speaking countries.

As a Border Patrol Agent, you'll find that speaking Spanish well will be an invaluable aid in doing your job. First, the probability of miscommunication is greatly reduced when both parties speak the same language. Second, speaking in another person's native language demonstrates your goodwill and a basic respect for that person. Since every Border Patrol Agent is required to know Spanish, you're ahead of the game if you already have a working knowledge of the language.

This chapter assumes you have that working knowledge. It will give you some tips on how to review your Spanish, if necessary. It reviews some of the essential grammar rules you may have forgotten—this section could be essential if you are a native speaker of Spanish who never really had to learn the rules. In this chapter, you'll also find some sample questions with tips on how to answer them, as well as a list of resources you can use to review.

▶ Some Helpful Hints for Reviewing

Learning or reviewing Spanish effectively is mostly a matter of establishing a set of good habits and then practicing, practicing, practicing. Here are some useful hints to help you get started.

- Schedule study time in small units. If you need to do a lot of studying, study for a half hour, then do something else, then study for another half hour, and so on.
- If you know a native Spanish speaker who speaks the language well, see if you can arrange practice sessions with that person. If that is not possible, the next best thing is to listen to a reading of someone who speaks Spanish well.
- Study out loud. It is important to hear yourself speaking Spanish. Doing this will enable you to speak more comfortably and easily. If possible, try to study with a friend. That way, you can check each other's pronunciation and grammar. You will find that this will enable you to learn the material more quickly, and the learning process will be more interesting.
- Spend extra time memorizing vocabulary. This is very important. There are a number of books available in bookstores or libraries that have vocabulary lists. A good choice would be *Master-*

ing Spanish Vocabulary: A Thematic Approach by José Navarro and Axel Navarro Ramil.

- Spend extra time on pronunciation. Be sure to get it right. This is essential, because, as in English, many Spanish words have different meanings when pronounced differently; for example, *paso* (I am passing by) is very different from *pasó* (he/she/you passed by). Correct pronunciation will help you choose the correct written word on the test.
- Always think of the meaning. When practicing, as you repeat basic sentences, think about their meanings and try to speak with feeling; that is, try to make your expression match the meaning. This will reinforce your learning, and practice won't become mere mechanical repetition.
- Continually review earlier material as you progress through the lessons. When you go back and review earlier, easier lessons, you will reinforce what you have already memorized.
- Use what is called *the pattern sentence technique.* This is a good way to systematically learn or review material. Pattern sentences can be used to practice verb conjugations, pronoun usage, and adjective endings. When practicing, alone or with a friend, try using this technique. Here's how it works:

> Take a correct sentence that uses a regular *-ar*, *-er*, or *-ir* verb form, then change the subject and repeat the new sentence aloud. For instance, if you say *¿Habla Ud. con él?* (Do you speak with him?), you or another person, could respond *Sí, hablo con él* (Yes, I speak with him).

> Practice correct pronoun and adjective usage this way too. If you asked the person *¿Ud. le dio el libro a mi hermano?* (Did you give the book to my brother?) They could answer *Sí, se lo di* (Yes, I gave it to him).

▶ Some Essential Grammatical Rules

Following is a list of grammatical rules you'll need to know. Supplement the information here by finding a good Spanish grammar book and studying it to be sure you understand the terms. A solid understanding of these rules of correct usage is the key to doing well on the Spanish Language portion of the Border Patrol Exam.

Nouns and Gender

A noun is a word that denotes a person, place, or thing. All nouns in Spanish are either masculine or feminine in gender.

- Masculine nouns require a masculine article, *el* (the) or *un* (a or an). Masculine nouns usually end in *-o*. An important exception is *la mano* (hand).
- Feminine nouns require a feminine article, *la* (the) or *una* (a or an). Feminine nouns usually end in *-a, -ción, -umbre, -dad, -tad,* or *-tud*.
- Always memorize the noun together with its masculine or feminine article: *el padre, la madre*. This is essential. It will also make learning the irregular ones easier. For instance, *El mapa* (the map) is an example of an irregular noun.

Types of Pronouns

A pronoun is a word that takes the place of a noun.

Subject Pronouns

Subject pronouns take the place of the subject of the sentence. The subject pronouns are *yo, tú, usted, él, ella, nosotros, nosotras, ustedes, ellos,* and *ellas*.

- Subject pronouns may be omitted when the form of the verb identifies the subject. An example is *Yo voy. Voy* can only mean *I go*, so *yo* can be omitted.
- However, subject pronouns may be added for greater clarity, emphasis, or contrast, as in the sentence *Yo voy no tú* (I am going, not you).
- In the polite form of address, the third person, *Usted* and *Ustedes* (abbreviated *Ud.* or *Vd.* and *Uds.* or *Vds.*), are often kept to avoid confusion with *él, ella, ellos, ellas.* That's why *Usted* and *Ustedes* are repeated so often.

Direct Object Pronoun

A direct object pronoun takes the place of a person or thing that directly receives the action of the verb. The direct object pronouns are *me, te, nos, la, las, lo,* and *los.* An example is *Los veo* (I see them).

Indirect Object Pronoun

The indirect object pronoun takes the place of a person to whom, or for whom, an action is performed. It is the ultimate receiver of the action of a verb. The indirect object pronouns are *me, te nos, le,* and *les.* An example is *Les habla* (he speaks to them).

Prepositional Pronoun

Prepositional pronouns are pronouns that come after a preposition. Prepositional pronouns are the same as regular pronouns, except for *me,* which becomes *mí,* and *te,* which becomes *ti:* for example, *para ti* (for you). When the preposition *con* appears before *mí* or *ti,* the two words are contracted and become *conmigo* and *contigo.*

Reflexive Direct and Indirect Object Pronouns

Reflexive direct and indirect objects are used when the subject performs the action to, or on, itself. The reflexive direct and indirect object pronouns are *me, te, se, nos,* and *se.* An example is *El se sienta* (he sits down, or more literally, he sits himself down).

Correct Position of Object Pronouns

Object pronouns come before conjugated verb forms. They should be placed in the following order: reflexive pronoun first, followed by the indirect object pronoun, then the direct object pronoun, and finally the verb. There is a device that will help you remember this correct order—it goes like this:

Indirect before direct, reflexive first of all.

Although it is quite common to have an indirect object pronoun followed by a direct object pronoun, it is rare to encounter a reflexive, a direct, and an indirect object pronoun all together. When it does happen, though, this device will help you remember the right order.

Object pronouns are placed after, and attached to, both infinitives and affirmative commands, making all one word. An example is *Mándamelo* (order it for me).

Adjectives

Adjectives modify or give specific information about nouns in a sentence. They tell qualities such as size, weight, color, and so forth. Some examples are *La casa es blanca* (the house is white), and *Los muchachos son simpáticos* (the boys are nice). Adjectives must agree in number and gender with the nouns they modify.

Verbs

Verbs are words that tell "action" or "state of being" in a sentence. For example, *Ellos llegan mañana* (they arrive tomorrow) is an example of a verb that tells "action," whereas *Es su hermano* (he is your brother) tells "state of being."

- Spanish verbs have three regular conjugations ending in: -*ar* (e.g., *cantar*), -*er* (e.g., *vender*), or -*ir* (e.g., *recibir*).
- Usually, verbs are formed by dropping the last two letters of the infinitive and adding the endings in their place. However, there are a number of quite common irregular verbs that must be memorized.

- The future and conditional tenses are formed by adding the endings to the entire infinitive.
- Two of the most frequently encountered verbs are *ser* (to be) and *estar* (to be). It will be easier to know which one to use if you remember this:

  Ser is used for a characteristic or essence of something.

  Estar is used for a location or condition.

Adverbs

An adverb is a word that gives additional information about a verb, an adjective, or another adverb. It tells how, when, or where the action or state is taking place.

- Adverbs are formed by adding -*mente* to the feminine form (ending in *a*) of the adjective. An example is when *rápido* becomes *rapidamente* (quickly).
- For adjectives ending in *e* or a consonant, just add -*mente* without changing it to an *a*. An example is when *gentil* becomes *gentilmente* (elegantly).

Conjunctions

Conjunctions are joining words. They link words, or groups of words, into more complex sentences. A few examples are *y* (and), *pero* (but), and *sin embargo* (although). *Que* (that) is a common connecting word that links clauses.

Personal *a*

In Spanish, an *a* must be used after a verb when the direct object is a person. An example would be *Conozco a su hermano* (I know your brother).

- The personal *a* may be used when referring to pets that one is especially fond of. *Quiero a Spot* (I love Spot) is an example. But it is mostly used only when people are the direct object of the verb.

- The only verb that the personal *a* is not used after is *tener*. Never use the personal *a* after *tener*: *Tengo un hermano mayor.*

▶ Practice Questions with Tips

The practice questions that follow are like those in the practice exam in this book—and like those in the real exam. There are four different kinds of questions. Study each sample carefully and use the information provided to create your own winning strategy.

Part A

The best way to prepare for the vocabulary part of the test is to memorize, memorize, memorize. Using flash cards or a book of vocabulary lists, spend time every day drilling your vocabulary. This is an effective way to increase your Spanish comprehension and reinforce what you have already learned.

The surest way to do well on the test is to study your vocabulary as much as possible. However, even then, you may run across a key word or a choice you don't know. How do you proceed? A useful tip is to look not only for the meaning of the word but also for its part of speech. For example, is the word a noun, a pronoun, or a verb? Often, several choices can be eliminated just by observing that they are the wrong number and gender for the noun, the wrong pronoun, or the wrong form of the verb. In example 1 that follows, three of the choices are the wrong verb forms to match the sentence. This leaves only two possibilities. Now you can make an educated guess about the right one. However, the best approach is to know your vocabulary.

For practice questions 1–3, find the suggested answer, of the five choices, that is closest in meaning to the key (italicized) word.

1. *Deseamos* oir todo la historia.
  a. Vienen
  b. Le dijo
  c. Robaremos
  d. Queremos
  e. Habló

The correct answer is **d**, *Queremos* (we want), because it is closer in meaning to *Deseamos* (we wish) than the other choices—*Vienen* (they come), *Le dijo* (she said), *Robaremos* (we will steal), and *Habló* (he spoke)—and because it has the correct verb form.

2. *El director* de la organización es nuevo.
  a. El jefe
  b. Los hermanos
  c. La secretaria
  d. Los curas
  e. La madre

The correct answer is **a**. *El jefe* (the boss) is closest in meaning to *El director* (the director). In this case, the word in question is a noun. You will observe that incorrect number or gender combinations rule out all possibilities except choice **a**.

In the vocabulary section, if you already know the meaning of the word in question, look at it from a grammatical point of view only to check your work.

3. *La mujer* del presidente es gorda.
   a. Los muebles
   b. El mono
   c. La señora
   d. Las hijas
   e. La jira

Choice **c** is the one that is closest in meaning and has the correct number and gender.

Part B-I

For this part of the test, the important thing to focus on is the grammar. Look for the combination of words that not only has an appropriate meaning, but also matches grammatically. Look for obvious errors such as choices using the wrong number and gender or an incorrect verb form.

When evaluating verbs, begin by looking for the one with a form that matches the subject, which may be either a noun or a pronoun. Then look for one that uses the appropriate tense. This will quickly eliminate several possibilities. As in the following examples, it may not even be necessary to know the meaning of the verb to be able to choose the correct answer using this technique.

Supply the correct words that should be used in place of the blanks within a sentence.

1. Ellos _____ en el jardín cuando _____ la música.
   a. está, oyo
   b. estaban, oyeron
   c. estarán, vienen
   d. han estado, oían
   e. estuvieron, oí

Choice **b** is the correct use of the imperfect and the preterit verb tenses. The other choices use a wrong verb form.

2. Las _____ fueron completamente _____ por la bomba.
   a. está, destruida
   b. cartas, encontrados
   c. casas, destruidas
   d. días, perdidos
   e. ventana, nueva

Choice **c** uses the correct verb form. The other possibilities are wrong because of incorrect verb form or gender agreement—not to mention that some of them, such as choice **e**, would simply make no sense in this context no matter what their forms.

3. Ellos _____ en el jardín cuando _____ la música.
   a. está, oyo
   b. estaban, oyeron
   c. estaran, vienen
   d. han estado, oían
   e. estuvieron, oí

Choice **b** is the only one that uses correct verb forms.

Part B-II

This section requires you to "put it all together." It tests your ability to recognize various language elements and incorporate them into a complete picture, the correct sentence. To do well on this portion of the Spanish Language exam, look for errors of grammar, sentence structure, or incorrect word usage.

1. a. Señor Garcia nos enviamos las papeles.
   b. Eso no valen la pena.
   c. Hay muchas flores en el jardín.
   d. Hay un gato dormiendo en la ventana.

Choice **c** is the only choice that does not have mistakes in verb form.

2. a. Más tarde la señora Smith y yo van a tomar café en el restaurante.
   b. Ella estaba llorando sin saber por qué.
   c. Me gusto el pollo frito.
   d. Juan nos invité a tomar algo.

The only correct sentence is choice **b**. The other possibilities use incorrect verb forms.

3. a. ¿Vimos Uds. al Presidente de México?
   b. Fuimos a un café.
   c. El muchacha es pequeña.
   d. ¿Es aburrido la examen?

The correct answer is **b**. It is the only choice that does not have an error in verb form or gender agreement.

Part B-III

This section also tests your overall comprehension. It requires you to decide whether or not a selection is correct. If it is incorrect, you will need to choose an alternative to the key word.

First, decide if the key word is used correctly in the sentence. Having a strong vocabulary will help you here! If the word seems to have an appropriate meaning, then look for the right grammatical structure. If the key word is a noun, look for matching number and gender; if it is a verb, look for correct form and tense. This is where the time you spend studying Spanish grammar will pay off! If the key word passes both of these tests, choice **e** is the right one—the sentence does not need any correction.

What if you spot an error, as in the first example below? In this case, proceed as you would in the earlier sections and evaluate the choices according to meaning, grammatical correctness, and complete sentence structure.

1. El fútbol y el béisbol son dos ejemplos de *montañas*.
   a. alfombras
   b. escuelas
   c. maderas
   d. deportes
   e. No es necesario hacer ninguna corrección.

Choice **d**, *deportes* (sports), is correct. The key word, *montañas* (mountains), is an example of wrong word usage and incorrect matching of gender. The other choices have no relationship to the subjects of the sentence, *el fútbol y el béisbol,* so choice **d** is the only correct one.

2. Comprendo por qué él *establecen* de los gatos.
  a. tiene miedo
  b. entiendo
  c. niegan
  d. establecemos
  e. No es necesario hacer ninguna corrección

The correct choice is **a** because it is the only one that will make a grammatically correct sentence. The other options use incorrect verb forms.

3. Esta *flor* es para mi abuela.
  a. regalos
  b. melón
  c. numero
  d. moscas
  e. No es necesario hacer ninguna corrección.

The right answer is **e** because the sentence is correct. The other choices use the wrong number or gender agreement.

▶ Conclusion

Spanish, like any language, is nothing more than a code or set of symbols that have definite meanings. All you have to do is learn the code in order to open up a whole new world of opportunity.

Learning and speaking Spanish is a rewarding experience. When you can speak Spanish fluently, you are better able to understand the culture and perspective of its native speakers. Improved understanding will make your job as a Border Patrol Agent easier and more rewarding. In fact, such understanding can lead to greater cooperation not only between individuals, but also between nations.

Making use of the tips and methods presented in this chapter, along with diligent study and practice, ensures that you will do well on the Spanish Language portion of the Border Patrol Exam.

▶ Resources

There are many resources for the person who wants to learn, or brush up on, the Spanish language. The traditional methods of using a textbook and conversational practice are today augmented by a range of new methods. The widespread use of the computer has created many new opportunities for learning. It is now possible to learn Spanish online, and interactive compact disks, some of which will even correct your pronunciation, are also available.

What follow are just some of the many widely available resources that will help you to confidently prepare for the Spanish Language portion of the Border Patrol Exam.

Conversation

Most of the following books come with an audio CD that provides essential practice in the sounds and pronunciation of Spanish words and phrases. Check online or at your local bookstore for more information.

Conversational Spanish, 3rd Edition by Juan Kattan-Ibarra (McGraw-Hill: 1997).

Conversational Spanish in Nothing Flat (Language Dynamics: 2002).

Instant Immersion Spanish Audio Deluxe (Topics Entertainment: 2006).

Mastering Spanish: Conversation Basics (Penton Overseas Inc.: 2005).

Spanish Conversation Study Cards (Visual Education Association: 1997).

Spanish (Instant Conversation) (Pimsleur: 2002).

Teach Yourself Spanish Conversation by Juan Kattan-Ibarra and Angela Howkins (Teach Yourself: 2005).

Grammar

The Everything Spanish Grammar Book: All The Rules You Need To Master Español by Julie Gutin (Adams Media Corporation: 2005).

Interactive Spanish Grammar Made Easy by Mike Zollo (McGraw-Hill: 2006).

Mastering Spanish Grammar by Pilar Munoz and Mike Thacker (McGraw-Hill: 2006).

Modern Spanish Grammar: A Practical Guide, 2nd Edition by Juan Kattan-Ibarra and Chris Pountain (Routledge: 2003).

Practice Makes Perfect: Complete Spanish Grammar by Gilda Nissenberg (McGraw-Hill: 2004).

Spanish Grammar and Verb Tables, 3rd Edition (HarperCollins: 2005).

Spanish Grammar the Easy Way by Boris Corredor, Ph.D. (Barron's Educational Series: 2003).

10 ▶ Border Patrol Practice Exam 1

CHAPTER SUMMARY

Here is a sample test based on the Border Patrol Exam. After reviewing the sample questions in Chapters 5 and 6, take this test to see how much your score has improved.

L ike the real Border Patrol Exam, the exam that follows tests your logical reasoning abilities and your Spanish-language ability or aptitude. There are three sections, and you must take two: Logical Reasoning, and **either** Spanish Language **or** Artificial Language. Take the Spanish test if you speak and read Spanish; otherwise, take the Artificial Language test.

For this exam, you should simulate the actual test-taking experience as closely as you can. Find a quiet place to work where you won't be disturbed. Tear out the answer sheet on the next page and find some number 2 pencils to fill in the circles. You will have three hours to complete the Logical Reasoning section and the Spanish Language or the Artificial Language test. Set a timer or stopwatch for practice, but do not worry too much if you go over the allotted time on this practice exam. You can work more on timing when you take the second practice exam in Chapter 11.

After the exam, use the answer key that follows to see how you did, and to find out why the right answers are right and the wrong ones are wrong.

► Section 1: Logical Reasoning

1.	ⓐ ⓑ ⓒ ⓓ ⓔ	11.	ⓐ ⓑ ⓒ ⓓ ⓔ	21.	ⓐ ⓑ ⓒ ⓓ ⓔ
2.	ⓐ ⓑ ⓒ ⓓ ⓔ	12.	ⓐ ⓑ ⓒ ⓓ ⓔ	22.	ⓐ ⓑ ⓒ ⓓ ⓔ
3.	ⓐ ⓑ ⓒ ⓓ ⓔ	13.	ⓐ ⓑ ⓒ ⓓ ⓔ	23.	ⓐ ⓑ ⓒ ⓓ ⓔ
4.	ⓐ ⓑ ⓒ ⓓ ⓔ	14.	ⓐ ⓑ ⓒ ⓓ ⓔ	24.	ⓐ ⓑ ⓒ ⓓ ⓔ
5.	ⓐ ⓑ ⓒ ⓓ ⓔ	15.	ⓐ ⓑ ⓒ ⓓ ⓔ	25.	ⓐ ⓑ ⓒ ⓓ ⓔ
6.	ⓐ ⓑ ⓒ ⓓ ⓔ	16.	ⓐ ⓑ ⓒ ⓓ ⓔ	26.	ⓐ ⓑ ⓒ ⓓ ⓔ
7.	ⓐ ⓑ ⓒ ⓓ ⓔ	17.	ⓐ ⓑ ⓒ ⓓ ⓔ	27.	ⓐ ⓑ ⓒ ⓓ ⓔ
8.	ⓐ ⓑ ⓒ ⓓ ⓔ	18.	ⓐ ⓑ ⓒ ⓓ ⓔ	28.	ⓐ ⓑ ⓒ ⓓ ⓔ
9.	ⓐ ⓑ ⓒ ⓓ ⓔ	19.	ⓐ ⓑ ⓒ ⓓ ⓔ	29.	ⓐ ⓑ ⓒ ⓓ ⓔ
10.	ⓐ ⓑ ⓒ ⓓ ⓔ	20.	ⓐ ⓑ ⓒ ⓓ ⓔ	30.	ⓐ ⓑ ⓒ ⓓ ⓔ

► Section 2: Spanish Language

1.	ⓐ ⓑ ⓒ ⓓ ⓔ	18.	ⓐ ⓑ ⓒ ⓓ ⓔ	35.	ⓐ ⓑ ⓒ ⓓ
2.	ⓐ ⓑ ⓒ ⓓ ⓔ	19.	ⓐ ⓑ ⓒ ⓓ ⓔ	36.	ⓐ ⓑ ⓒ ⓓ
3.	ⓐ ⓑ ⓒ ⓓ ⓔ	20.	ⓐ ⓑ ⓒ ⓓ ⓔ	37.	ⓐ ⓑ ⓒ ⓓ
4.	ⓐ ⓑ ⓒ ⓓ ⓔ	21.	ⓐ ⓑ ⓒ ⓓ ⓔ	38.	ⓐ ⓑ ⓒ ⓓ
5.	ⓐ ⓑ ⓒ ⓓ ⓔ	22.	ⓐ ⓑ ⓒ ⓓ ⓔ	39.	ⓐ ⓑ ⓒ ⓓ
6.	ⓐ ⓑ ⓒ ⓓ ⓔ	23.	ⓐ ⓑ ⓒ ⓓ ⓔ	40.	ⓐ ⓑ ⓒ ⓓ
7.	ⓐ ⓑ ⓒ ⓓ ⓔ	24.	ⓐ ⓑ ⓒ ⓓ ⓔ	41.	ⓐ ⓑ ⓒ ⓓ ⓔ
8.	ⓐ ⓑ ⓒ ⓓ ⓔ	25.	ⓐ ⓑ ⓒ ⓓ ⓔ	42.	ⓐ ⓑ ⓒ ⓓ ⓔ
9.	ⓐ ⓑ ⓒ ⓓ ⓔ	26.	ⓐ ⓑ ⓒ ⓓ ⓔ	43.	ⓐ ⓑ ⓒ ⓓ ⓔ
10.	ⓐ ⓑ ⓒ ⓓ ⓔ	27.	ⓐ ⓑ ⓒ ⓓ ⓔ	44.	ⓐ ⓑ ⓒ ⓓ ⓔ
11.	ⓐ ⓑ ⓒ ⓓ ⓔ	28.	ⓐ ⓑ ⓒ ⓓ ⓔ	45.	ⓐ ⓑ ⓒ ⓓ ⓔ
12.	ⓐ ⓑ ⓒ ⓓ ⓔ	29.	ⓐ ⓑ ⓒ ⓓ ⓔ	46.	ⓐ ⓑ ⓒ ⓓ ⓔ
13.	ⓐ ⓑ ⓒ ⓓ ⓔ	30.	ⓐ ⓑ ⓒ ⓓ ⓔ	47.	ⓐ ⓑ ⓒ ⓓ ⓔ
14.	ⓐ ⓑ ⓒ ⓓ ⓔ	31.	ⓐ ⓑ ⓒ ⓓ ⓔ	48.	ⓐ ⓑ ⓒ ⓓ ⓔ
15.	ⓐ ⓑ ⓒ ⓓ ⓔ	32.	ⓐ ⓑ ⓒ ⓓ ⓔ	49.	ⓐ ⓑ ⓒ ⓓ ⓔ
16.	ⓐ ⓑ ⓒ ⓓ ⓔ	33.	ⓐ ⓑ ⓒ ⓓ	50.	ⓐ ⓑ ⓒ ⓓ ⓔ
17.	ⓐ ⓑ ⓒ ⓓ ⓔ	34.	ⓐ ⓑ ⓒ ⓓ		

► Section 2: Artificial Language

1.	ⓐ ⓑ ⓒ ⓓ ⓔ	18.	ⓐ ⓑ ⓒ ⓓ ⓔ	35.	ⓐ ⓑ ⓒ ⓓ ⓔ
2.	ⓐ ⓑ ⓒ ⓓ ⓔ	19.	ⓐ ⓑ ⓒ ⓓ ⓔ	36.	ⓐ ⓑ ⓒ ⓓ ⓔ
3.	ⓐ ⓑ ⓒ ⓓ ⓔ	20.	ⓐ ⓑ ⓒ ⓓ ⓔ	37.	ⓐ ⓑ ⓒ ⓓ ⓔ
4.	ⓐ ⓑ ⓒ ⓓ ⓔ	21.	ⓐ ⓑ ⓒ ⓓ ⓔ	38.	ⓐ ⓑ ⓒ ⓓ ⓔ
5.	ⓐ ⓑ ⓒ ⓓ ⓔ	22.	ⓐ ⓑ ⓒ ⓓ ⓔ	39.	ⓐ ⓑ ⓒ ⓓ ⓔ
6.	ⓐ ⓑ ⓒ ⓓ ⓔ	23.	ⓐ ⓑ ⓒ ⓓ ⓔ	40.	ⓐ ⓑ ⓒ ⓓ ⓔ
7.	ⓐ ⓑ ⓒ ⓓ ⓔ	24.	ⓐ ⓑ ⓒ ⓓ ⓔ		
8.	ⓐ ⓑ ⓒ ⓓ ⓔ	25.	ⓐ ⓑ ⓒ ⓓ ⓔ		
9.	ⓐ ⓑ ⓒ ⓓ ⓔ	26.	ⓐ ⓑ ⓒ ⓓ ⓔ		
10.	ⓐ ⓑ ⓒ ⓓ ⓔ	27.	ⓐ ⓑ ⓒ ⓓ ⓔ		
11.	ⓐ ⓑ ⓒ ⓓ ⓔ	28.	ⓐ ⓑ ⓒ ⓓ ⓔ		
12.	ⓐ ⓑ ⓒ ⓓ ⓔ	29.	ⓐ ⓑ ⓒ ⓓ ⓔ		
13.	ⓐ ⓑ ⓒ ⓓ ⓔ	30.	ⓐ ⓑ ⓒ ⓓ ⓔ		
14.	ⓐ ⓑ ⓒ ⓓ ⓔ	31.	ⓐ ⓑ ⓒ ⓓ ⓔ		
15.	ⓐ ⓑ ⓒ ⓓ ⓔ	32.	ⓐ ⓑ ⓒ ⓓ ⓔ		
16.	ⓐ ⓑ ⓒ ⓓ ⓔ	33.	ⓐ ⓑ ⓒ ⓓ ⓔ		
17.	ⓐ ⓑ ⓒ ⓓ ⓔ	34.	ⓐ ⓑ ⓒ ⓓ ⓔ		

▶ Section 1: Logical Reasoning

1. Among other requirements, an applicant for citizenship must show that he or she is "attached to the principles of the Constitution of the United States and well-disposed to the good order and happiness of the United States." The courts have defined attachment to the Constitution as a belief in representative democracy, a commitment to the ideals embodied in the Bill of Rights, a belief that political change should be affected only in an orderly way, and general satisfaction with life in the United States. These requirements do NOT, however, preclude a belief that it might be desirable to make a change in our form of government as long as the change is made within constitutional limits.

   From the information given above, it can be validly concluded that

   a. all persons who want the U.S. government to change should be denied citizenship.

   b. only persons who believe that it might be desirable to work toward change in the U.S. government should be granted citizenship.

   c. all persons who work within constitutional limits toward change in the U.S. government should be granted citizenship.

   d. a commitment to the ideals embodied in the Bill of Rights is only one aspect of "attachment to the Constitution."

   e. "attachment to the Constitution" cannot include a belief that it might be desirable to change the form of government of the United States.

2. The United States is a country of immigrants who came to inherit the land neither by divine right nor by open immigration policy. Since the land was taken from indigenous inhabitants, it is wrong for current citizens to exclude future immigrants. On the other hand, some people believe that too much immigration may compromise the standard of living in the United States. As a result, jobs and resources may be taken from persons who are already citizens, so that the very reasons immigrants were historically attracted to the United States—that is, all its advantages and opportunities—may be threatened if the country becomes overcrowded.

   From the information given above, it can be validly concluded that

   a. since current citizens did not inherit this land by divine right, too much immigration may compromise the United States' standard of living.

   b. if too much immigration would compromise the United States' standard of living, then its citizens should want an open immigration policy.

   c. if the citizens of the United States want an open immigration policy, then the United States standard of living would not be compromised.

   d. if the United States does not have an open immigration policy, then the land was taken away from its indigenous inhabitants.

   e. some people believe the very reasons immigrants were historically attracted to the United States will be compromised by an open immigration policy.

3. The Model Penal Code (1969) says that the court shall not sentence a defendant to pay a fine in addition to a sentence of imprisonment or probation unless the defendant has derived a monetary gain from the crime. The only exception is when the court is of the opinion that a fine is specially adapted to deterrence of the crime committed or to the correction of the offender. The court shall not sentence a defendant to pay a fine unless the defendant is or will be able to pay the fine, and the fine will not prevent the defendant from making restitution or reparation to the victim of the crime.

From the information given above, it can be validly concluded that a fine, in addition to imprisonment or probation,

  a. must be imposed if the person convicted has made monetary gain from the crime.
  b. cannot be imposed if the person convicted has made restitution or reparation to the victim.
  c. can be imposed if the court believes it will teach the person not to commit the same crime again.
  d. must be imposed if a person convicted of a crime would be able to pay the fine.
  e. can be imposed only if the court believes it will teach the person not to commit the same crime again.

4. If a state has the final authority to determine citizenship, this can result in some persons having dual nationalities and others being stateless. A child can be born stateless when two situations arise simultaneously—the state in which the child is born only recognizes the child as receiving the nationality of the parents, and the parents' home state only recognizes the nationality of the state where the child is born.

From the information given above, it can be validly concluded that, in the case of a child named Jon, who is born in a state other than his parents' home state, then

  a. the parent's home state recognizes only the nationality of the state where a child is born and then Jon has dual nationality.
  b. Jon is considered to have dual nationality, and the state in which he is born only recognizes a child as receiving the nationality of the parents.
  c. Jon is considered stateless because the state in which he is born and the parents' home state each only recognizes a child as receiving the nationality of the parents.
  d. Jon's parents' home state only recognizes the child as receiving the nationality of the parents, and Jon is considered stateless.
  e. Jon is considered to have dual nationality; the state where he was born recognizes the birthplace of the child and his parents' home state recognizes the nationality of the parents.

5. According to psychiatrists, there are several categories of "personality disorder," among them a subcategory called *antisocial personality disorder*. Most criminals do not have antisocial personality disorder, but people who do are more likely than average to engage in unlawful behavior (although they may be clever enough to stay out of reach of the authorities). People with this disorder have a pervasive pattern of deceitfulness and disregard for the rights of others, reckless disregard for the safety of self or others, and lack of remorse for mistreatment of others. When this type of personality disorder is discussed, the emphasis tends to be on unlawful behavior; however, actually only a small percentage of people in the category engage in illegal behavior. The rest fit into the mainstream, displaying their characteristics in ways that are socially acceptable in jobs and professions where their negative traits can be masked as "shrewdness," "toughness," or "hard-headed realism."

*From the information given, it **CANNOT** be validly concluded that*

a. all persons diagnosed as having antisocial personality disorder fall under a subcategory of personality disorder.

b. some persons who are characterized by tough, hardheaded realism suffer from antisocial personality disorder.

c. antisocial personality disorder is not a characteristic of most criminals.

d. all persons who commit illegal acts suffer from antisocial personality disorder.

e. persons who behave in socially acceptable ways may suffer from antisocial personality disorder.

6. Criminals should be held accountable for their behavior. If holding criminals accountable for their behavior requires harsh sentencing, then so be it. However, no person should be held accountable for behavior in which he or she had no control.

From the information given above, it can be validly concluded that

a. criminals should not be held accountable for the behavior of other people.

b. people have control of their own behavior.

c. people cannot control the behavior of other people.

d. behavior that cannot be controlled should not be punished.

e. criminals have control over their own behavior that may subject them to harsh punishment.

7. Under INA law, any alien who is believed likely to become a public charge is excludable at the time of application. However, in *Matter of Kohama* (1978), it was decided that an immigrating couple who had no means of support other than reliance on their daughter and son-in-law, who were U.S. residents, could not be excluded as likely to become public charges. The daughter and son-in-law gave depositions and submitted affidavits as evidence of their ability and willingness to support the couple. The court held that such evidence was sufficient to overcome the belief that they would become charges of the state.

From the information given above, it can be validly concluded that

a. persons may be permitted to immigrate to the United States if they have relatives in their home country willing to support them.

b. for the court to accept a claim that relatives will support an immigrant to the United States, the relatives must submit evidence supporting their ability to do so.

c. if relatives agree to support a person and can submit evidence supporting their ability to do so, then that person must immigrate to the United States.

d. if a person wishes to immigrate to the United States and has no relative willing and able to financially support him or her, then that person may not immigrate to the United States.

e. if a person immigrates to the United States, he or she has relatives willing and able to support him or her.

8. There is clear evidence that the mandated use of safety seats by children under age four has resulted in fewer child fatalities over the past five years. Compared to the five-year period prior to the passage of laws requiring the use of safety seats, fatalities of children under age four have decreased by 30%.

From the information given above, it can be validly concluded that

a. the number of serious automobile accidents involving children under the age of four has remained steady over the past five years.

b. automobile accidents involving children have decreased sharply over the past five years.

c. the use of air bags in automobiles has increased by 30% during the past five years.

d. most fatal automobile accidents involving children under the age of four occur in driveways of their homes.

e. the number of teenage drivers has increased by 30% over the past five years.

9. Retaliating against others for what is perceived as hurtful acts, a person with paranoid personality disorder may sometimes find himself or herself in trouble with the law. A person with this diagnosis shows a pervasive suspiciousness of other people, and usually without grounds can perceive the motives of others as malevolent. Such a person is usually reluctant to confide in others because of an unfounded fear that the information will be used maliciously. Such a person may bear a persistent grudge against another for an imagined wrong. To fall into this category, the distrustful and suspicious behavior must not occur exclusively during an episode of schizophrenia or other psychotic disorder and must not be due to the direct physiological effects of a general medical condition.

From the information given, it can be validly concluded that

a. all persons who suffer from paranoid personality disorder are mistrustful of others.

b. some persons with paranoid personality disorder only exhibit symptoms of that disorder when in an episode of schizophrenia.

c. no person diagnosed with paranoid personality disorder can ever become schizophrenic.

d. all persons with paranoid personality disorder will at some point find themselves in trouble with the law.

e. all persons who are reluctant to confide in others suffer from paranoid personality disorder.

10. The reasonable suspicion standard has never been clearly defined. Reasonable suspicion is a lesser level of proof than probable cause, a less stringent analysis, yet it is far more than just a hunch or a gut feeling. Allowing police officers to stop motorists based solely on hunches does not fulfill the reasonable suspicion standard and is an unfounded invasion of an individual's liberty. To permit police officers to make traffic stops based simply on their hunches would "leave law abiding citizens at the mercy of the officers' whim or caprice." So while reasonable suspicion generally requires less than probable cause to make a stop, it is not so lenient as to permit any stops. It is based on an officer's observations, and the reasonable inference that can be drawn, based on the training and experience that lead the officer to believe the suspect is acting on unlawful design. An officer making a stop must be able to "point to specific articulable facts which taken together with rational inferences from those facts reasonably warrant the intrusion." The U.S. Supreme Court has invalidated totally random stops of automobiles. Nor do the courts permit officers to rely on a "hunch" that is based on perfectly noncriminal circumstances or characteristics. This practice is exactly what courts should prohibit. However, police officers may stop a motor vehicle when circumstances are beyond the ordinary, even if they are not criminally suspicious. An officer must be able to point to specific, identifiable, objective facts that lead him or her to believe that a person is of unlawful design. Whether specific facts exist to justify the particular traffic stop must be determined from the totality of the circumstances that led the officer to stop the vehicle.

From the information given, it can be validly concluded that reasonable suspicion

a. allows police officers to make random stops on motorists.
b. requires a far more stringent standard than does probable cause.
c. is comparable to a hunch or a gut feeling.
d. exists when an officer is able to point to specific, identifiable, objective facts.
e. is a skill developed by officers over time.

11. The legal authority of a Border Patrol Agent is derived from congressional legislation; this is called *statutory authority*. However, Congress does not have the final word regarding the interpretation and application of legislation, as this power is reserved for the judicial branch of government. Following the codification of statutory authority, written guidance regarding the codified statutory authority is created by federal agencies and published and updated annually in the Federal Register; this is known as the *Code of Federal Regulations*. However, Border Patrol Agents are ultimately required to operate in accordance with agency regulations or directives that are more restrictive than a plain reading of statutory law. Agency regulations and directives are promulgated by an agency to provide field level guidance to agents

to use when exercising their statutory authority. These regulations comply with the requirements of both statutory legislation and the Code of Federal Regulations. Additionally, the American judicial system is constantly rendering decisions that affect the interpretation and application of legislation enacted by Congress. Border Patrol Agents routinely receive legal updates regarding judicial decisions that ultimately decide how agents exercise their statutory authority in the field.

From the information given, it can be validly concluded that

a. the legal authority of a Border Patrol Agent is derived from agency directives.
b. the legal authority of an agency to publish written guidance in the Federal Register is derived from statutory authority.
c. the courts interpret and apply the Code of Federal Regulations in legal matters.
d. statutory authority is interpreted through field level agency regulations and directives.
e. the judicial system ultimately interprets and applies congressional legislation, and these decisions affect the method and means by which Border Patrol Agents exercise their statutory authority.

12. The Model Code (EC 5-18) states:

A LAWYER EMPLOYED OR RETAINED BY A CORPORA-
TION OR SIMILAR ENTITY OWES HIS ALLEGIANCE TO
THE ENTITY AND NOT TO THE STOCKHOLDER,
DIRECTOR, OFFICER, EMPLOYEE, REPRESENTATIVE,
OR OTHER PERSON CONNECTED TO THE ENTITY. THE
LAWYER SHOULD NOT BE INFLUENCED BY THE PER-
SONAL DESIRES OF ANY PERSON OR ORGANIZATION.
IF A LAWYER FOR AN ENTITY IS REQUESTED BY A
STOCKHOLDER, DIRECTOR, OFFICER, EMPLOYEE,
REPRESENTATIVE, OR OTHER PERSON CONNECTED
TO THE ENTITY TO REPRESENT HIM/HER IN AN INDI-
VIDUAL CAPACITY, THE LAWYER MAY SERVE THE
INDIVIDUAL ONLY IF THE LAWYER IS CONVINCED
THAT DIFFERING INTERESTS ARE NOT PRESENT.

*From the information given above, it can be
validly concluded that*
a. no lawyer convinced that differing interests
   are present may represent a stockholder,
   director, officer, employee, representative, or
   other person connected to an entity that he
   or she represents.
b. if a lawyer feels allegiance to a corporation
   or similar entity, that lawyer has been
   employed or retained by that entity.
c. no stockholder, director, officer, employee,
   representative, or other person connected to
   an entity may require that a lawyer
   employed or retained by that entity represent him or her individually.
d. no lawyer who represents a stockholder,
   director, officer, employee, representative, or
   other person connected to an entity may
   represent that entity.
e. any lawyer who represents a stockholder,
   director, officer, employee, representative, or
   other person connected to an entity may
   represent that entity.

13. Contracts by and of parties are formed by
intentions. However, mere intentions alone are
insufficient. Parties to a contract must objec-
tively manifest their intentions in a contract,
written or verbal, to enter into an agreement.
Intentions concealed by any party to a contract
do not form a contract.

*From the information given above, it can be
validly concluded that*
a. concealed intentions may form a contract.
b. all intentions by any party to a contract
   must be written into a contract.
c. verbal agreements do not constitute a
   contract.
d. contracts must be formed by more than two
   parties.
e. disclosed intentions form the basis of a
   contract.

14. Under INA law, unless an applicant for citizenship is physically unable to do so through
blindness or deafness, an applicant for naturalization must be able to speak, understand, read,
and write simple English. Before 1978, the act
provided an exemption to the literacy requirement for persons who, on the effective date of
this chapter (1952), were over 50 years of age
and had been residing in the United States for
periods totaling at least 20 years. In 1978, Congress amended the provision to exempt any
person who was over the age of 50 at the time
of filing a petition and who had been lawfully
admitted for permanent residence for periods
totaling 20 years.

*From the information given above, it can be
validly concluded that,* on the effective date in
1952, all people over 50 years of age

a. became exempt from the literacy requirement unless they had lived in the United States for 20 years.

b. could become exempt from the literacy requirement if they had lived in the United States for 20 years.

c. had to meet the literacy requirements if they had lived in the United States for 20 years.

d. met the literacy requirements if they had lived in the United States for 20 years.

e. who had been in the United States at least 20 years, met the literacy requirements.

15. Any time the Senate and House of Representatives vote together on an order, resolution, or another issue besides a bill, that vote must be approved by the president before it becomes effective. If the president rejects the vote of Congress, the vote will still be effective if $\frac{2}{3}$ of both houses agree to override the president's veto (similar to the rules governing bills).

From the information given above, it CAN-NOT be validly concluded that

a. the Senate and House vote on orders and resolutions.

b. the president must approve any vote on an order or resolution voted on by the Senate and House.

c. although a president may veto a bill, he or she can never veto a resolution.

d. if the president vetoes a congressional order, a majority vote by both houses of Congress will override the veto.

e. the president may reject a vote of Congress.

16. There are limited exceptions to the requirement that law enforcement officers first obtain a search warrant prior to conducting a search of a person. One of the most common exceptions involves a search of a person incidental to arrest. In this exception, a warrantless search of the person being arrested, incidental to a lawful arrest, provides that a search may be conducted for weapons or evidence of the crime even if no probable cause for the search itself exists. This exception is primarily for officer safety and is tightly regulated by agency regulations. However, this exception does not apply to searches that would require intrusion into a person's body (e.g., body cavity search). It is important to note that evidence obtained in a body search that arose from an unlawful arrest is normally not admissible, regardless of its significance.

From the information given above, it can be validly concluded that

a. body searches also involve searches of body cavities.

b. probable cause, normally derived from a lawful arrest, is required to conduct a body search incidental to arrest.

c. an arrest must be lawful to conduct a search of a person.

d. a citizens arrest justifies a search of the person being arrested.

e. exceptions to constitutional protections are warranted when officer safety is involved.

17. Police Sergeant O'Malley reports that all police precincts in the city of Garrison have drug-seeking dogs, and that some police precincts in the same city have search-and-rescue dogs. Sergeant O'Malley professes to know all about dogs. Search-and-rescue dogs, he says, are better at tracking, but are disobedient, whereas drug-sniffing dogs are obedient. All the precincts, Sergeant O'Malley maintains, have discontinued the use of attack dogs, because they are too dangerous.

*From the information given, it **CANNOT** be validly concluded that,* according to Sergeant O'Malley,
a. all police precincts have disobedient dogs.
b. some police precincts have disobedient dogs.
c. all police precincts have obedient dogs.
d. no police precincts have attack dogs.
e. no police precincts have dangerous dogs.

18. When a verdict is appealed to a higher court, on the basis of an error that was made by a judge during trial in a lower court, the appellate court must decide if the error was a "harmless error" that would not have made a difference to the outcome, or whether the error might have made a difference to the outcome. In criminal cases where constitutional issues are involved, the error must be proved harmless beyond a reasonable doubt. For example, if, in a criminal case, the prosecutor comments on the defendant's failure to take the stand, the comment violates the defendant's Fifth and Fourteenth Amendment rights, and so a new trial would be granted.

From the information given above, it can be validly concluded that a new trial will likely be ordered in cases

a. where an error is held to be harmless beyond a reasonable doubt.
b. where an error is not held to be harmless beyond a reasonable doubt.
c. that involve constitutional issues that are harmless beyond a reasonable doubt.
d. that do not involve constitutional issues that are not harmless beyond a reasonable doubt.
e. where constitutional issues are not involved.

19. Defense against biological terrorism is a priority of law enforcement officials. There are two types of assault that terrorists might make—ejecting disease-causing bacteria and ejecting viruses. Bacteria are one-celled organisms, able to reproduce and metabolize completely on their own. They can be harmful parasites, infiltrating an animal (called the host) and can cause injury or death. Many bacteria, however, even parasitic ones, are actually beneficial to the host. On the other hand, viruses are, in some ways, more terrifying than bacteria. First of all, there is a debate over whether they can even truly be called "live," since they are able to reproduce and metabolize only within the living cell of a host. Viruses are parasites too small to be filtered out, and are always harmful, using the host cell to replicate themselves and thereby destroying that cell. Antibiotics do not work against them.

*From the information given above, it **CANNOT** be validly concluded that*
a. no bacteria are unable to metabolize on their own.
b. no viruses are susceptible to antibiotics.
c. some bacteria are beneficial parasites.
d. all viruses are harmful parasites.
e. harmful parasites are always viruses.

20. On the witness stand, Harry (who was known to always tell the truth) said, "Charlie and me both had guns, but it was Charlie that knocked down that family of four when he ran past." When Charlie (who was known to sometimes lie and had twice committed perjury in other trials) took the witness stand, he said, "I didn't have a gun; that's a lie. Harry's the one that had the gun, but yes, your Honor, it was me that knocked down that family of four. They got in my way, so it wasn't my fault."

From the information given, it can be validly concluded that
a. only Charlie had a gun.
b. only Harry had a gun.
c. it was Harry who knocked over the family of four.
d. maybe the family of four did not get in Charlie's way.
e. neither Charlie nor Harry had guns.

21. A certain police department is planning to give an Outstanding Service award to the officer who made the most drug busts in a single year. Officer Grimsley made fewer drug busts than Officer Abdalla but more drug busts than Officer Paradis. Officer Sanchez has made more than Officer Grimsley, but fewer than Officer Abdalla. Officer Abdalla, a maverick, has announced he will not accept the award, because he does not believe awards should be given to people simply for doing their jobs. Who will receive the award?
a. Officer Sanchez
b. Officer Abdalla
c. Officer Grimsley
d. Officer Paradis
e. There will be a tie.

22. The officers in a certain big-city police department unofficially rank the different divisions of the department as "more important" and "less important." They rank Labor Relations as less important than Narcotics, but more important than Public Affairs. Administrative Vice is more important than Public Affairs but less important than Organized Crime. Narcotics is less important than Organized Crime, and less important than Administrative Vice.

From the information given above, it can be validly concluded that, based on this unofficial ranking, the division that is second most important is
a. Narcotics.
b. Administrative Vice.
c. Public Affairs.
d. Labor Relations.
e. Organized Crime.

23. The length of prison terms and the standards for and duration of parole are set by law. Prisoners who have not been given life sentences are subject to three years on parole (if parole is granted); however, they can be discharged after one year if they commit no parole violations. Prisoners who have been given life sentences (except for those who are sentenced to life without the possibility of parole and receive no hearing) are subject to five years on parole (if parole is granted); however, they can be discharged after three years if they commit no parole violations. A parole hearing is mandatory, even for those given life imprisonment, but the granting of parole is far from automatic. A careful review must be done by the Board of Prison Terms, and a high percentage of this population is not granted parole.

From the information given above, it can be validly concluded that, with the exception of persons sentenced to life without the possibility of parole,

a. at some point, even for lifers, parole is mandatory.
b. non-lifers can be released from parole after one year.
c. the sentence a person will receive is the sentence he or she will serve.
d. all lifers receive a mandatory parole hearing after three years.
e. a large percentage of lifers never receive a parole hearing.

24. Five officers are chasing a burglary suspect on foot down a busy street. Officer Corona is directly behind the burglar. Officers Jabar and Bertonelli are side by side behind Officer Corona. Zelig is behind Jabar and Bertonelli. Officer Yong is side by side with Zelig. Corona grabs the suspect by the jacket, but the jacket tears, and Corona trips and falls. Zelig trips over Corona but recovers and darts ahead past Jabar and Bertonelli. One of the officers is now able to grab the suspect and pull him to the ground. Which officer is most likely the one who makes the capture?

a. Officer Bertonelli
b. Officer Zelig
c. Officer Jabar
d. Officer Corona
e. Officer Yong

25. Five police officers want a promotion, but promotion is based strictly on seniority. Officer Robbins has been with the department two months longer than Officer Gimcrack, who has been with the department three months less than Officer Nardil. Officer Kachaski has been with the department one month longer than Officer Gimcrack. Officer Xavier has been with the department one month longer than Officer Kachaski. Who will get the promotion?

a. Officer Xavier
b. Officer Kachaski
c. Officer Nardil
d. Officer Gimcrack
e. Officer Robbins

26. All the prisoners in Cell Block D have killed someone. Some of the prisoners have committed manslaughter. All those convicted of manslaughter will be eligible for parole at some future date. Some prisoners who have committed second-degree murder will be eligible for parole at some future date.

From the information given above, it can be validly concluded that, of the prisoners in Cell Block D,

a. all will be eligible for parole.

b. all who have committed second-degree murder will be ineligible for parole.

c. none who has been convicted of manslaughter will be ineligible for parole.

d. all who have committed second-degree murder will be eligible for parole.

e. none who is eligible for parole has committed manslaughter.

27. Under immigration law, one way a child under age 16 can receive a visa and be adopted is if that child is an orphan. A child is considered an orphan if both parents have died, disappeared, or abandoned the child, or if the sole or surviving parent is incapable of providing the child with proper care, and if that parent has irrevocably released the child for emigration and adoption. The orphan must be adopted by, or be traveling to the United States to be adopted by, a U.S. citizen and spouse jointly, or by an unmarried U.S. citizen at least 25 years of age.

    From the information given above, it can be validly concluded that a child named Mary would be considered an orphan only if

    a. her parents are unable to care for her but will not relinquish her for emigration or adoption.

    b. her parents are alive but have disappeared or abandoned her.

    c. she is adopted by spouses jointly.

    d. she is adopted by an unmarried single person over 25.

    e. she is under age 16 and her parents are dead.

28. Attorney-client privilege holds that a client has the right not to disclose (and to prevent his or her lawyer from disclosing) any confidential communication between them that relates to their professional relationship. Some people say that the attorney-client privilege is

one way in which important evidence is suppressed. Furthermore, if the client were innocent, disclosure would not hurt the client, and if the client is guilty, that fact should be brought out. A counterargument says that, if there were no privilege, clients simply would not consult attorneys. Furthermore, if attorneys were required to take the stand to give damaging evidence against the client, there would be no one to represent the client during cross-examination, and the client could not receive the fair trial guaranteed by the Constitution.

    From the information given above, it can be validly concluded that one argument against privileged communication is that, if there were no privilege,

    a. disclosure could not hurt the client.

    b. no evidence against the client could be suppressed.

    c. the client could receive a more fair trial.

    d. disclosure could not hurt an innocent client.

    e. no evidence could be used against the client.

29. I have never been arrested, but all of the people who live with me have been. Some of the people who live with me work nights. All of the people who live with me pay their rent on time. No murderers live with me.

    From the information given above, it can be validly concluded that

    a. all the people who work nights have been arrested.

    b. some of the people who work nights have never been arrested.

    c. none of the people who has been arrested works nights.

    d. none of the people who pays rent on time works nights.

    e. all murderers who live with me work nights.

30. Some people regularly experience what psychiatrists call *depersonalization disorder*—that is, periods of detachment from one's self. The commission of crimes while in this state is rare. More often, persons who claim to have had an episode of depersonalization while committing a crime are being deceitful. The sense of depersonalization is not considered a disorder if it occurs during a schizophrenic episode, during a time of great stress, or if it is part of a meditative trance practiced in the person's culture or religion.

From the information given above, it can be validly concluded that

a. no crimes are committed by persons with depersonalization disorder.

b. some religious trance states are instances of depersonalization disorder.

c. some persons with depersonalization disorder can commit crimes while in a depersonalized state.

d. some instances of schizophrenia are also instances of depersonalization disorder.

e. all persons with depersonalization disorder are deceitful.

▶ Section 2

If you are taking the Artificial Language Test, turn to page 111.

Spanish Language (Part A)

Find the suggested answer, of the five choices, that is closest in meaning to the key (italicized) word.

1. Es muy *sensillo* conducer un coche.
   a. fácil
   b. difícil
   c. divertido
   d. compilado
   e. comparado

2. Es muy difícil *oír* lo que el agente esta diciendo.
   a. responder
   b. comprobar
   c. entender
   d. pretender
   e. desentender

3. Estas bajo *detención*.
   a. encontrar
   b. concentrar
   c. aclarar
   d. custodia
   e. aplastar

4. Examinaremos la evidencia *antes* de corte.
   a. después de
   b. anteriormente
   c. estipendios
   d. cortesias
   e. ofrendas

5. Mi casa está *al lado de* la iglesia.
   a. a caudillo por
   b. lejos de
   c. por aqui
   d. menos de
   e. cerca de

6. ¡Por favor, *siéntense* en el sofá!
   a. piensen
   b. sitúense
   c. váyanse
   d. echen
   e. quítense

7. Sólo está abierta *por la mañana*.
   a. hasta mediodía
   b. dentro de tarde
   c. por la madera
   d. hasta la noche
   e. hoy día

8. Ella está *enferma*.
   a. mentirosa
   b. infeliz
   c. temblorosa
   d. mala
   e. enfadosa

9. *Buscamos* una secretaria que hable inglés.
   a. Necesitamos
   b. Pegamos
   c. Pagamos
   d. Presentamos
   e. Escuchamos

10. ¿Y tu *alcoba* dónde está?
   a. guayaba
   b. cuchillo
   c. jardín
   d. dormitorio
   e. cuchara

11. Yo soy de Nuevo México, y mi amigo es de Colorado; somos *norteamericanos*.
   a. japonés
   b. noruegos
   c. de españa
   d. espaldas
   e. yanquis

12. *Quiero* presentar a mi hermano.
   a. Deseo
   b. Odio
   c. Quedo
   d. Amo
   e. Necesito

13. En la bandera de México hay un emblema interesante: un *águila* sobre un nopal devorando una serpiente.
   a. gato
   b. zozobra
   c. zorro
   d. tortuga
   e. pájaro

14. La Cruz Roja pidió *donaciones* para las víctimas del terremoto.
   a. piedras
   b. contribuciones
   c. nieves
   d. contrabandos
   e. domicilios

15. En México, el padre Hidalgo, como Jorge Washington en los Estados Unidos, es llamado el "Padre *de la Patria*."
   a. del Patológico
   b. de la Armada
   c. del País
   d. del Pato
   e. del Pavo

16. Hemos trabajado *bastante* hoy.
   a. ilegítimo
   b. harto
   c. batalla
   d. bizcocho
   e. vendaje

17. ¡*Vámonos* ahorita!
   a. Gritemos
   b. Descansemos
   c. Traduzcamos
   d. Salguemos
   e. Vistámonos

18. Ellos se encontraron diez años *después* en la playa.
   a. antes
   b. frecuente
   c. más tarde
   d. despacio
   e. brevemente

19. El jai alai, un juego de pelota de origen español, *se parece* a nuestro juego de handball.
   a. es diferente
   b. es similar
   c. se aburre
   d. se habla
   e. espera

20. Si *la gente* tiene miedo todos los días, el gobierno no está bién.
   a. el pueblo
   b. la ciudad
   c. el gerente
   d. el conejo
   e. el general

Spanish Language (Part B-I)

Supply the correct words that should be used in place of the blanks within a sentence.

21. Me entrar _____ el edificio _____ través de la oficina.
   a. a, sobre
   b. en, desde
   c. con, bajo
   d. en, al lado
   e. en, a

22. La viuda me _____ que ella _____ los documentos apropiados.
   a. dijo, entregara
   b. dice, entregue
   c. dirá, entrar
   d. traido, entregue
   e. habra traido, entrar

23. Los officiales _____ usan la sala de reunions para discutir asuntos _____.
   a. sumariamente, difícil
   b. frecuentemente, variadas
   c. normalmente, diversos
   d. rara vez, personal
   e. ocasionalmente, unilateral

24. _____ a los detendios y _____ al tanto de los resultados.
   a. visita, ponlos
   b. visite, ponerlos
   c. visitare, ponga
   d. habre visitado, pondre
   e. visitando, habia puesto

25. Los agentes _____ con cada _____ en el avión.
   a. volando, droga
   b. llegan, espeja
   c. hablaban, persona
   d. harto, especialista
   e. habían, choque

26. _____ piden permiso para _____ una llamada por teléfono.
   a. Ella, hagan
   b. Yo, haga
   c. Nuestro, hacer
   d. Nosotros, hablando
   e. Ellos, hacer

27. Este _____ no _____ entrar legalmente.
   a. niña, podía
   b. muchacho, quiso
   c. niña, quiso
   d. joven, pudieron
   e. muchacha, pudieron

28. ¿Quién _____ ha recibido los paquetes _____ Colombia?
   a. aquí, de
   b. aquel, por
   c. aquella, por
   d. ustedes, de
   e. usted, hasta

29. Yo _____ un hermano menor y _____ hermana menor también.
   a. traigo, mucha
   b. tuvo, una
   c. tengo, una
   d. tenemos, mucha
   e. perdiden, una

30. ¿Van _____ a la iglesia el domingo _____ nosotros?
   a. Ud., el
   b. somos, de
   c. tú, para
   d. tú, de
   e. Uds., con

Spanish Language (Part B-II)

Of the four choices given for each of the following questions, select the only one that is correct.

31. **a.** Los oficiales entran en la casa el frente y el sospechoso.
   b. Los oficiales convenidos entrarían en la casa del sospechoso delantero.
   c. Que los oficiales convinieron que entrarían en la casa del frente y que rodearían a sospechoso.
   d. Los sospechosos acordaron incorporar el frente de la casa y rodearlo.

32. **a.** El contrabando de extranjeros ilegales plantea un gran riesgo a nuestro país.
   b. Contrabando del riesgo a nuestro país.
   c. Nuestro país es a los contrabandistas y al país.
   d. Los contrabandistas del extranjero ilegal podrían ser un riesgo al país.

33. **a.** El juez conviene con veredicto.
   b. El juez no convino con el veredicto del jurado hasta más adelante.
   c. El veredicto del juez convino con más adelante.
   d. El veredicto del jurado no convino con el juez.

34. **a.** El tratado fue firmado por muchos países que rechazaron firmar el país que el tratado fue firmado en ese entonces.
   b. Muchos países firmaron el tratado en efecto a la hora del tratado.
   c. Aunque muchos países firmaron el tratado en efecto hasta tiempo todos los países firmaron.
   d. Aunque muchos países firmaron el tratado, el tratado no es en efecto hasta tal hora que todos los países han firmado el tratado.

35. **a.** Déjales somos esperiendo.
   b. Dígales que esperen.
   c. No me dicho él.
   d. No tú hablo hoy.

36. **a.** Ud. tengo la responsibilidad.
   b. Ahora es la tiempo.
   c. El no quiero esa papel.
   d. Es una lástima que ella no goce de la vida.

37. **a.** Le terminó tú para la mañana.
   b. El terminaré todo sus trabajo.
   c. Me avisó que llegaría tarde.
   d. Nunca estaría en la pasado otra vez.

38. **a.** ¡Monos arriba!
   b. ¡Firme Ud. la tarjeta!
   c. ¿Que passa?
   d. ¿A dónde hora es?

39. **a.** Tú no está la acordar con Ud.
   b. No estoy de acuerdo con Ud.
   c. No ha está en acuerdo contigo.
   d. Tenemos que acuerdo con Ud.

40. a. Todos piensan la mismo cosas.
    b. Una gran jefe fue el director del empresa.
    c. Lástima que ella no vine temprano.
    d. Un gran caudillo de la independencia sudameri-
    cana fue el general argentino José de San Martín.

Spanish Language (Part B-III)

Read each sentence carefully, and supply the word that will correctly replace the italicized word. If the italicized word is correct, select choice **e**.

41. No es *fácil* aprobar el examen de la academia.
    a. entendido
    b. difícil
    c. divertido
    d. complicado
    e. No es necesario hacer ninguna corrección.

42. El agente no *entendía* lo que dijo el extranjero ilegal.
    a. responder
    b. comprendió
    c. vio
    d. sentía
    e. No es necesario hacer ninguna corrección.

43. Debemos *informar* al sospechoso las sus dere-chas cuando lo arrestan.
    a. encontrar
    b. concentrar
    c. decir
    d. empeorar
    e. No es necesario hacer ninguna corrección.

44. Los Estados Unidos *proporcionan* la ayuda exte-rior a los países en desarrollo.
    a. dan
    b. cuentas
    c. ventas
    d. perdido
    e. No es necesario hacer ninguna corrección.

45. Los ingleses tienen *la cálido* de beber mucho té.
    a. la cuenta
    b. el cuento
    c. la cuesta
    d. la costumbre
    e. No es necesario hacer ninguna corrección.

46. La comida mexicana es más *carne* que la americana.
    a. máiz
    b. queso
    c. picante
    d. asado
    e. No es necesario hacer ninguna corrección.

47. En esta tienda todo *está* barato.
    a. este
    b. sed
    c. soccoro
    d. es
    e. No es necesario hacer ninguna corrección.

48. Mi abuelita *era* ochenta y cinco años cuando murió.
    a. tenía
    b. ten
    c. tuve
    d. salía
    e. No es necesario hacer ninguna corrección.

49. ¿Dónde *fuiste* ayer cuando te llamé a las cuatro de la tarde?
    a. son
    b. estabas
    c. tendrían
    d. salimos
    e. No es necesario hacer ninguna corrección.

50. El fútbol y el béisbol son dos ejemplos de *muñecas*.
    a. alfombras
    b. deportes
    c. escuelas
    d. maderas
    e. No es necesario hacer ninguna corrección.

▶ Supplemental Booklet

In order to answer the Artificial Language questions, refer to the sections in this Supplemental Booklet: *Vocabulary Lists* and *Grammatical Rules*. (See Chapter 8 of this book for additional information.)

The words given in the following Vocabulary Lists are not exactly the same as those that will be given in the actual Border Patrol exam (some are and some are not). Therefore, it is best not to try to memorize them before taking the actual test. The Grammatical Rules are the same as those used in the actual test, except that some of the suffixes (word endings) used in the real test differ from those used in the manual and in this supplemental booklet. You may also need to refer to the Glossary of Grammatical Terms as you take the practice exams. The manual will be given to you at the time of the real test, as well.

▶ Vocabulary Lists for the Artificial Language

ARRANGED ALPHABETICALLY BY THE ENGLISH WORD			
English	**Artificial Language**	**English**	**Artificial Language**
a, an	bex*	skillful	autile
alien	huslek	that	velle
and	cre	the	ric**
boy	ekaplek	this	volle
country	failek	to be	synbar
difficult	brale	to border	regbar
enemy	avelek	to cross	chonbar
friend	kometlek	to drive	arbar
from	mor	to escape	pirbar
government	almanlek	to guard	bonbar
he, him	yev	to have	tulbar
jeep	cublek	to identify	kalenbar
legal	colle	to injure	liabar
loyal	inle	to inspect	zelbar
man	kaplek	to shoot	degbar
of	quea	to spy	tatbar
paper	trenedlek	to station	lexbar
river	browlek	to work	frigbar

* *Applies to all genders*
** *Applies to all genders and numbers*

ARRANGED ALPHABETICALLY BY THE ARTIFICIAL LANGUAGE WORD			
Artificial Language	**English**	**Artificial Language**	**English**
almanlek	government	kalenbar	to identify
arbar	to drive	kaplek	man
autile	skillful	kometlek	friend
avelek	enemy	lexbar	to station
bex	a, an*	liabar	to injure
bonbar	to guard	mor	from
brale	difficult	pirbar	to escape
browlek	river	quea	of
chonbar	to cross	regbar	to border
colle	legal	ric	the**
cre	and	synbar	to be
cublek	jeep	tatbar	to spy
degbar	to shoot	trenedlek	paper
ekaplek	boy	tulbar	to have
failek	country	velle	that
frigbar	to work	volle	this
huslek	alien	yev	he, him
inle	loyal	zelbar	to inspect

  * *Applies to all genders*
** *Applies to all genders and numbers*

▶ Grammatical Rules for the Artificial Language

The grammatical rules given here are the same as those used in the Border Patrol Exam, with the only exception being that some of the suffixes (word endings) and prefixes (word beginnings) used in the exam differ from those used here.

During the exam, you will have access to the rules at all times. Consequently, it is important that you under-stand these rules, but it is not necessary that you memorize them. In fact, memorizing them will hinder rather than help you, since the endings of words are different in the version of the Artificial Language that appears in this manual than the one that appears in the actual test.

You should note that Part Three of the Artificial Language Manual contains a glossary of grammatical terms to assist you if you are not thoroughly familiar with the meanings of these grammatical terms.

Rule 1

To form the feminine singular of a noun, a pronoun, or an adjective, add the suffix *-zof* to the masculine singular form of the noun. In the Artificial Language, there are only masculine and feminine forms for these words. There are no neuter forms.

> Example: If a male eagle is a *verlek*, a female eagle is a *verlekzof*. If an ambitious man is a *tosle* man, an ambitious woman is a *toslezof* woman.

Rule 2

To form the plural of nouns, pronouns, and adjectives, add the suffix *-ax* to the correct singular form.

> Example: If one male eagle is a *verlek*, several male eagles are *verlekax*. If an ambitious woman is a *toslezof* woman, several ambitious women are *toslezofax* women.

Rule 3

Adjectives modifying nouns and pronouns with feminine and/or plural endings must have endings that agree with the words they modify.

> Example: If an active male eagle is a *sojle verlek*, several active male eagles are *sojleax verlekax*. If an active female eagle is *sojlezof verlekzof*, several active female eagles are *sojlezofax verlekzofax*.

Rule 4

The stem of the verb is obtained by omitting the suffix *-bar* from the infinitive form of the verb.

> Example: The stem of the verb *tirbar* is *tir*.

Rule 5

All subjects and their verbs must agree in number; that is, singular subjects require singular verbs and plural subjects require plural verbs. (See Rules 6 and 7).

Rule 6

To form the present tense of a verb, add the suffix *-ot* to the stem for the singular form or the suffix *-et* to the stem for the plural.

> Example: If to bark is *nalbar*, then *nalot* is the present singular (the dog barks) and *nalet* is the present tense for the plural (the dogs bark).

Rule 7

To form the past tense of a verb, first add the suffix *-rem* to the stem, and then add the suffix *-ot* if the verb is singular or the suffix *-et* if the verb is plural.

> Example: If to bark is *nalbar*, then *nalremot* is the past tense for the singular (the dog barked), and *nalremet* is the past tense for the plural (the dogs barked).

Rule 8

To form a noun from a verb, add the suffix *-lek* to the stem of the verb.

> Example: If *longbar* is to write, then a writer is a *longlek*.

Rule 9

To form an adjective from a noun, substitute the suffix *-le* for the suffix *-lek*.

> Example: If *pellek* is *beauty*, then a beautiful male eagle is a *pelle verlek*, and a beautiful female eagle is a *pellezof verlekzof*. (Note the feminine ending *-zof*).

Rule 10

To form an adverb from an adjective, add the suffix *-de* to the masculine form of the adjective. (Note that adverbs do not change their form to agree in number or gender with the word they modify.)

> Example: If *pelle* is beautiful, then beautifully is *pellede.*

Rule 11

To form the possessive of a noun or pronoun, add the suffix *-oe* to the noun or pronoun.

> Example: If a *boglek* is a dog, then a dog's collar is a *boglekoe* collar. If he is *yev*, then his book is *yevoe* book.

Rule 12

To make a word negative, add the prefix *poh-* to the correct affirmative form.

> *Example:* An inactive male eagle is a *pohsojle verlek.* If the dog barks is *boglek nalot,* then the dog does not bark is *boglek pohnalot.*

▶ Section 2: Artificial Language

Use the Supplemental Booklet on pages 111–114 to help you answer these questions. You may refer to the vocabulary and grammatical rules throughout this test section.

For questions 1 through 20, make a check mark beside each numbered word that is correctly translated into the Artificial Language. When you have finished this process, fill out your answer sheet by marking:

a. if only the word numbered 1 is checked as correctly translated.

b. if only the word numbered 2 is checked as correctly translated.

c. if only the word numbered 3 is checked as correctly translated.

d. if two or more of the numbered words are checked as correctly translated.

e. if none of the words is checked as correctly translated.

Be sure to check only the **numbered** words that are **correctly** translated. Study the sample question below before going on to the test questions.

Sample Sentence

This woman crossed the river.

Sample Translation

Bex kaplekzof chonremet ric browlek.
1   2   3

The word numbered 1, *bex*, is incorrect because the translation of *bex* is *a*. The word *volle* should have been used. The word numbered 2 is correct and should be checked. *Kaplekzof* has been correctly formed by adding the feminine ending to the masculine noun, applying Rule 1. The word numbered 3, *chonremet*, is incorrect because the singular form, *chonremot*, should have been used. Since the word numbered 2 has been checked, the answer to the sample question is **b**.

Now go on with questions 1 through 20 and answer them in the manner indicated. Be sure to record your answers on the separate answer sheet found at the beginning of the test.

Sentence

1. He identifies the driver.

2. She is an alien.

3. The guard is a friend.

4. The women drove the jeep.

5. That government is legal.

Translation

1. Volle kalenim wir arlek.
    1   2   3

2. Wir bonlek synem bex kometlek.
    1   2   3

3. Wir bonlek synem bex kometlek.
    1   2   3

4. Wir kapleknef arzotem wir daqlek.
        1   2   3

5. Velle almanlek synzotim colleki.
    1   2   3

Sentence	Translation

Sentence

6. The men and women escaped.

7. The alien's friend injured him.

8. This boy is from that country.

9. Those were difficult inspections.

10. Spies are disloyal.

11. She was a skillful inspector.

12. Those aliens are not enemies of the government.

13. Guards have to identify illegal workers.

14. The government identified these girls.

15. She crossed the river to work illegally.

16. The boys' escape was difficult.

17. The identified shooter worked illegally.

18. Those guards have loyal friends from the country.

19. The inspectors injured her.

20. Illegal papers are difficult to identify.

Translation

6. Wir kaplek loa wir kapleknef pirker.
  1   2   3

7. Wir huslekae kometlek liazotim yevae.
  1   2   3

8. Volle ekaplek synem mor volle failek.
  1   2   3

9. Velle synzotim glasle zelkeroz.
  1   2   3

10. Tatleknef synzotem inlefer.
  1   2   3

11. Yevnef synzotem bex janlenef zelnef.
                1   2   3

12. Velle huslekoz synimfer avelekoz quea wir almanlek.
  1   2   3

13. Bonlekoz tulim kalenker fercolle friglekoz.
  1   2   3

14. Ric almanlek kalenremot volle ekaplekzofax.
  1   2   3

15. Yevoe chonremot ric browlek frigbar pohcolle.
  1   2   3

16. Ric ekaplekax piret synbar brale.
       1   2   3

17. Ric kalenle deglek zelremot collede.
       1   2   3

18. Velleax bonlekax tulet inle kometlekax mor bex failek.
  1   2   3

19. Ric zelek liaremot yevzof.
       1   2   3

20. Pohcolle trenedlekax synret brale kalenbar.
  1   2   3

For questions 21 through 30, select the correct translation of the numbered, italicized word or group of words in the paragraph below. Mark on your answer sheet the letter of the correct translation.

Study the sample question below before going on to the test questions. Select the correct translation for the words in italics, which are numbered 22.

Where are *the papers*?
       22

    a. bex trenedlek
    b. ric trenedlek
    c. ricax trenedlekax
    d. ric trenedlekax
    e. bex trenedlekax

Choice **d** is the correct translation of the numbered, italicized words, *the papers*, because the definite article, *ric*, does not change its ending to agree with the noun (see note to the vocabulary list), and the noun *trenedlekax* has the proper plural suffix (rule 2).

Now proceed according to the directions you just read. Base your answers on the following paragraph.

The men and women who *guard the country's border* have *difficult work*. Unlike
                  21   22

guards who work only in *a border station*, they patrol difficult country on foot or in
                  23

their jeeps. They *have to identify* aliens who attempt *to cross rivers* and desolate
   24   25   26

terrain. The danger of their job often tests how *loyally they guard* the country, for
                                27

they are sometimes put in situations such as *the shooting of spies*, and they risk
                            28

injury from this work. In addition to the bravery needed to patrol, the border guard
                      29

has to be very intelligent. He or she has to be skilled in the *identification of illegal papers*.
                      30

21. a. bonlek ric failek regbar
    b. bonet ric failek reglek
    c. bonet ric failekoe reglek
    d. bonot ric failekoe reglek
    e. bonlek ric failekoe reglek

22. a. brale friglekax
    b. brale friglek
    c. brale frigbar
    d. braleax friglekax
    e. bralek friglek

23. a. bex reglek lexlek
  b. cre regle lexlek
  c. cre reglek lexlek
  d. bex reglek lexbar
  e. bex regle lexlek

24. a. yevaxoe cublekax
  b. yevax cublek
  c. yevaxoe cublek
  d. yev cublekax
  e. yevoe cublekoe

25. a. tulet kalenet
  b. tulot kalenot
  c. tulot kalenbar
  d. tulet kalenbar
  e. tulremet kalenbar

26. a. chonet browlekax
  b. chonbar browlekax
  c. chonbarax browlekax
  d. chonbar browlek
  e. chonet browlek

27. a. inle yevax bonet
  b. inle yevzof bonet
  c. inlede yevax bonot
  d. inlede yevax bonet
  e. inle yev bonot

28. a. ric deget quea tatlekax
  b. ric deglek mor tatlekax
  c. ric degbar quea tatlekax
  d. ric deglek mor tatlekax
  e. ric deglek quea tatlekax

29. a. liale mor volleoe friglek
  b. lialek mor volle friget
  c. lialek mor volle frigot
  d. liale mor volle friget
  e. lialek mor volle friglek

30. a. kalenlekax quea colleax trenedlekax
  b. kalenlek quea pohcolle trenedlekax
  c. kalenlek quea pohcolleax trenedlekax
  d. kalenet quea pohcolleax trenedlekax
  e. kalenlek quea colleax trenedlekax

Of the five suggested answers to questions 31–36, select the one that correctly translates the English word or words in parentheses into the Artificial Language. You should translate the entire sentence in order to determine what form should be used. Study the following sample question before going on to the test questions.

That government's spies (crossed the border).
  a. chonremet bex reglek
  b. chonremot ric reglek
  c. chonremet ric reglek
  d. chonremet ric regbar
  e. chonremot bex reglek

Since *chonremet ric reglek* is the only one of these expressions that means *crossed the border*, choice **c** is the correct answer to the sample question.

31. The guard inspected (his friends' papers).
  a. yevoe kometlekaxoe trenedlek
  b. yevzofoe kometlekaxoe trenedlekax
  c. yevoe kometlekoe trenedlek
  d. yev kometlekax trenedlekax
  e. yevoe kometlekaxoe trenedlekax

32. The woman (drove the jeep skillfully).
  a. arremot ric cublek autilede
  b. aret ric cublek autile
  c. arremet ric cublekzof autilek
  d. arremet mor cublek autilede
  e. arremet ric cublekzof autilede

33. (The governments of those countries) have spies.
   a. Ricax almanlekax quea velleax failekax
   b. Ric almanlekax quea velleax failekax
   c. Ric almanlekax mor velleax failekax
   d. Ric almanlekax quea velle failekax
   e. Ricax almanlekax queax velleax failekax

34. (Those girls crossed) the river illegally.
   a. Velleax ekaplekax chonremet
   b. Vollezofax kaplekzofax chonremet
   c. Vellezofax ekaplekzofax chonremet
   d. Vellezofax kaplekzofax chonremet
   e. Vellezof ekaplekzof chonremot

35. The border guards work (loyally from their government) station.
   a. inle mor yevoe almanle
   b. inlede mor yevaxoe almanlek
   c. inle mor yevaxoe almanlek
   d. inlede mor yevaxoe almanle
   e. inlede mor yevoe almanle

36. (The identification of illegal aliens) is a difficult task.
   a. Ric kalenbar quea pohcolleax huslekax
   b. Ric kalenlek quea pohcolleax pohuslekax
   c. Ric kalenle quea colleax huslekax
   d. Ric kalenlek quea pohcolleax huslekax
   e. Ric kalenlek quea pohcolle huslekax

Choose the correct form of the italicized word or words.

37. Vellezofax kaplekzofax *autile* pirremet ric bonlekax. (adverb)
   a. autilezofaxde
   b. autilekzofax
   c. autilede
   d. autile
   e. autiledezofax

38. Ric kaplekax quea velle failek *synbar kometlek*. (past tense—plural adjective)
   a. synremot—kometleax
   b. synremet—kometlekax
   c. synremot—kometlek
   d. synremet—kometlek
   e. synremet—kometleax

39. Bonlekax tulet zelbar mor *colle* trenedlekax. (negative plural masculine adjective)
   a. colleax
   b. pohcollezofax
   c. colle
   d. pohcolleax
   e. pohcolle

40. Ric ekaplekzof *piret* mor ric *degbar*. (singular past tense—masculine singular noun)
   a. pirremot—deglek
   b. piremet—deglek
   c. pirremot—degle
   d. piremot—deglek
   e. pirremet—deglek

► Answers

Section 1: Logical Reasoning

1. d. Sentence 2 in the passage lists several additional beliefs that fall under "attachment to the Constitution" (supporting choice **d**). Choice **a** is ruled out by the final sentence of the passage, which says that an applicant cannot be excluded simply because he or she believes *it might be desirable to make a change in our form of government.* However, it does not say that a person *must* have a desire to change the government, ruling out choices **b** and **c**. Choice **e** is ruled out by the final sentence of the passage.

2. e. Choice **e** is correct because the passage states in sentence 3 that *some people believe that too much immigration may compromise the United States' standard of living.* Choice **a** is illogical because its two parts have nothing to do with one another. Choice **b** is illogical, because the chances are good that citizens would not want the United States' standard of living lowered (because it would affect them adversely); therefore, they would tend not to want an open immigration policy. Choice **c** is illogical because what the citizens want has nothing to do with immigration's compromising the United States' standard of living. Choice **d** is incorrect because the historical fact cannot be changed; in addition, the U.S. immigration policy is unrelated to past treatment of people who already lived here.

3. c. Finding the right answer to this question depends on close reading of small words, such as *must, unless,* and *only.* The first sentence states that the court shall *not sentence the defendant to pay a fine . . . unless . . . the fine is specially adapted to deterrence of the crime,* supporting choice **c**. Nothing in the passage suggests that the court *must* impose the sentence of a fine (ruling out choices **a** and **d**). Choice **b** is not in the passage (the only reference to restitution is in the final sentence). Choice **e** contains the words *only if,* which makes that answer false.

4. e. Choice **e** is right because, if Jon is considered to have dual nationality, then he must have met the criteria for citizenship in the state in which he was born *and* in his parents' home state—the situation described in choice **e**. Choice **a** is wrong because in this instance the child cannot be a citizen of the parents' home state and have dual nationality. Choice **b** is wrong because in this instance, the child cannot be a citizen of the state where he was born. Choice **c** is wrong because in this instance, the child will be a citizen of the parents' home state and, therefore, will not be stateless. Choice **d** is wrong because in this instance, the child will be a citizen of his parents' home state.

5. d. This question asks you to identify what is *not* in the passage. The third sentence states that, *Most criminals do not have antisocial personality disorder,* supporting choice **d** (correct because it is not in the passage). The first sentence rules out choice **a** (because it is in the passage). The second sentence rules out choice **c**. The final sentence rules out choices **b** and **e**.

6. b. Choice **b** includes the following premises: People are accountable for their own behavior, and people are not accountable for behavior they cannot control. The logical conclusion based on these premises is that people can control their own behavior. Choice **a** would require that criminals never have control over the behavior of other people, which the argument does not prove. Choice **c** requires that people should not be held accountable for the behavior of other people. Choice **d** is not a conclusion, as it simply reiterates a premise of the argument. Choice **e** provides for the possibility that a criminal might not have control over another person's behavior, which is subject to harsh criminal sentencing.

7. b. Choice **b** is supported by the fact that, in *Kohama,* the relatives submitted evidence that they were willing and able to support the couple, and the court *accepted the evidence as sufficient.* The example in the passage is of relatives who lived in the United States; the passage does not discuss people with relatives in their *home country* (ruling out choice **a**). Choice **c** is made illogical by the word *must*—the relatives cannot force the person to immigrate. The passage simply states that aliens will be excluded if they are likely to become a public charge—there are obviously other ways to avoid becoming a public charge (such as employment), ruling out choice **e**.

8. a. Choice **a** strengthens the argument and provides support for the major assumption of the argument that there are no significant differences between the five-year period preceding the passage of laws and the five-year period since the passage of the new laws. Choice **b** undermines the major assumption. Choices **c**, **d**, and **e** offer no support for the major assumption of the argument and do not provide suitable conclusions.

9. a. The second sentence states that *a person with this diagnosis shows a pervasive suspiciousness of others,* supporting choice **a**. The first sentence states that the person with paranoid personality disorder *may sometimes* be in trouble with the law, ruling out choice **d**. The final sentence states that, in order to fall into the category of paranoid personality disorder, the symptoms of that disorder *must not occur exclusively during the course of schizophrenia,*

ruling out choice **b**. Choice **c** is not in the passage, and it is doubtful that anyone could voice such an opinion with certainty about the future of a patient. Choice **e** takes the true statement, that persons with paranoid personality disorder are reluctant to confide in others, and reverses it so that it becomes invalid. (An analogous logic problem would be: *True: All horses are animals. Invalid: Therefore, all animals are horses.*)

10. c. Choice **c** is supported by the very first sentence of the first paragraph, which reads, "The reasonable suspicion standard has never been clearly defined." Choice **a** is incorrect because the passage states that the courts should prohibit the stopping of motor vehicles by police officers who rely on hunches. Choice **b** is incorrect since the third sentence of the second paragraph states that police officers may stop a motor vehicle when circumstances are beyond the ordinary, even if circumstances are not criminally suspicious. Choice **d** is incorrect because it is the making of vehicle stops based solely on hunches that put law-abiding citizens at the mercy of an officer's whim, while requiring reasonable suspicion prevents this. Choice **e** is unsupported by the passage.

11. e. Choice **e** is correct because it is directly supported by the second and last sentence in the paragraph. The information in choice **a** is specifically contradicted by the first sentence. Choices **b** and **c** are incorrect because there is no supporting statement in the paragraph. Choice **d** is incorrect since the passage clearly states that agency regulations and directives provide field level guidance to agents and that the judicial branch of government interprets statutory law.

12. a. Choice **a** is supported by the third sentence of the passage. It says the same thing as choice **a**, except that it is stated in the positive: The lawyer may serve the individual *only if* the lawyer is convinced that differing interests are not present. Choice **b** is ruled out by the phrase *feels allegiance,* which is not the same thing as the phrase used in the passage, *has allegiance.* (A lawyer may *feel* allegiance to her father's firm, for example, just because of the parent-child relationship—but she may *have* no allegiance in the legal sense.) Choices **c** and **d** are wrong, because the final sentence says that *the lawyer may serve the individual only if the lawyer is convinced that differing interests are not present.* Choice **e** is not in the passage.

13. e. Choice **e** accurately reflects the premise of the paragraph and is directly supported by the third statement. Choices **a, b, c,** and **d** are all unsupported by the paragraph. This is an example that draws on preconceived, yet invalid notions of law (e.g., intentions must be written and contracts must be written).

14. b. Choice **b** accurately reflects the third sentence of the passage. The small word *unless* rules out choice **a.** Choices **c, d,** and **e** all erroneously apply the criteria for *becoming exempt* from the literacy requirements to *meeting* the literacy requirements.

15. d. This is an example of a test question with a negative lead-in statement. It asks for the conclusion that is not supported by the paragraph. That means that four of the statements are valid conclusions from the paragraph, while one is not. Based solely on the information presented in this paragraph, the only statement not supported by the information is **d.** All the other statements are supported by the information either directly or indirectly.

16. c. The only choice accurately reflected in the information is **c.** The answer is supported by the statement "incidental to a lawful arrest" in

the third sentence of the paragraph. Choice **a** draws an inaccurate conclusion. Choice **b** is incorrect in that probable cause is not required to conduct a search if the search is incidental to a lawful arrest. The provided information makes no reference to a citizen's arrest. Choice **e** is too broad in that it addresses constitutional protections that are not referenced in the information.

17. a. The question asks that you identify what is not in the passage. Since the search-and-rescue dogs are labeled disobedient, and only *some* (not all) of the precincts have search-and-rescue dogs, it is *not* true that all precincts have disobedient dogs (supporting choice **a**). The other choices can be found in the passage and are therefore incorrect answers to this *cannot* question.

18. b. Turned into a positive statement, choice **b** says that a new trial will be granted where an error is held to be harmful beyond a reasonable doubt, which matches the information in the passage (so choice **b** is supported and choice **a** is ruled out). Choices **d** and **e** are wrong because they speak as if the *constitutional issues* (rather than the judicial errors) must be found harmless. Choice **e** is wrong because the example given is one in which a constitutional issue is involved.

19. e. The question asks you to identify what is *not* in the passage. Choice **e** is the correct answer because the passage states that bacteria (as well as viruses) *can be harmful parasites.* Choice **a** is tricky because it is a double negative; however, turned around, it really says that *All bacteria are able to metabolize on their own,* which is correct, according to the passage. Choices **b, c,** and **d** are clearly expressed in the passage. (Note that choice **d** is a reversal of choice **e,** and that choice **d** is valid, but choice **e** is invalid.)

20. d. Charlie says that the family of four got in his way, but the passage notes that Charlie *sometimes lies,* so choice **d** can be validly concluded. Harry always tells the truth, and Harry says they both had guns, ruling out choices **a**, **b**, and **e**. Nobody suggested that Harry knocked over the family of four, ruling out choice **c**.

21. a. Officer Abdalla would get the award except that he has taken himself out of the race. After making a list, carefully following the ranking described in the passage, you will find that Officer Sanchez will get the award.

22. b. Instead of trying to figure the problem out in your head, make a simple list. You will find that Administrative Vice (choice **b**) is the correct answer. Note that at the end of the problem, there are two "less importants" in a row. Also, do not forget while you are working the problem out that the question asks for the *second* most important division.

23. b. See the second sentence of the passage. Choice **a** is ruled out by the last sentence of the passage. (According to the passage, a parole *hearing* is mandatory, but parole is not.) Choice **c** is ruled out by the fact that the length of parole can be shortened for both lifers and non-lifers if they commit no violations while on parole. Choice **d** is wrong because those sentenced to life without possibility of parole are not granted a hearing. Choice **e** is ruled out by the final sentence in the passage.

24. b. Again, make a list, following the content of the passage carefully. Remember that two of the officers trip and fall, but one recovers. You will find that choice **b**, Officer Zelig, is the correct answer.

25. c. After making your list by carefully following the context of the passage, you will find that, although Officer Robbins and Officer Xavier tie, Officer Nardil wins the promotion.

26. c. Choice **c** is a little confusing because it is stated in the negative; restated in the positive, it means *all who have been convicted of manslaughter will be eligible for parole,* which is verified by the second sentence of the passage (supporting choice **c** and ruling out choice **e**). Choice **a** is ruled out by the third and fourth sentences, which tells about groups that are eligible for parole. Choices **b** and **d** are ruled out by the final sentence (a *some* statement that rules out both of these two *all* statements, even though the *all* statements express ideas that are opposite one another).

27. b. The second sentence says that a child is an orphan if her parents have disappeared or abandoned her, suggesting that the parents may still be alive. Choice **a** is wrong, because one of the conditions specified in the second sentence is that, in order to be considered an orphan, the parents must have *irrevocably released the child for emigration and adoption.* Choices **c** and **d** are irrelevant to the matter of who is an orphan. Choice **e** is ruled out by the second sentence, which lists ways a child can become an orphan, even if the parents are still alive.

28. d. In theory, if a client is innocent, no communication between client and lawyer could hurt the client (see the second sentence of the passage). The final sentence indicates that a client could be hurt by lack of privilege—for one thing, the client could not receive a fair trial (this rules out choices **a** and **c**). Choice **b** is wrong, because the passage says that attorney-client privilege is *one* way evidence can be suppressed—the passage does not say it is the *only* way evidence could be suppressed. Choice **e** is illogical and is not in the passage.

29. a. Since all of the people who live with me have been arrested, and some of them work nights, choice **a** is true, and **b** and **c** cannot be true. Since all of the people have been arrested and all pay their rent on time, **d** cannot be true. Since no murderers live with me, **e** cannot be true.

30. c. The passage states that such crimes are rare, indicating that they *can* occur, supporting choice **c** and ruling out choice **a**. Choices **b** and **d** are refuted by the last sentence of the passage. Although the passage states that *some* persons who say they were in a depersonalized state are *being* deceitful, it does not state that *all* persons with depersonalization disorder are deceitful, ruling out choice **e**.

Section 2: Spanish Language

1. a. *Fácil* (easy) is the closest match for *sensillo* (easy to use).

2. c. *Entender* (to understand) is the closest to *oír* (hear).

3. d. *Custodia* (custody) is the choice that best matches *detención* (arrest).

4. b. *Anteriormente* (prior) is the best synonym that matches *antes* (before).

5. e. The only appropriate match for *al lado de* (next to) is *cerca de* (near).

6. b. *Sitúense* (place yourselves) most nearly means *siéntense* (sit down).

7. a. The best choice for *por la mañana* (in the morning) is *hasta mediodía* (until noon).

8. d. *Mala* (bad, ill) most nearly means *enferma* (sick).

9. a. The correct choice to match the meaning of *buscamos* (we are searching for) is *necesitamos* (we need).

10. d. The nearest match for *alcoba* (bedroom) is *dormitorio* (sleeping room).

11. e. *Yanquis* (Yankees) most nearly matches the meaning of *norteamericanos* (North Americans).

12. a. The best match for *Quiero* (I want) is *Deseo* (I wish).

13. e. The nearest match for *águila* (eagle) is *pájaro* (bird).

14. b. The appropriate choice to match *donaciones* (donations) is *contribuciones* (contributions).

15. c. The correct choice for *de la patria* (of the native land) is *del país* (of the country).

16. b. The choice that most nearly matches *bastante* (enough) is *harto* (quite a lot).

17. d. The best match for *vámonos* (let's go) is *salguemos* (let's leave).

18. c. The correct choice for *después* (later) is *más tarde,* which also means later.

19. b. For *se parece* (resembles), the nearest match is *es similar* (is similar).

20. a. The correct match for *la gente* (the people) is *el pueblo* (the people).

21. e. Choices **a, b, c,** and **d** all use incorrect prepositions.

22. a. Both verbs in choice **a** represent the correct past tense in the indicative mood. In choices **b, c, d,** and **e,** the wrong verb or wrong forms of the verb have been used.

23. c. This choice correctly modifies the verb *usan* and *diversos.*

24. a. In this choice, the two verbs are in agreement.

25. c. This choice is the one that uses the correct verb and noun combinations.

26. e. Here there is agreement of number and verb form.

27. b. This is the correct choice because of agreement of gender and of verb usage.

28. a. This is the only match because it is the only one that makes sense.

29. c. This is the right choice because it has both correct verb usage and gender agreement.

30. e. This is the only combination that correctly matches the third person plural verb form *Van* (are you going) and has an appropriate preposition, *con* (with).

31. c. The other possibilities contain various errors including incorrect prepositions, illogical structures, and incorrect verb forms.

32. a. The other possibilities contain various errors including incorrect terms, illogical structure, and incorrect verb forms.

33. b. The other possibilities contain various errors, including incorrect terms, misplaced clauses, and disagreement of verb tenses.

34. d. This is the only choice that uses the correct verb form, number, and gender.

35. b. This is the only correctly phrased command.

36. d. This is the only choice with the correct combination of verb form, gender, and word usage.

37. d. The other choices have incorrect verb form, number, or gender.

38. b. The other choices use a wrong word, a misspelled word, or an incorrect verb form.

39. b. This is the only choice that correctly uses the construction *estar + de + acuerdo* (to be in agreement).

40. d. This is the only choice that has correct verb usage, number, and gender agreement.

41. e. No change necessary.

42. b. *Entendía* means to understand something. Therefore, choice **b**, *comprendió* ("to comprehend"), is the best choice. Choice **e** is simply incorrect. Choices **a**, **c**, and **d** ("to respond," "to see," and "to feel") are completely unrelated to the meaning of *entendía*.

43. c. *Informar* means to inform. Therefore, choice **c**, *decir* ("to tell"), is the best choice. Choices **a**, **b**, and **d** ("to find," "to concentrate," and "to worsen") are completely unrelated.

44. a. *Proporcionan* means to provide. Therefore, choice **a**, *dan* ("give"), is the best choice. Choices **b**, **c**, and **d** ("counts," "sells," and "lost") are completely unrelated.

45. d. *La costumbre* (the custom) is correct. The other choices make no sense.

46. c. The only choice that makes a correct sentence is *picante* (spicy hot).

47. d. *Es* (is) is the third person singular form of the verb *ser*. The verb *ser* (to be) is used instead of *estar* (to be) when expressing a characteristic. In this case, it is a characteristic of the store that it is *barato* (cheap in price).

48. a. *Tenía* (had) is the right choice because the construction *tener + años* is used to express age.

49. b. *Estabas* (were you) is the correct usage because the imperfect is used to show a continuing action in the past.

50. b. *Deportes* (sports) is the only choice that correctly completes the sentence.

Section 2: Artificial Language

1. c. Word 1, *Volle*, is incorrect since the translation of *Volle* is *this*. The word numbered 2, *kalenim*, is also incorrect because the singular form *Kalenem* should have been used. Word 3 is correct. *Arlek* has been correctly formed from the infinitive *arker* (to drive) by applying Rules 4 and 8. Since the word numbered 3 has been identified as the only word translated correctly, the answer is **c**.

2. b. Word 1, *yev*, is incorrect because it means he, not she. Word 2, *synem*, is correct. According to Rules 4 and 6, to form the present tense of a verb, you should add the suffix *-em* to the stem of the verb when the verb has a singular subject. Word 3, *huslek*, is incorrect. According to Rule 1, a feminine noun must take the ending *-nef*. Accordingly, the word numbered 3 should have been *husleknef*.

3. d. Word 1, *wir*, is correct. The vocabulary lists state that *wir* is the translation for *the*, and that it applies equally to both genders and both numbers. Word 2, *bonlek*, is correct. According to Rule 8, to form a noun from a verb, the suffix *-lek* should be added to the stem of the infinitive. The infinitive (as it appears in the vocabulary list) is *bonker*, and its stem is *bon* (note that all infinitives in the vocabulary list have the suffix *-ker* and are distinguished only by their respective stems). The word numbered 3, *kometlek*, is correct. This is the word for *friend* as it appears in the vocabulary lists. Since the feminine gender is not specified in the sentence, *kometlek* does not take a feminine ending.

4. d. The word numbered 1, *kapleknef*, is correct. According to Rule 1, the feminine singular of a noun is formed by adding the suffix *-nef* to the masculine singular. Accordingly, to form the word *woman*, the suffix *-nef* should be added to the word *kaplek* (*man*). The word numbered 2, *arzotem*, is correct. According to Rule 4, the stem of the infinitive *to drive* is *ar* (since the infinitive form is *arker* in the vocabulary list). Since according to Rule 7 (page 113) the past tense is formed by adding the suffix *-zot* to the stem of the verb and then adding the suffix *-em* when the verb is singular, the correct translation of *drove* is *arzotem*.

5. a. Word 1, *almanlek*, is the correct translation for the word *government* in the vocabulary list. The word numbered 2, *synzotim*, is incorrect. The correct way to form the present tense singular according to Rule 6 is to add the suffix *-em* to the stem of the verb. Accordingly, the correct translation for *is* would be *synem*. The erroneous word *synzotim* is actually the past tense in the plural form, *were* (see Rule 7). The word numbered 3, *colleki*, is incorrect. The correct translation for the word *legal*, an adjective, is *colle* (see vocabulary lists). The erroneous word *colleki* is actually the word *legally*, which is formed by adding the suffix *-ki* to the adjectival form (see Rule 11).

6. e. Since none of the numbered words is correct, the answer is **e**. The word numbered 1, *kaplek*, is incorrect. *Kaplek* is the word for the singular noun man. Since the word *men* is a plural noun, the correct translation according to Rule 2 would have been *kaplekoz*. As Rule 2 states, in the Artificial Language, the plural of nouns is formed by adding the suffix *-oz* to the correct singular form. The word numbered 2, *kapleknef*, is incorrect. *Kapleknef* is the word for the singular noun *woman*. Consequently, the word *kapleknef* correctly includes the suffix *-nef* for the feminine form (Rule 1), but incorrectly neglects the suffix *-oz* for the plural form (Rule 2). The correct translation of *women* is *kapleknefoz*. The word numbered 3, *pirker*, is incorrect. *Pirker* (*to escape*) is the infinitive form of the verb, whereas the sentence calls for the past tense *escaped*. To form the past tense (Rule 7), the suffix *-zot* should be added to the stem of the verb, and then the suffix *-im* should be added when the verb refers to a plural subject (*men and women*). Accordingly, the correct translation is *pirzotim*.

7. a. Since only the word numbered 1 is correct, the answer is **a**. The word numbered 1, *huslekae*, is correct. Since *alien's* is a possessive form, the word *huslek* (*alien*) must take the possessive suffix *ae* (Rule 12). The word numbered 2, *liazotim*, is incorrect. *Liazotim* correctly applies Rule 4 to form the stem of the verb and correctly applies the suffix for the past tense, *-zot*, but it incorrectly applies the plural suffix *-im*. The correct translation for *injured* in this sentence would be *liazotem* since the verb refers to a singular subject and, therefore, takes the suffix *-em* (see Rule 7). The word numbered 3, *yevae*, is incorrect. The possessive ending *yevae* would apply to the possessive pronoun *his*, whereas the pronoun used in the sentence is *him*. According to the vocabulary list, the translation for *him* is *yev*. Accordingly, *yev* should have been used in the sentence.

8. d. Since two of the numbered words are correct, the answer is **d**. The word numbered 1, *volle*, is correct. According to the vocabulary lists, the correct translation for *this* is *volle*. The word numbered 2, *mor*, is correct. According to the vocabulary lists, the correct translation for *from* is *mor*. You should note that it is not always necessary to apply the grammatical rules, as is the case with these two words. In the case of these words, it is sufficient to consult the vocabulary lists. It is necessary to apply the grammatical rules only when the word in question cannot be used exactly as it appears in the vocabulary lists. The word numbered 3, *volle*, is incorrect. According to the vocabulary lists, the correct translation for *that* is *velle* (*volle* means *this*, as seen in the case of the word numbered 1).

9. e. Since none of the numbered words is correct, the answer is **e**. The word numbered 1, *velle*, is incorrect. The correct translation of *those* would be *velleoz*, since *those* is the plural of *that*, and according to Rule 2, the plural form for pronouns must take the suffix *-oz*. The word numbered 2, *glasle*, is incorrect. *Glasle* means *difficult* (as can be seen in the vocabulary lists), but according to Rule 2, adjectives take the ending *-oz* when they are modifying a plural noun. Since the adjective *difficult* in the sentence is modifying the plural noun *inspections*, it must take the suffix *-oz*. Accordingly, the correct form to use is *glasleoz*. The word numbered 3, *zelkeroz*, is incorrect. According to Rule 9, to form a noun from a verb, the suffix *-lek* should be added to the stem of the verb (in this case *zel*, which according to Rule 4 is the stem of

the infinitive *zelker, to inspect*). Thus, the noun *inspection* (singular) is *zellek*, but in the sentence, this noun appears in the plural (*inspections*). Consequently, according to Rule 2, *zellek* must take the ending *-oz*, thus making it the plural *zellekoz*.

10. e. Since none of the numbered words is correct, the answer is **e**. The word numbered 1, *tatleknef*, is incorrect. *Tatleknef* is the correct word for a *female spy* (Rules 4, 9, and 1), whereas the word numbered 1 in the sentence refers to *spies*, in the plural and with no specification as to gender. Therefore, the correct translation would be *tatlekoz*, which first forms a noun (*tatlek*) from the infinitive verb (*tatker*) according to Rules 4 and 9, and then forms the plural *tatlekoz* according to Rule 2. The word numbered 2, *synzotem*, is incorrect. The verb in the English sentence is in the present tense and plural form (*are*). The correct translation in this case must be *synim*, according to Rule 6, which states that, to form the present tense in the plural form, you should add the suffix *-im* to the stem of the infinitive (which is itself formed by applying Rule 4). The word numbered 3, *inlefer*, is incorrect. According to Rule 13, the adjective *disloyal* must be formed by adding the negative prefix *fer-* to the adjective *inle* (*loyal*). The word numbered 3, *inlefer*, erroneously uses *fer* as a negative suffix rather than as a negative prefix. In addition, the adjective must have a plural ending according to Rule 2, since it refers to the plural noun *spies*. Consequently, the correct translation must be *ferinleoz*.

11. b. Since only the word numbered 2 is correct, the answer is **b**. The word numbered 1, *bex*, is incorrect. In the Artificial Language, the article *bex* (in English *a/an*) takes a feminine ending (see Rules 1 and 3). The correct word is *bexnef*. The word numbered 2, *janlenef*, is correct. *Janle* (*skillful*) is an adjective, and as such must take a feminine ending when referring to a feminine subject (see Rules 1 and 3). The word numbered 3, *zelnef*, is incorrect. Since it is a noun (*inspector* in English), it must first take the ending -*lek*—this is required by Rules 4 and 9, which state that to form a noun from a verb, the suffix -*lek* should replace the infinitive suffix -*ker* (note that the infinitive form appears in the vocabulary lists: *zelker*). Once the noun (*zellek*) has been formed, then the feminine suffix -*nef* must be added because the sentence has a feminine subject. Accordingly, the correct word would be *zelleknef*.

12. c. Since only the word numbered 3 is correct, the answer is **c**. The word numbered 1, *velle*, is incorrect. *Velle* means *that*, whereas the word in the sentence is the plural *those*. Accordingly, *velle* must appear in the plural, which would be *velleoz* (see Rule 2, which states that the plural of adjectives must be formed by adding the suffix -*oz* to the singular form). The word numbered 2, *synimfer*, is incorrect. The first portion of the word *synim* is the correct form *are* in the plural (see Rules 4 and 6), but the negative form *fer* must be used as a prefix rather than as a suffix (see Rule 13). Accordingly, the correct form for *are not* in the plural must be *fersynim*. The word numbered 3, *avelekoz*, is correct. According to the vocabulary lists, the correct translation of the noun *enemy* is *avelek*, and according to Rule 2, the plural of nouns is formed by adding the suffix *oz* to the singular.

13. d. Since two of the numbered words are correct, the answer is **d**. The word numbered 1, *bonlekoz*, is correct. *Bonlekoz* (which means *guards*) is formed by first changing the infinitive verb *to guard* (*bonker*) into the singular noun *bonlek* (see Rules 4 and 9, which state

that to form a noun from a verb, you should add the suffix -*lek* to the stem of the verb). Next, to make the noun plural (*guards*), the suffix -*oz* should be added to the singular form. The word numbered 2, *fercolle*, is incorrect. According to Rule 13, the adjective *illegal* must be formed by adding the prefix *fer*- to the adjective *colle* (*legal*). According to Rules 2 and 3, the ending -*oz* must be added to make the adjective plural because it is modifying a plural noun (*workers*). Accordingly, the correct word would be *fercolleoz*. The word numbered 3, *friglekoz*, is correct. The first portion of the noun, *friglek*, means *worker*; you form this noun (according to Rules 4 and 9) by adding the suffix -*lek* to the stem of the infinitive *frigker* (*to work*). Next, according to Rule 2, to make the noun plural, you add the suffix -*oz* to the singular.

14. d. Word 1, *almanlek*, is the correct masculine singular form of the noun, *government*. Word 2, *volle* (*this*), is incorrect because it is an adjective and must have the feminine plural ending to agree with the noun, *girls* (Rules 2 and 3). Word 3, *ekaplekzofax* (*girls*), is the correct feminine plural form of the noun (Rule 2).

15. b. Word 1, *yevoe*, is incorrect because it is the possessive pronoun *her*; the correct translation is the feminine singular pronoun, *yevzof* (*she*), formed by adding the feminine singular ending to the pronoun, *yev* (*he*), following Rule 1. Word 2, *chonremot* (*crossed*), is the correct past singular conjugation of the verb, *chonbar* (Rules 4, 5, and 7). Word 3, *pohcolle*, is incorrect because it is the adjectival form of the word; the correct translation is the adverbial form, *pohcollede* (*illegally*), following Rule 10.

16. e. Word 1, *ekaplekax*, is incorrect because it is the masculine plural noun, but it lacks the required possessive ending to be translated properly; the correct translation is the possessive noun, *ekaplekaxoe* (*boys'*), formed according to Rules 2 and 11. Word 2, *piret*, is incorrect because it is translated as a verb; the word *escape* in the sentence is a noun, and should be translated *pirlek* (*escape*) from the verb, *pirbar* (Rule 8). Word 3, *synbar*, is incorrect because the verb is in the unconjugated infinitive; the verb should be in the past singular conjugation, *synremot* (*was*), to agree with the subject of the sentence, *escape* (Rules 4, 5, and 7).

17. a. Word 1, *kalenle* (*identified*), is an adjective correctly formed from the infinitive, *kalenbar* (*to identify*), according to Rule 10. Word 2, *zelremot* (*inspected*), is incorrect; although *zelremot* has the correct past singular conjugation (Rules 4, 5, and 7), it is an incorrect translation of the verb, *worked*. The correct translation is *frigremot*. Word 3, *collede* (*legally*), is an incorrect translation of the word *illegally* because it is lacking the negative prefix (Rule 12); the correct translation is *pohcollede*.

18. a. Word 1, *velleax* (*those*), is correct because it is an adjective that has the masculine plural suffix to agree with the noun *guards* (Rules 2 and 3). Word 2, *inle* (*loyal*), is incorrect because it is an adjective that should have the masculine plural suffix to agree with the noun, *friends*; the correct translation is *inleax* (Rules 2 and 3). Word 3, *bex* (*a, an*), is an incorrect translation of the word *the* (*ric*).

19. c. Word 1, *zelek* (*guard*), is incorrect because it lacks the masculine plural ending required to translate the plural noun, *inspectors* (Rule 2); the correct translation is *zelekax*. Word 2, *liaremot*, is incorrect because it is the past singular conjugation of the verb; it should be the past plural conjugation of the verb to agree

with the plural subject, *inspectors* (Rules 4, 5, and 7); the correct translation is *liaremet*. Word 3, *yevzof* (*her*), is the correctly translated feminine form of the pronoun, *yev* (*him*), because it has the feminine ending (Rule 1).

20. b. Word 1, *pohcolle*, is incorrect because it is an adjective that requires the plural ending to agree with the noun *papers* (Rules 2 and 3); the correct translation is *pohcolleax*. Word 2, *trenedlekax* (*papers*), is correct because it has the masculine plural ending on the noun (Rule 2). Word 3, *brale*, is incorrect because it is an adjective modifying the plural noun, *papers*. It should, therefore, take the masculine plural ending (Rule 2); the correct translation is *braleax*.

21. c. The verb, *bonet*, is in the present tense plural (Rules 4 and 6). The possessive noun, *country's*, is correctly formed with the possessive suffix added to the noun (Rule 11), and the noun, *border* (*reglek*), has been correctly formed from the infinitive *regbar* according to Rule 8.

22. b. The word *difficult* is correctly translated as *brale*, and the noun, *work* (*friglek*), is correctly formed from the infinitive (Rule 8).

23. e. The article, *a*, is correctly translated *bex*; the adjective, *border* (*regle*), is correctly formed from the infinitive *regbar*, according to Rules 8 and 9; and the noun, *station* (*lexlek*), is correctly formed from the infinitive *lexbar* (Rule 8).

24. a. The plural possessive pronoun, *their* (*yevaxoe*), has been correctly formed from the singular pronoun, *he* (*yev*), by adding the plural and possessive endings (Rules 2 and 11); and the plural noun, *jeeps* (*cublekax*), has been correctly formed following Rule 2.

25. d. The verb, *have* (*tulet*), is in the correct plural present form to agree with the subject of the sentence, *they* (Rules 4, 5, and 6). The infinitive, *to identify,* is correctly translated *kalenbar.*

26. b. The infinitive, *to cross* (*chonbar*), is correctly translated, and the plural noun, *rivers* (*browlekax*), is correctly formed according to Rule 2.

27. d. The adverb, *loyally* (*inlede*), is correctly formed according to Rule 10. The plural pronoun, *they* (*yevax*), is correctly formed from the singular pronoun *he* (*yev*) by adding the plural suffix (Rule 2). The verb, *guard* (*bonet*), is in the correct plural present form to agree with the subject, *they* (Rules 4, 5, and 6).

28. e. The word *the* is correctly translated *ric*; the noun, *shooting* (*deglek*), is correctly formed from the infinitive (Rule 8). The word *of* is correctly translated *quea*, and the plural noun, *spies* (*tatlekax*) is correctly formed according to Rules 2 and 8.

29. e. The noun, *injury* (*lialek*), is correctly formed from the infinitive, *liabar,* according to Rule 8. The word *from* is correctly translated *mor.* The pronoun, *this* (*volle*), is correctly formed according to Rule 11, and the noun, *work* (*friglek*), is correctly formed from the infinitive, *frigbar* (Rule 8).

30. c. The noun, *identification* (*kalenlek*), is correctly formed from the infinitive, *kalenbar,* according to Rule 8. The word *of* is correctly translated *quea.* The adjective, *illegal* (*pohcolleax*), is correctly formed by adding the negative prefix to the word for legal, and it is in the plural form to agree with the noun, *papers* (Rules 2 and 12). The plural noun, *papers* (*trenedlekax*), is correctly formed with the plural suffix according to Rule 2.

31. e. *Yevoe kometlekaxoe trenedlekax* is the only one of these expressions that means *his friends' papers,* employing the possessive ending on the possessive pronoun and noun,

yevoe and *kometlekaxoe* (Rule 11), and attaching the masculine plural ending to the noun, *trenedlekax* (Rule 2).

32. a. *Arremot ric cublek autilede* is the only one of these expressions that means *drove the jeep skillfully,* employing the past singular conjugation of the verb, *arremot* (Rules 4, 5, and 7) and the adverbial suffix to form the adverb, *autilede* (Rule 10).

33. b. *Ric almanlekax quea velleax failekax* is the only one of these expressions that properly translates *the governments of those countries,* using the correct masculine plural endings on the nouns, *almanlekax* and *failekax* (Rule 2), and the masculine plural ending on the adjective, *velleax* (Rules 2 and 3).

34. c. *Vellezofax ekaplekzofax chonremet* is the only one of these expressions that properly translates *those girls crossed,* using the correct feminine plural endings for the adjective, *vellezofax,* and noun, *ekaplekzofax* (Rule 2), as well as the past plural conjugation of the verb, *chonremet* (Rules 4, 5, and 7).

35. d. *Inlede mor yevaxoe almanle* is the only one of these expressions that properly translates *loyally from their government.* The adverb, *inlede,* is correctly formed using the adverbial ending (Rule 10); the possessive pronoun, *yevaxoe,* is correctly formed by adding the plural ending and the possessive suffix (Rules 2 and 11); and the adjective, *almanle,* is correctly formed from the noun, *almanlek,* using Rule 9.

36. d. *Ric kalenlek quea pohcolleax huslekax* is the only one of these expressions that properly translates *the identification of illegal aliens.* The noun, *kalenlek,* is formed correctly from the infinitive, *kalenbar* (Rule 8); the adjective, *pohcolleax,* is correctly formed, agreeing in number and gender with the noun and using the negative prefix (Rules 2, 3, and 12); the noun, *huslekax*, has the necessary plural ending (Rule 2).

37. c. Choices **a**, **b**, and **e** are incorrect because they all include feminine plural endings; however, adverbs do not take gendered or numbered suffixes. Choice **d** is incorrect because it lacks the adverbial ending, *-de*, required for the formation of adverbs (Rule 10).

38. e. Choices **a** and **c** are incorrect because the verb, *synremot*, is in the past singular conjugation; it should be in the past plural, *synremet*, to agree in number with the subject of the verb, *kaplekax* (Rules 4, 5, and 7). In addition, choice **c** is incorrect because the word *kometlek* is a masculine singular noun, not an adjective. While choice **b** has the correct verb form, the word *kometlekax* is a masculine plural noun, not an adjective. Choice **d** also has the correct verb form, but the word *kometlek* is a masculine singular noun, not an adjective. Choice **e** has the correct verb form, and the correct form of the adjective, *kometleax* (Rule 9).

39. d. Choices **a** and **c** are incorrect because they are both lacking the negative prefix (Rule 12). Choice **b** is incorrect because it includes the feminine suffix when the noun that the adjective modifies is masculine plural (Rule 3). Choice **e** is incorrect because it is in the masculine singular form, but it should be in the masculine plural form to agree with the noun, *trenedlekax* (Rules 2 and 3). Choice **d** is the correct answer.

40. a. In choices **b** and **d**, the verb form is misspelled. In choice **c**, the verb is in the correct past singular form, *pirremot* (Rules 4, 5, and 7), to agree with the singular subject, *ekaplekzof*. However, the word *degle* is the adjectival form, not a noun. In choice **e**, the verb is in the incorrect past plural form.

► Scoring

To evaluate how you did on this practice exam, start by totaling the number of correct responses on the two sections of the exam—Logical Reasoning and Spanish or Artificial Language (whichever you chose to take). First, find the number of questions you got right in each part. Questions you skipped or got wrong don't count; just add up the number of correct answers.

If at least 70% of your responses on the two parts are correct, you will most likely pass the Border Patrol Exam.

Keep in mind that what's much more important than your scores, for now, is how you did on each of the basic skills tested by the exam. Diagnose your strengths and weaknesses so that you can concentrate your efforts as you prepare for the exam. Turn again to the instructional chapters that cover each of the basic skills tested on the Border Patrol Exam, and review the areas that gave you the most trouble.

If you didn't score as well as you would like, ask yourself the following: Did I run out of time before I could answer all the questions? Did I go back and change my answers from right to wrong? Did I get flustered and sit staring at a difficult question for what seemed like hours? If you had any of these problems, once again, be sure to go over the LearningExpress Test Preparation System in Chapter 3 again to learn how to avoid them.

After working more on the instructional chapters, take the second practice exam in Chapter 11 to see how much you've improved.

CHAPTER

11 ▶ Border Patrol Practice Exam 2

CHAPTER SUMMARY

This is the second of the two practice tests in this book based on the
Border Patrol Agent Exam. Use this test for more practice with Logical Reasoning and Language questions.

For this exam, once again simulate the actual test-taking experience as closely as possible. Work in a
quiet place, away from interruptions. Tear out the answer sheet on the next page, and use your
number 2 pencil to fill in the circles. Use a timer or stopwatch and allow yourself three hours to complete all sections of the exam.

After the exam, use the answer key that follows it to see your progress on each section and to find out why
the correct answers are correct and the incorrect ones incorrect. Then use the scoring section at the end of the
exam to see how you did overall.

► Section 1: Logical Reasoning

1. ⓐ ⓑ ⓒ ⓓ ⓔ	11. ⓐ ⓑ ⓒ ⓓ ⓔ	21. ⓐ ⓑ ⓒ ⓓ ⓔ
2. ⓐ ⓑ ⓒ ⓓ ⓔ	12. ⓐ ⓑ ⓒ ⓓ ⓔ	22. ⓐ ⓑ ⓒ ⓓ ⓔ
3. ⓐ ⓑ ⓒ ⓓ ⓔ	13. ⓐ ⓑ ⓒ ⓓ ⓔ	23. ⓐ ⓑ ⓒ ⓓ ⓔ
4. ⓐ ⓑ ⓒ ⓓ ⓔ	14. ⓐ ⓑ ⓒ ⓓ ⓔ	24. ⓐ ⓑ ⓒ ⓓ ⓔ
5. ⓐ ⓑ ⓒ ⓓ ⓔ	15. ⓐ ⓑ ⓒ ⓓ ⓔ	25. ⓐ ⓑ ⓒ ⓓ ⓔ
6. ⓐ ⓑ ⓒ ⓓ ⓔ	16. ⓐ ⓑ ⓒ ⓓ ⓔ	26. ⓐ ⓑ ⓒ ⓓ ⓔ
7. ⓐ ⓑ ⓒ ⓓ ⓔ	17. ⓐ ⓑ ⓒ ⓓ ⓔ	27. ⓐ ⓑ ⓒ ⓓ ⓔ
8. ⓐ ⓑ ⓒ ⓓ ⓔ	18. ⓐ ⓑ ⓒ ⓓ ⓔ	28. ⓐ ⓑ ⓒ ⓓ ⓔ
9. ⓐ ⓑ ⓒ ⓓ ⓔ	19. ⓐ ⓑ ⓒ ⓓ ⓔ	29. ⓐ ⓑ ⓒ ⓓ ⓔ
10. ⓐ ⓑ ⓒ ⓓ ⓔ	20. ⓐ ⓑ ⓒ ⓓ ⓔ	30. ⓐ ⓑ ⓒ ⓓ ⓔ

► Section 2: Spanish Language

1. ⓐ ⓑ ⓒ ⓓ ⓔ	18. ⓐ ⓑ ⓒ ⓓ ⓔ	35. ⓐ ⓑ ⓒ ⓓ
2. ⓐ ⓑ ⓒ ⓓ ⓔ	19. ⓐ ⓑ ⓒ ⓓ ⓔ	36. ⓐ ⓑ ⓒ ⓓ
3. ⓐ ⓑ ⓒ ⓓ ⓔ	20. ⓐ ⓑ ⓒ ⓓ ⓔ	37. ⓐ ⓑ ⓒ ⓓ
4. ⓐ ⓑ ⓒ ⓓ ⓔ	21. ⓐ ⓑ ⓒ ⓓ ⓔ	38. ⓐ ⓑ ⓒ ⓓ
5. ⓐ ⓑ ⓒ ⓓ ⓔ	22. ⓐ ⓑ ⓒ ⓓ ⓔ	39. ⓐ ⓑ ⓒ ⓓ
6. ⓐ ⓑ ⓒ ⓓ ⓔ	23. ⓐ ⓑ ⓒ ⓓ ⓔ	40. ⓐ ⓑ ⓒ ⓓ
7. ⓐ ⓑ ⓒ ⓓ ⓔ	24. ⓐ ⓑ ⓒ ⓓ ⓔ	41. ⓐ ⓑ ⓒ ⓓ ⓔ
8. ⓐ ⓑ ⓒ ⓓ ⓔ	25. ⓐ ⓑ ⓒ ⓓ ⓔ	42. ⓐ ⓑ ⓒ ⓓ ⓔ
9. ⓐ ⓑ ⓒ ⓓ ⓔ	26. ⓐ ⓑ ⓒ ⓓ ⓔ	43. ⓐ ⓑ ⓒ ⓓ ⓔ
10. ⓐ ⓑ ⓒ ⓓ ⓔ	27. ⓐ ⓑ ⓒ ⓓ ⓔ	44. ⓐ ⓑ ⓒ ⓓ ⓔ
11. ⓐ ⓑ ⓒ ⓓ ⓔ	28. ⓐ ⓑ ⓒ ⓓ ⓔ	45. ⓐ ⓑ ⓒ ⓓ ⓔ
12. ⓐ ⓑ ⓒ ⓓ ⓔ	29. ⓐ ⓑ ⓒ ⓓ ⓔ	46. ⓐ ⓑ ⓒ ⓓ ⓔ
13. ⓐ ⓑ ⓒ ⓓ ⓔ	30. ⓐ ⓑ ⓒ ⓓ ⓔ	47. ⓐ ⓑ ⓒ ⓓ ⓔ
14. ⓐ ⓑ ⓒ ⓓ ⓔ	31. ⓐ ⓑ ⓒ ⓓ	48. ⓐ ⓑ ⓒ ⓓ ⓔ
15. ⓐ ⓑ ⓒ ⓓ ⓔ	32. ⓐ ⓑ ⓒ ⓓ	49. ⓐ ⓑ ⓒ ⓓ ⓔ
16. ⓐ ⓑ ⓒ ⓓ ⓔ	33. ⓐ ⓑ ⓒ ⓓ	50. ⓐ ⓑ ⓒ ⓓ ⓔ
17. ⓐ ⓑ ⓒ ⓓ ⓔ	34. ⓐ ⓑ ⓒ ⓓ	

► Section 2: Artificial Language

1. ⓐ ⓑ ⓒ ⓓ ⓔ	18. ⓐ ⓑ ⓒ ⓓ ⓔ	35. ⓐ ⓑ ⓒ ⓓ ⓔ
2. ⓐ ⓑ ⓒ ⓓ ⓔ	19. ⓐ ⓑ ⓒ ⓓ ⓔ	36. ⓐ ⓑ ⓒ ⓓ ⓔ
3. ⓐ ⓑ ⓒ ⓓ ⓔ	20. ⓐ ⓑ ⓒ ⓓ ⓔ	37. ⓐ ⓑ ⓒ ⓓ ⓔ
4. ⓐ ⓑ ⓒ ⓓ ⓔ	21. ⓐ ⓑ ⓒ ⓓ ⓔ	38. ⓐ ⓑ ⓒ ⓓ ⓔ
5. ⓐ ⓑ ⓒ ⓓ ⓔ	22. ⓐ ⓑ ⓒ ⓓ ⓔ	39. ⓐ ⓑ ⓒ ⓓ ⓔ
6. ⓐ ⓑ ⓒ ⓓ ⓔ	23. ⓐ ⓑ ⓒ ⓓ ⓔ	40. ⓐ ⓑ ⓒ ⓓ ⓔ
7. ⓐ ⓑ ⓒ ⓓ ⓔ	24. ⓐ ⓑ ⓒ ⓓ ⓔ	
8. ⓐ ⓑ ⓒ ⓓ ⓔ	25. ⓐ ⓑ ⓒ ⓓ ⓔ	
9. ⓐ ⓑ ⓒ ⓓ ⓔ	26. ⓐ ⓑ ⓒ ⓓ ⓔ	
10. ⓐ ⓑ ⓒ ⓓ ⓔ	27. ⓐ ⓑ ⓒ ⓓ ⓔ	
11. ⓐ ⓑ ⓒ ⓓ ⓔ	28. ⓐ ⓑ ⓒ ⓓ ⓔ	
12. ⓐ ⓑ ⓒ ⓓ ⓔ	29. ⓐ ⓑ ⓒ ⓓ ⓔ	
13. ⓐ ⓑ ⓒ ⓓ ⓔ	30. ⓐ ⓑ ⓒ ⓓ ⓔ	
14. ⓐ ⓑ ⓒ ⓓ ⓔ	31. ⓐ ⓑ ⓒ ⓓ ⓔ	
15. ⓐ ⓑ ⓒ ⓓ ⓔ	32. ⓐ ⓑ ⓒ ⓓ ⓔ	
16. ⓐ ⓑ ⓒ ⓓ ⓔ	33. ⓐ ⓑ ⓒ ⓓ ⓔ	
17. ⓐ ⓑ ⓒ ⓓ ⓔ	34. ⓐ ⓑ ⓒ ⓓ ⓔ	

▶ Section 1: Logical Reasoning

1. Law enforcement agencies use scientific techniques to identify suspects or to establish guilt. One obvious application of such techniques is the examination of a crime scene. Some substances found at a crime scene yield valuable clues under microscopic examination. Clothing fibers, dirt particles, and even pollen grains may reveal important information to the careful investigator. Nothing can be overlooked because all substances found at a crime scene are potential sources of evidence.

From the information given above, it can be validly concluded that

a. all substances that yield valuable clues under microscopic examination are substances found at a crime scene.

b. some potential sources of evidence are substances that yield valuable clues under microscopic examination.

c. some substances found at a crime scene are not potential sources of evidence.

d. no potential sources of evidence are substances at a crime scene.

e. some substances that yield valuable clues under microscopic examination are not substances found at a crime scene.

2. Patrol car E0110 leaves the station traveling west on Highway 9. After three miles, the car makes a right turn onto Route 21. Two miles up Route 21, a dirt road forks off in a diagonal right. Patrol car E0110 turns onto the dirt road and continues until the road reaches a farmhouse on the right-hand side of the road. The car turns into the driveway, and both agents get out.

From the information given above, it can be validly concluded that when the agents exit the car at the farmhouse, they will be facing

a. northeast.

b. southwest.

c. east.

d. south.

e. insufficient information provided

3. The alphanumeric coding of a fingerprint is a systemic description of the main patterns on the print. Within a certain metropolitan district, 90% of the population has fingerprints that can be alphanumerically coded.

From the information given above, it can be validly concluded that the fingerprints of a person from this district, selected at random,

a. can be alphanumerically coded, with a probability of 10%.

b. can be alphanumerically coded, with a probability of less than 90%.

c. cannot be alphanumerically coded, with a probability of 10%.

d. cannot be alphanumerically coded, with a probability of up to 90%.

e. may be coded alphanumerically, but the probability is unknown.

4. The printed output of some computer-driven printers can be recognized by forensic analysts. The Acme Model 200 printer was manufactured using two different inking mechanisms, one of which yields a Type A micro pattern of ink spray around its characters. Of all Acme Model 200 printers, 70% produce this Type A micro pattern, which is also characteristic of some models of other printers. Forensic analysts at a crime lab have been examining a kidnap ransom note that clearly exhibits the Type A micro pattern.

From the information given above, it can be validly concluded that this note

a. was printed on an Acme Model 200 printer, with a probability of 70%.

b. was printed on an Acme Model 200 printer, with a probability of 30%.

c. was not printed on an Acme Model 200 printer, with a probability of 70%.

d. was not printed on an Acme Model 200 printer, with a probability of 30%.

e. may have been printed on an Acme Model 200 printer, but the probability cannot be estimated.

5. Quite often, a Border Patrol Agent is required to give assistance to an injured person. Upon responding to a call to assist an injured person, an agent should be guided by the following procedure:

- Administer first aid.
- Call for medical assistance.
- Call the ambulance again if it fails to arrive within 20 minutes.
- Accompany the injured person to hospital if he or she is unidentified or unconscious.
- Witness search of unidentified or unconscious person.
- Attempt to identify unconscious person by searching belongings.

While on patrol, Agent Maguire observes a man lying ten yards from the international boundary in Imperial Beach, CA. Upon questioning, the man reveals he fell while scaling the border fence. He claims he is in a great deal of pain and is unable to move. Agent Maguire requests an ambulance and provides immediate first aid. He then requests the man provide his name. However, the man refuses. The ambulance arrives in 15 minutes when a Supervisory Border Patrol Agent guides it to the remote area. Agent Maguire resumes his normal patrol duties immediately east of the area.

From the information given, it can be validly concluded that Agent Maguire failed to fulfill his obligations in this incident because he

a. did not make a second call for the ambulance when the man was in great pain.

b. failed to accompany the man to the hospital.

c. did not attempt to locate a doctor while waiting for the ambulance.

d. failed to relieve the injured man's pain through proper first aid.

e. failed to notify a Supervisory Border Patrol Agent.

6. Homicide is the killing of one human being by the act, procurement, or omission of another. The term *homicide* is a neutral term and may refer to what is called voluntary, willful, or criminal homicide; homicide by accident; homicide in the administration of justice or execution of a sentence; and homicide from inevitable necessity, such as in self-defense. The first type is felonious homicide; the latter types are either justifiable (importing no error or fault) or excusable (importing some error or fault that does not rise to the level of a felony).

From the information given above, it can be validly concluded that homicide is

a. a neutral act.
b. always felonious.
c. always willful.
d. sometimes legal.
e. never exempt from punishment.

7. A person (called the *actor*) is guilty of solicitation to commit a crime if, by words or actions, he or she commands, encourages, or persuades another to commit the crime. However, if, after such solicitation, the actor persuades or attempts to persuade the other person not to follow through with the crime, or prevents the other person from following through, this may be used in the actor's defense. On the other hand, if the actor makes no attempt to stop the crime, he or she is guilty of solicitation, whether or not the crime is committed. Under the Model Penal Code, solicitation is of the same grade and degree as the offense solicited.

From the information given above, it CANNOT be validly concluded that

a. solicitation to commit a crime is regarded as being as serious as committing the crime oneself.
b. for a person to be found guilty of the crime of solicitation, a crime must have been committed.
c. if a person attempts to stop the crime he orshe has solicited another to commit, this fact can be used in that person's defense.
d. solicitation need not entail a verbal request in order to be criminal.
e. there are varying degrees of solicitation.

8. *Slander* is the speaking of false and defamatory words tending to cause prejudice against a person and damage that person's reputation. In some cases, prosecution for slander may necessitate proof of a special kind of damage. However, in other cases, slander is considered *slander per se*—that is, slanderous in itself—and special damage need not be proven. Falling under the heading *slander per se* are utterances that charge the other person with commission of a crime; attributes to that person that he or she has some disease that would cause society to shun that person; or accusations that tend to injure a person in that person's occupation.

From the information given above, it can be validly concluded that a person can be prosecuted for slander only if that person's slanderous words

a. cause special damage to the slandered person.
b. damage the slandered person in that person's occupation.
c. deprive the slandered person of society.
d. entail false and defamatory statements.
e. charge the slandered person with a crime.

9. Grounds for deportation of aliens fall into two broad categories. The first covers prohibited acts committed at or prior to entry into the United States (which includes having entered the country illegally—for example, by falsifying documents or evading inspection at the border). The second covers prohibited acts committed since entry into the United States (for example, committing a criminal offense or engaging in activity whose purpose is the overthrow of the United States government by force). In regard to the former category, the Immigration and Nationality Act permits the DHS to "look back" and deport aliens who should not have been admitted in the first place, had their prohibited acts been known.

From the information given above, it can be validly concluded that

a. only aliens who have committed a deportable offense prior to entering the United States may be deported.

b. some aliens who have not committed a deportable offense prior to entering the United States may be deported.

c. aliens may be deported only if they commit prohibited acts both before and after entering the United States.

d. only aliens who have falsified documents or evaded inspection of the border may be deported.

e. only aliens who have committed criminal acts or advocated the overthrow of the U.S. government by force may be deported.

10. The Supreme Court has consistently held that the decision to admit an alien to the United States or to exclude an alien from the United States lies entirely with Congress and that Congress can set whatever terms it chooses. Congress has the authority to discriminate on the basis of nationality, race, political belief, moral character, or mental or physical disability. In addition, Congress can grant special preference to relatives of U.S. residents, and to persons possessing work skills that would tend to boost the U.S. economy. On the other hand, once admitted to the United States, aliens can claim most of the protections guaranteed by the Constitution—for example, freedom of speech and religion, freedom from unreasonable search and seizure, but not the right to hold federal elective office. Persons who are undergoing proceedings to expel them from the United States are likewise granted the safeguards of due process under the Fifth Amendment and cannot be compelled to incriminate themselves.

*From the information given above, it **CANNOT** be validly concluded that*

a. a person seeking to enter the United States has virtually no legal rights.

b. a person, once admitted to the United States, cannot hold any elected office.

c. some noncitizens are guaranteed certain constitutional rights, even if they engage in criminal activities.

d. persons pending deportation have a right to due process without regard to the opinion Congress may hold of that person.

e. a person seeking to enter the United States can be excluded on the basis of nationality or race.

11. In terms of criminal activity, *mitigating circumstances* are those which reduce the moral blameworthiness of the action. It is a term used for the sake of fairness and mercy and does not constitute justification for the offense, nor does it excuse the offense. For example, a person who kills in the heat of passion may be said to have killed under mitigating circumstances— but that person will still be prosecuted, though perhaps for manslaughter rather than murder. Another example would be that of a defendant in a civil suit who is accused of slander but who had spoken in good faith, with honesty and purpose, rather than maliciously for the sake of harming another.

From the information given above, it can be validly concluded that mitigating circumstances

a. can result in a decreased sentence.
b. are only looked at in heat-of-passion defenses.
c. are only looked at in criminal proceedings.
d. are only looked at in civil proceedings.
e. constitute a justification for a crime.

12. As a student at the U.S. Border Patrol Academy, you are provided with the following scenario: Agent Dassaro, while on routine patrol in the area of the South Levee, just feet from the international border and miles from any residential area, discovers that the door to a water plant storage building is unlocked. He carefully opens the door and hears sounds from inside. Prudently, he steps away and radios for backup because he knows there are tools inside that can be used as weapons. Three Border Patrol Agents immediately respond to back up Agent Dassaro. The agents open the door and tactically enter the storage building. The illegal aliens hiding inside the building are surprised and immediately surrender without a struggle. Both suspects admit to being Mexican nationals and entering the United States without proper documentation or examination. Here are the details:

Location:	South Levee, water plant storage building
Date:	Tuesday, July 25, 2006
Time:	1:20 A.M.
Event:	Illegal entry
Agents involved:	Brian Henderson, Peter Maguire, Claudio De La O
Suspects involved:	Roberto Martinez, Raul Contreras

Agent Dassaro must file a report on the incident. You are the Supervisory Border Patrol Agent who must review the report. From the information given above, it can be validly concluded that

a. Martinez and Contreras broke into a storage shed at 1:20 A.M. on Tuesday, July 25. Brian Henderson, Peter Maguire, Claudio De La O, and Dassaro captured them.
b. at 1:20 A.M. on Tuesday, July 25, an illegal entry into the United States was discovered at the water plant storage building on the South Levee. With the assistance of Henderson, Maguire, and De La O, the suspects Contreras and Martinez were arrested by Agent Dassaro without incident.
c. Henderson, Maguire, and De La O assisted Dassaro in taking Martinez and Contreras into custody following their illegal entry into the United States.
d. The illegal entry of two illegal aliens was averted at the South Levee on Tuesday, July 25 at 1:20 A.M. when the suspects, Maguire and De La O, were surprised and did not shoot at Henderson or Dassaro.
e. Dassaro, Henderson, Maguire, and De La O all violated Border Patrol policy because they are not allowed to enter private premises to make arrests.

13. In several states, the crime of arson is divided into three degrees: first, second, and third. First-degree arson is the burning at night of an inhabited dwelling. Second-degree arson is the burning at night of a building other than an inhabited dwelling but close enough to such a dwelling as to endanger it. Third-degree arson is the burning of a building, not subject to arson in the first or second degree, whether one's own or another's, for the purpose of defrauding an insurance company.

From the information given above, it can be validly concluded that

a. the crime of arson is always divided into three degrees and sometimes entails the burning of a building that belongs to another.

b. the crime of arson is sometimes divided into three degrees and always entails the burning at night of an inhabited dwelling.

c. the crime of arson is always divided into three degrees and can entail the burning of a building of one's own or of another person.

d. the crime of arson is sometimes divided into three degrees and can entail the burning of a building of one's own or of another.

e. the crime of arson is always divided into three degrees and entails the burning of an inhabited dwelling at night.

14. Hearsay is a statement made outside of court and repeated in court for the purpose of asserting the truth of the facts stated. As hearsay, the statement is inadmissible. For example, Bill runs into the back of a trailer being pulled by Raina's car, and maintains that Raina was at fault because the red lights on the back of the trailer were broken. Raina's brother tells the insurance investigator that those lights have been broken for a month. The statement is inadmissible in court as testimony because it is hearsay asserting the fact that the lights were broken. A statement made out of court is not necessarily hearsay, however. David trips over a broken piece of sidewalk in front of Sasha's house, and sues Sasha for negligence. Sasha offers the testimony of her cousin who says that just before David tripped, he shouted a warning, "Watch out!" This is not hearsay, because the testimony is not offered for the purpose of asserting the fact that there was a dip in the sidewalk, only for the purpose of declaring that the injured party was forewarned.

From the information given above, it can be validly concluded that the term *hearsay* refers to

a. any statement made out of court and repeated in court.

b. some statements made out of court and repeated in court.

c. an untrue statement made under oath.

d. any statement made out of court to an insurance investigator.

e. a true statement overheard at a crime scene.

15. Attorney-client privilege gives a client the right not to disclose, and to prevent his or her lawyer from disclosing, any confidential communication that takes place between them relating to their professional relationship. However, if the client freely tells an outside third party the details of the consultation, the privilege is presumed waived. If a third party is present, the privilege is also presumed waived, unless that third person is deemed helpful to the consultation (for example, a law clerk or a translator for client who does not speak English). If client and lawyer take reasonable precautions and are still eavesdropped upon, this does not waive the attorney-client privilege. If, however, their business is discussed in a crowded elevator, where they have no reasonable expectation of privacy, the attorney-client privilege is waived.

*From the information given above, it **CANNOT** be validly concluded that* attorney-client privilege is presumed waived if

a. a third party is present who is unnecessary to the consultation.

b. a lawyer and client fail to take all precautions and are overheard by an eavesdropper.

c. a lawyer and client choose to speak of confidential matters in a small space crowded with other people.

d. a third person is present who is helpful to the consultation.

e. the client freely tells a third person about the consultation.

16. The common law application of criminal intent requires that a defendant have the general or specific intent to commit a crime. This distinction has never been clear. However, the courts have attempted to fill the void left by the legislature because legislation does not always explicitly delineate with regard to the type of intent required for conviction. Over time, the courts have determined that a defendant who acts with general intent means to perform the crime but does not necessarily mean to accomplish a result, whereas a defendant who acts with specific intent not only intends to perform the criminal act but also intends to accomplish the result. Crimes requiring specific intent for conviction include larceny and burglary. While specific intent is more subjective in its analysis, general intent is more objective and is based on the perspective of a reasonable person. Both types of intent are not weighted in terms of morality. This should not be confused with the traditional *mens rea* approach used by the courts to assess moral blameworthiness as it has evolved into a much more specific and objective approach in determining guilt.

From the information given above, it can be validly concluded that

a. general intent is subjectively determined by a court.

b. specific intent and general intent are mutually exclusive.

c. the legislature intentionally delegated the standards for intent to the courts to avoid the traditional issues of morality in American jurisprudence.

d. if a defendant achieved the desired result in the commission of a crime, he or she acted with specific intent.

e. both types of intent are weighted on the morality of the crime.

17. When judging witnesses, courts customarily find the testimony of an expert witness appropriate where the witness is called to interpret facts which lay persons are not usually called upon to evaluate. An example would be fingerprint or ballistic interpretation. Courts are less likely to find the testimony of an expert witness appropriate when its purpose is to help the jury make the kinds of evaluations juries are usually asked to make. Statements about the reliability of eyewitness testimony, for example, or testimony about whether a witness is being truthful fall into this category. Eyewitness testimony has repeatedly been shown to be unreliable, yet judges generally presume that juries are intelligent enough to judge whether the eyewitness is lying or mistaken. Similarly, judges trust juries to be able to intelligently evaluate the credibility of a witness.

From the information given above, it can be validly concluded that eyewitness testimony

a. is unreliable unless it is backed up by expert testimony.

b. reliable in most cases unless contradicted by expert testimony.

c. inappropriate and unreliable according to most judges.

d. often wrong but allowed by most judges as appropriate.

e. most reliable if the eyewitness is an expert.

18. Ivan is on trial for the murder of Shamus in a hunting accident. The prosecutor has elicited testimony from a forest ranger. According to the ranger, Shamus said, "I'm gonna die. It was Ivan that shot me," at the scene of the accident. Later, Ivan's attorney elicited testimony from Larry, who sat beside Shamus in the hospital the day after the accident, just before he took a turn for the worse. Shamus told Larry that Corina, an old girlfriend who had been lying in wait in a duck blind, had shot him. The judge ruled that Shamus's statement to the forest ranger was admissible as a dying declaration, but that Ivan's attorney could try to impeach (throw doubt upon) Shamus's dying statement, just as if it were the testimony of a living witness.

*From the information given above, it **CANNOT** be validly concluded that* a witness who is dead at the time of trial can be

a. cross-examined just as if the witness were alive.

b. impeached just as if the witness were alive.

c. quoted in court as part of the testimony.

d. detrimental to the prosecution.

e. useful to the defense.

19. Karla sued Madeleine for assault at a bar called Rico's. At trial, a witness, Bill, testified that Madeleine had jumped Karla, who was sitting peacefully on a barstool sipping her beer, and that the attack was completely unprovoked. On cross-examination, Karla's attorney asked Bill about a prior bad act, having evaded income tax for the past three years. Madeleine's attorney objected. The judge rightly ruled the question proper, because the prior bad act was brought out on cross-examination, rather than through presenting extrinsic evidence. It was relevant, the judge said, because it showed the witness's character as being sometimes untruthful.

From the information given above, it can be validly concluded that, during a trial, questioning a witness about a prior bad act is
a. always proper.
b. never proper.
c. proper as long as it is not elicited on cross-examination.
d. sometimes proper and sometimes not.
e. proper as long as evidence is presented.

20. Bob Hinkley, an accountant, is on trial for embezzlement from the company he works for, Grandma's Homemade Cookies. He offers to bring in testimony by his neighbors of his peace-loving nature. The judge will not admit the testimony, saying that a criminal defendant is not allowed to offer into evidence testimony about his or her good character, unless the character trait bears directly upon the crime at issue. Because the defendant is accused of embezzlement, testimony regarding his peace-loving, nonviolent nature is irrelevant. Specifically, the crime has everything to do with his truthfulness, but nothing to do with his lack of a tendency toward violence.

From the information given above, it can be validly concluded that testimony about any defendant's good character is likely to be
a. admissible in court only if it can be proven.
b. not admissible in court unless it bears directly on the crime.
c. admissible in court only if it does not bear directly on the crime.
d. not admissible in court unless it is related to truthfulness.
e. admissible in court with no restrictions.

21. A-1 and A-2 visas to the United States are valid for as long as the Secretary of State extends recognition to the holder. A-3 visas are valid for not more than three years but may be extended in increments of not more than two years. In 2000, A-1 visas are given to Adara Janus, her husband, and their two children, because Adara is an ambassador from her country. At the same time, an A-3 visa is given to Oden Wolf, Adara's personal assistant. Also in 2000, an A-2 visa is given to Hedrick Yuli, an employee of his country's government, and an A-3 visa is given to Ron Tripp, Hedrick's personal secretary.

From the information given above, it can be validly concluded that, if Hedrick asks Ron Tripp to remain in the United States for nine years, until the year 2009, Ron
a. could not do this because his visa is only valid for three years.
b. could not do this because his visa is only valid for five years (three years plus an extension of two years).
c. could do this as long as the Secretary of State extended recognition to him.
d. could do this if he were granted three more two-year extensions.
e. could do this because of a request by his employer.

22. Roy Pfeifer is arrested on a drunk driving charge, taken to the police station, booked, and videotaped. The tape reveals that he slurs his speech and insults officers. At trial, the prosecutor properly identifies the tape and asks that it be admitted into evidence. The judge says that, although the tape could conceivably be excluded if its value as evidence were outweighed by the danger that it would be unfairly prejudicial to the defendant, in this case it would be allowed, because the prejudice it may cause is not unfair. The tape is, in fact, evidence that Roy was drunk.

From the information given above, it can be validly concluded that at trial, videotapes of the defendant misbehaving

a. cannot be used unless they have probative value and are unfairly prejudicial.

b. will always be used if they are not unfairly prejudicial and have no value as evidence.

c. cannot be used unless they have value as evidence and are not unfairly prejudicial.

d. will always be used if they have value as evidence and probative value.

e. cannot be used if they have value as evidence and are not unfairly prejudicial.

23. Bryce Camden sues Mavis Parmenter because he tripped over paint cans on the sidewalk out in front of Mavis's flower shop. Dr. Forke, a physician who has no prior knowledge of the case, but who sat through the entire trial listening, is called by Mavis's lawyer to give an opinion as to whether Bryce's injuries are permanent. The judge allows the testimony.

From the information given above, it can be validly concluded that the testimony of an expert witness

a. cannot be allowed unless the witness sits through the entire trial listening.

b. can be allowed only if the witness sits through the entire trial listening.

c. is only believed if the witness has sat and listened throughout the entire trial.

d. can sometimes be allowed even if the witness has sat through the entire trial listening.

e. is not believed unless the witness has sat through the entire trial listening.

24. The First Amendment to the Constitution guarantees freedom of religion, which embraces two concepts: the freedom to believe and the freedom to act on that belief. The first is absolute. The second is subject to regulation for the protection of society.

From the information given above, it can be validly concluded that under the First Amendment to the Constitution, if a religious belief is such that

a. it is not acted upon, it is a belief from which society needs protection.

b. if society does not need protection from it, then it can be acted upon.

c. if society does not act upon it, then it does not need protection.

d. it needs protection from society, then it cannot be acted upon.

e. it does not need protection from society, then it can be acted upon.

25. Although undercover work by the police or by government officials is allowed, it has limitations. For example, if an officer or agent of the government induces a person to commit a crime that the person has not contemplated committing, for the purpose of instituting criminal prosecution against that person, this is called *entrapment* and is illegal. Entrapment can occur in two ways: (1) by knowingly representing the crime in a false light, so that it will not be seen by the person as illegal; and (2) by employing persuasive tactics that will induce the person to commit the illegal act when that person originally had no intention of committing it.

From the information given above, it can be validly concluded that, if an undercover officer named Ron arrests a suspect named Sheryl for an act they have discussed beforehand,

a. Ron is not guilty of entrapment unless Sheryl was not intending to commit the crime until Ron suggested it.

b. Ron is guilty of entrapment if he suggested that the crime was not illegal, and Sheryl was already intending to commit it.

c. Sheryl is not the victim of entrapment if she was not intending to commit the crime until Ron suggested it.

d. Sheryl is not the victim of entrapment if she committed the crime suggested by Ron because he said it was not illegal.

e. Ron is not guilty of entrapment if he suggested committing a crime and Sheryl did it without contemplating it beforehand.

26. Embezzlement occurs when a person willfully and unlawfully converts another's money to his or her own use—money of which the wrong-doer initially acquired possession lawfully by reason of a position of trust, such as employment. For embezzlement to be proven in court, (1) the money must have been converted to the defendant's own use; (2) there has to have been a relationship of trust, such as employment, between the defendant and the money's owner; (3) the money must have come into the defendant's possession through that relationship; and (4) the conversion of the money to the defendant's use has to have been deliberate and knowingly fraudulent.

From the information given above, it can be validly concluded that if an administrative assistant, Jon, spends money that he got from the Green Valley Country Club travel fund on buying a new $1,000 blazer, it is very likely embezzlement if

a. the blazer was for Jon's wear on private social occasions and Jon does not manage country club funds.

b. Jon manages country club funds, the blazer bore the country club logo, and it was for wear to country club business funds only.

c. it is not part of Jon's job to manage country club funds, but he took the money anyway.

d. Jon manages country club funds and the blazer is for wear on private social occasions.

e. Jon believed he was authorized to buy the blazer so that he would look well groomed and prosperous at country club functions.

27. Pete is on trial for selling marijuana, a crime that took place four months ago. His new wife, Candi, is called by the prosecutor to testify about a meeting she saw before they were married, between Pete and a man named Ardis, during which Pete sold Ardis $\frac{1}{4}$ kilo of marijuana. Pete's lawyer objects, but the judge says that it is Candi's choice whether or not she wants to give adverse testimony. He points out, however, that spousal privilege (which says that a person cannot be forced to testify against his or her spouse) does not apply here, because the communication did not take place during the marriage.

From the information given above, it can be validly concluded that if Candi

a. testifies, she violates spousal privilege.

b. does not testify, the judge can compel her to do so.

c. does not testify, she will be implicated in the crime.

d. testifies, she will be implicated in the crime.

e. does not testify, the judge cannot compel her to do so.

28. The legal Rules of Evidence state that, at trial, all relevant evidence is admissable, but evidence that is irrelevant will not be admissable. Furthermore, evidence is relevant only if it has probative value—that is, if it tends toward proving a fact consequential to the case.

From the information given above, it can be validly concluded that, at trial, evidence that is

a. not irrelevant will be deemed not to have probative value.

b. not relevant will be deemed not to have probative value.

c. deemed to have probative value will be deemed not relevant.

d. not irrelevant will not be deemed to have probative value.

e. not deemed to have probative value will be deemed not irrelevant.

29. A U.S. citizen can lose his or her citizenship in one of two ways, by denaturalization (which applies to naturalized citizens only) or by expatriation (which can apply to both naturalized citizens and citizens by birth). Denaturalization takes place when a court revokes the naturalization order because it is found to have been illegally or fraudulently obtained. Expatriation takes place when any citizen voluntarily abandons his or her country and becomes a citizen or subject of another. The Supreme Court has said, however, that the expatriate must have voluntarily performed an expatriating act in order for loss of citizenship to occur (examples are becoming a citizen of another country, serving in the military of a hostile country, or formally renouncing nationality before a diplomatic officer of the United States).

From the information given above, it can be validly concluded that

a. no denaturalization takes place if the naturalization order is found not to have been obtained legally.

b. expatriation takes place only if the act of expatriating is not involuntary.

c. no expatriation takes place if the act of expatriating is voluntary.

d. no denaturalization takes place unless the naturalization order is found to have been obtained legally.

e. expatriation takes place unless the act of expatriating is not involuntary.

30. Probation is the releasing of a convicted person into the community rather than imprisoning him or her. Two basic rules of probation are that the convicted person must behave in a manner approved by the probation officer, and that the convicted person must report to him or her. It is an act of grace and clemency granted by judicial action to a deserving individual, from whom good behavior is expected—frequently a juvenile or a first offender. Parole is the release from imprisonment after actually serving part of a sentence. It is conditional freedom granted by executive action—that is, by a parole board that believes the parolee will be law-abiding after release.

From the information given, it can be validly concluded that if a person is placed on probation, that person
a. has shown good behavior while confined.
b. has not yet commenced his or her sentence.
c. is under executive order to abide by the law.
d. is always a juvenile or first offender.
e. has not committed a truly criminal act.

▶ Section 2

If you are taking the Artifical Language Test, turn to page 155.

Spanish Language (Part A)

Find the suggested answer, of the five choices, that is closest in meaning to the key (italicized) word.

1. Los hombres *labraban* la tierra durante el verano.
a. escuchaban
b. lloraban
c. cansaban
d. se lavaban
e. cultivaban

2. El sospechoso no *entregó* la arma al agente.
a. entregaron
b. comprobar
c. dio
d. llevó
e. desentender

3. *Comienzo* a trabajar a las cinco de la mañana todos los días.
a. Conozco
b. Empiezo
c. Como
d. Enojo
e. Traduzco

4. ¿Hay *alguna persona* aquí que pueda entender el español?
a. algodón
b. una nieta
c. alguien
d. un perico
e. una pesadilla

5. Los nacionales extranjeros no *entraron* a través del puerto de la entrada.
   a. venido
   b. venido adentro
   c. ir
   d. cortesias
   e. llegar

6. *El señor* tiene un perro.
   a. La ventana
   b. El helado
   c. La señora
   d. El hombre
   e. La mesa

7. Yo *mercaré* algunas cosas hoy en la tienda.
   a. hablaré
   b. daré
   c. enojaré
   d. leeré
   e. compraré

8. Ud. no tiene *la derecha* de entrar ilegalmente.
   a. la capacidad
   b. el honor
   c. el privilege
   d. la cierta
   e. la posible

9. El domingo voy a llevar mi *vestido nuevo*.
   a. perro nuevo
   b. piel nueva
   c. ropa nueva
   d. vestigo nuevo
   e. vía nueva

10. La gente *no podía cruzar* el río sin difículty.
   a. cruzo
   b. no podría cruzar
   c. cruzaran
   d. no se cruzaban
   e. habrían cruzando

11. ¿Es necesario tener pasaportes para *visitar* México?
   a. viajar a
   b. vigilar
   c. zurcir
   d. casar
   e. ayudar

12. ¿Qué tal?
   a. ¿Por qué?
   b. ¿Cómo estás?
   c. ¿Qué lástima?
   d. ¿Qué sorpresa?
   e. ¿Qué baste?

13. Ellos desaparecen en *aquella ciudad*.
   a. por allí
   b. los de abajo
   c. aquel cuervo
   d. por allá
   e. aquel pueblo

14. ¿Quiénes *preparaban* la comida ayer cuando Ud. llegó?
   a. tiraban
   b. se bañaban
   c. habían
   d. cocinaban
   e. les gustaba

15. Todos los *agentes* senalaron al mismo sospechosos cuando entro por la puerta.
  a. agentos
  b. senores
  c. policia
  d. extranjeros
  e. jefes

16. *El ferrocarril* es uno de los principales medios de transporte.
  a. El automóvil
  b. La ferretería
  c. El hipódromo
  d. El funicular
  e. El tren

17. *Caminamos* con los pies.
  a. Andamos
  b. Nadamos
  c. Jugamos
  d. Cantamos
  e. Votamos

18. Yo tengo un *arma*.
  a. instrumento
  b. cuchillo
  c. cuchara
  d. brazo
  e. dentaduras

19. Siempre se prohibe *hablar* inglés aquí.
  a. tocar
  b. ver
  c. oír
  d. pensar
  e. usar

20. Ellos son gigantes, y si tienes miedo *quítate* de ahí, que yo voy a entrar con ellos en desigual batalla.
  a. vete
  b. descansa
  c. implora
  d. lastímate
  e. límpiate

Spanish Language (Part B-I)
Supply the correct words that should be used in place of the blanks within a sentence.

21. Mi coche tiene _____ motor grande y _____ rápido.
  a. una, era
  b. una, fue
  c. un, es
  d. un, carro
  e. un, my

22. Muchas veces, cuando hace mucho ____, hace mucho _____ también.
  a. tiempo, valor
  b. sol, calor
  c. nieve, frijol
  d. sol, comer
  e. viento, calma

23. _____prefiero que _____ vengas por la tarde.
  a. Yo, tú
  b. Uds., tú
  c. Tú, Ud.
  d. Yo, nosotros
  e. Tú, Uds.

24. _____ evidencia escasa _____ procesar al contrabandista y a los extranjeros ilegales.
  a. Había, para
  b. No, es
  c. Hay, para
  d. No había, en orden
  e. Tienen, nosotros

25. Las _____ no le dijeron la _____ al agente.
  a. pájaros, comida
  b. pasajero, corrección
  c. farmacia, factura
  d. familias, verdad
  e. árboles, piensamiento

26. ¿Hay _____ pulgas aquí en _____?
  a. muchas, la playa
  b. muy, la ropa
  c. los mejores, esta hotel
  d. pulchras, el casa
  e. delicioso, la ventana

27. Siempre se lava _____ las manos antes de
_____.
  a. tú, comiendo
  b. Ud., comer
  c. Ud., comiendo
  d. tus, comiendo
  e. Uds., comer

28. Ramón acaba de _____ para _____.
  a. hablar, jamón
  b. quieran, dulces
  c. salir, casa
  d. sale, casar
  e. saliré, casa

29. _____ agua no está _____.
  a. La, correcto
  b. La, terminado
  c. El, feliz
  d. La, fresca
  e. El, fría

30. En 1808 España _____ invadida por los ejércitos de Napoleón y las colonias aprovecharon _____ momento para declarar su independencia.
  a. sería, este
  b. sera, este
  c. fue, este
  d. fueron, esta
  e. fuma, sera

Spanish Language (Part B-II)

Of the four choices given for each of the following questions, select the only one that is correct.

31. a. Antes de México la guerra iraron corregir la observación.
  b. Ahora día la Universidad de México es muy moderna.
  c. Vamos a olvidar la día de la independencia.
  d. En México la guerra por la independencia fue iniciada por el cura Miguel Hidalgo en 1810.

32. a. Minas Gerais es un ciudad muy hermoso.
  b. Con los descubrimientos de minas en la región de Minas Gerais, llegaron al Brasil millares de europeos en busca de fortuna.
  c. Los europeos han buscando la fuerza.
  d. ¡Quién conozco!

33. a. ¿Cómo estás Ud.?

b. ¿Dormes bien?

c. ¿En como busca aquí?

d. Prefiero jugo de naranja con azúcar.

34. a. Nosotros deben ser caudillos aquí.

b. Ustedes no puedas venir.

c. La mujer no tiene su pasaporte.

d. ¿Cúantos annos tiene Ud.?

35. a. ¿Quieres ir al sonrisa?

b. ¿Porqué no pregunta Ud. la papagayo?

c. Nosotros vamos al centro.

d. Hasta madona.

36. a. ¡Tráigame sus papeles, por favor!

b. Palabras magníficas es fácil decir difícil hacer.

c. ¡Es perro un minuto!

d. Tal vez tieno miedo.

37. a. ¿Cuál hora es abuelito querido?

b. Señor Garcia nos enviamos las papeles.

c. Eso no valen la pena.

d. Hay muchas flores en el jardín.

38. a. ¿Con quién somos hablan Ud.?

b. La verdad es una flora mucho delicado.

c. Ud. comía en aquel restaurante en esos tiempos, ¿no es verdad?

d. Todos los animaluchos estan esperiendo su comida.

39. a. Las mujeres dijeron que no podían oír en aquel sitio.

b. Los mayos sabía mucho de matemáticas y astronomía.

c. Ricardo Palma es uno de los excritores más célebres del Perú.

d. No tengo tiempo suficiente gastar en vacaciones.

40. a. Nosotros no sabemos la dirección de su oficina.

b. Ud. pueden entender bien el español.

c. Yo conoco a él.

d. Cuando regresaré Ud. podemos continuar la lección.

Spanish Language (Part B-III)

Read each sentence carefully and supply, from the five choices, the word that will correctly replace the italicized word. If no correction is necessary, select choice **e**.

41. El supervisor no *aprobó* la detención.

a. autorizó

b. negó

c. abriemos

d. abrio

e. No es necesario hacer ninguna corrección.

42. Te requieren *tener* todos los documentos necesarios.

a. tienes

b. tengo

c. tenéis

d. tienen

e. No es necesario hacer ninguna corrección.

43. Los manuales hemos *abarcado* un sinnumero de posibilidades y hemos *abreviado* el tiempo que se necesita para completar los tramites.

a. abarcando / abreviando

b. abarcados / abreviados

c. abarco / abrevio

d. abarcan / abrevian

e. No es necesario hacer ninguna corrección.

44. Los que *abastecen* las cocinas de las unidades de rescate anoche trajeron magnificas provisiones.
   a. habian abastecido / lentamente
   b. abasteciendo / no
   c. abastecieran / manana
   d. abastezco / arriba
   e. No es necesario hacer ninguna corrección.

45. Mi esposa y yo *viajaría* a España el verano pasado.
   a. viajaron
   b. viajamos
   c. viajaremos
   d. ven
   e. No es necesario hacer ninguna corrección.

46. En Cuba hace *mucha calma*, pero después de cuatro años me acostumbré al clima cálido.
   a. muy fuerte
   b. mucho calor
   c. mucha nieve
   d. muchas travesuras
   e. No es necesario hacer ninguna corrección.

47. La cocaína es *un* droga peligrosa.
   a. unos
   b. una
   c. el
   d. aquel
   e. No es necesario hacer ninguna corrección.

48. Usted no fumas tanto como antes.
   a. Ti
   b. Ustedes
   c. Nosotros
   d. Tú
   e. No es necesario hacer ninguna corrección.

49. *Las legumbres* quiere que sus estudiantes no lleguen tarde a clase.
   a. El professor
   b. La tarea
   c. El papel
   d. Los estudiantes
   e. No es necesario hacer ninguna corrección.

50. Tengo un *compromiso* con la señorita Martinez.
   a. playa
   b. hormiga
   c. mariposa
   d. arco iris
   e. No es necesario hacer ninguna corrección.

▶ Supplemental Booklet

To answer the Artificial Language questions, refer to the sections in this Supplemental Booklet: *Vocabulary Lists* and *Grammatical Rules*. (See Chapter 8 of this book for additional information.)

The words given in the following Vocabulary Lists are not exactly the same as those that will be given in the actual Border Patrol Exam (some are and some are not). Therefore, it is best not to try to memorize them before taking the actual test. The Grammatical Rules are the same as those used in the actual test, except that some of the suffixes (word endings) used in the real test differ from those used in the manual and in this supplemental booklet. You may also need to refer to the Glossary of Grammatical Terms as you take the practice exams. The manual will be given to you at the time of the real test, as well.

▶ Vocabulary Lists for the Artificial Language

ARRANGED ALPHABETICALLY BY THE ENGLISH WORD			
English	**Artificial Language**	**English**	**Artificial Language**
a, an	bex*	skillful	autile
alien	huslek	that	velle
and	cre	the	ric**
boy	ekaplek	this	volle
country	failek	to be	synbar
difficult	brale	to border	regbar
enemy	avelek	to cross	chonbar
friend	kometlek	to drive	arbar
from	mor	to escape	pirbar
government	almanlek	to guard	bonbar
he, him	yev	to have	tulbar
jeep	cublek	to identify	kalenbar
legal	colle	to injure	liabar
loyal	inle	to inspect	zelbar
man	kaplek	to shoot	degbar
of	quea	to spy	tatbar
paper	trenedlek	to station	lexbar
river	browlek	to work	frigbar

* *Applies to all genders*
** *Applies to all genders and numbers*

ARRANGED ALPHABETICALLY BY THE ARTIFICIAL LANGUAGE WORD			
Artificial Language	**English**	**Artificial Language**	**English**
almanlek	government	kalenbar	to identify
arbar	to drive	kaplek	man
autile	skillful	kometlek	friend
avelek	enemy	lexbar	to station
bex	a, an*	liabar	to injure
bonbar	to guard	mor	from
brale	difficult	pirbar	to escape
browlek	river	quea	of
chonbar	to cross	regbar	to border
colle	legal	ric	the**
cre	and	synbar	to be
cublek	jeep	tatbar	to spy
degbar	to shoot	trenedlek	paper
ekaplek	boy	tulbar	to have
failek	country	velle	that
frigbar	to work	volle	this
huslek	alien	yev	he, him
inle	loyal	zelbar	to inspect

* *Applies to all genders*
** *Applies to all genders and numbers*

▶ Grammatical Rules for the Artificial Language

The grammatical rules given here are the same as those used in the Border Patrol Exam, with the only exception being that some of the suffixes (word endings) and prefixes (word beginnings) used in the exam differ from those used here.

During the exam, you will have access to the rules at all times. Consequently, it is important that you understand these rules, but it is not necessary that you memorize them. In fact, memorizing them will hinder rather than help you, since the endings of words are different in the version of the Artificial Language that appears in this manual than the one that appears in the actual test.

You should note that Part Three of the Artificial Language Manual contains a glossary of grammatical terms to assist you if you are not thoroughly familiar with the meanings of these grammatical terms.

Rule 1

To form the feminine singular of a noun, a pronoun, or an adjective, add the suffix *-zof* to the masculine singular form of the noun. In the Artificial Language, there are only masculine and feminine forms for these words. There are no neuter forms.

> Example: If a male eagle is a *verlek*, a female eagle is a *verlekzof*. If an ambitious man is a *tosle* man, an ambitious woman is a *toslezof* woman.

Rule 2

To form the plural of nouns, pronouns, and adjectives, add the suffix *-ax* to the correct singular form.

> Example: If one male eagle is a *verlek*, several male eagles are *verlekax*. If an ambitious woman is a *toslezof* woman, several ambitious women are *toslezofax* women.

Rule 3

Adjectives modifying nouns and pronouns with feminine and/or plural endings must have endings that agree with the words they modify.

> Example: If an active male eagle is a *sojle verlek*, several active male eagles are *sojleax verlekax*. If an active female eagle is *sojlezof verlekzof*, several active female eagles are *sojlezofax verlekzofax*.

Rule 4

The stem of the verb is obtained by omitting the suffix *-bar* from the infinitive form of the verb.

> Example: The stem of the verb *tirbar* is *tir*.

Rule 5

All subjects and their verbs must agree in number; that is, singular subjects require singular verbs and plural subjects require plural verbs. (See Rules 6 and 7.)

Rule 6

To form the present tense of a verb, add the suffix *-ot* to the stem for the singular form or the suffix *-et* to the stem for the plural.

> Example: If to bark is *nalbar*, then *nalot* is the present singular (the dog barks) and *nalet* is the present tense for the plural (the dogs bark).

Rule 7

To form the past tense of a verb, first add the suffix *-rem* to the stem, and then add the suffix *-ot* if the verb is singular or the suffix *-et* if the verb is plural.

> Example: If to bark is *nalbar*, then *nalremot* is the past tense for the singular (the dog barked), and *nalremet* is the past tense for the plural (the dogs barked).

Rule 8

To form a noun from a verb, add the suffix *-lek* to the stem of the verb.

> Example: If *longbar* is to write, then a writer is a *longlek*.

Rule 9

To form an adjective from a noun, substitute the suffix *-le* for the suffix *-lek*.

> Example: If *pellek* is beauty, then a beautiful male eagle is a *pelle verlek*, and a beautiful female eagle is a *pellezof verlekzof*. (Note the feminine ending *-zof*.)

Rule 10

To form an adverb from an adjective, add the suffix *-de* to the masculine form of the adjective. (Note that adverbs do not change their form to agree in number or gender with the word they modify.)

> Example: If *pelle* is beautiful, then beautifully is *pellede*.

Rule 11

To form the possessive of a noun or pronoun, add the suffix *-oe* to the noun or pronoun.

> Example: If a *boglek* is a dog, then a dog's collar is a *boglekoe* collar. If he is *yev*, then his book is *yevoe* book.

Rule 12

To make a word negative, add the prefix *poh-* to the correct affirmative form.

> Example: An inactive male eagle is a *pohsojle verlek*. If the dog barks is *boglek nalot*, then the dog does not bark is *boglek pohnalot*.

▶ Section 2: Artificial Language

Use the Supplemental Booklet on pages 155–158 to help you answer these questions. You may refer to the vocabulary and grammatical rules throughout this test section.

For questions 1 through 20, make a check mark beside each numbered word that is correctly translated into the Artificial Language. When you have finished this process, fill out your answer sheet by marking:

a. if only the word numbered 1 is checked as correctly translated.

b. if only the word numbered 2 is checked as correctly translated.

c. if only the word numbered 3 is checked as correctly translated.

d. if two or more of the numbered words are checked as correctly translated.

e. if none of the words is checked as correctly translated.

Be sure to check only the **numbered** words that are **correctly** translated.

Sentence

Translation

1. The guard inspects identification papers.

1. Ric bonlek zelremot kalenleax trenedlekax.
                1   2   3

2. Those drivers are not illegal aliens.

2. Velle arlekax pohsynet pohcolleax huslek.
      1   2   3

3. She is a loyal friend of the government.

3. Yevzof synet bex inlezof kometlekzof quea ric
         1   2
almanlek.
   3

4. The skillful inspector identifies those papers.

4. Ric autileax zellekax kalenot vellezof trenedlekax.
        1   2   3

5. This friendly girl is an enemy spy.

5. Volle kometlezof ekaplekzof synremot bex avelezof
     1   2
tatlekzof.
   3

6. The driver of the jeep was from this country.

6. Bex arlek quea ric cublek synremet mor volle failek.
       1   2   3

7. Those boys crossed the river.

7. Velleax ekaplekax regremet ricax browlek.
           1   2   3

8. The man shot him from the jeep.

8. Ric ekaplek degremot yev mor ric cublek.
         1   2   3

9. These women worked illegally.

9. Vollezof kaplekzof frigremet pohcolle.
      1   2   3

Sentence	Translation

10. She is disloyal to spy.

10. Kaplekzof synot pohinlezof tatlekzof.
           1   2   3

11. The enemies shot the driver.

11. Ric avelekax degremet ric arle.
        1   2   3

12. She is from the border station.

12. Yevzof synot mor ric reglek lexot.
           1   2   3

13. He has to guard the river.

13. Yev tulremot bonot ric browlekoe.
        1   2   3

14. The government inspected his papers.

14. Ric almanlek zelbremot yevoe trenedlek.
           1   2   3

15. These aliens escaped from his station.

15. Velleax huslekax piret mor yevoe lexlek.
       1   2   3

16. This man and boy have illegal papers.

16. Volle kaplek cre ekaplek tulet pohcolleax
           1   2
trenedlekax.
  3

17. The men are friends of the disloyal guard.

17. Ric kaplekax synet kometlekax quea ric inle bonlek.
       1   2   3

18. These women work illegally.

18. Volleoz kapleknefoz frigim fercollekinef.
      1   2   3

19. The illegal aliens were not injured.

19. Wir fercolle huslekoz synim fer liazotim.
     1   2   3

20. Those women are not aliens from that country.

20. Vellenefoz kapleknefoz fersynem huslekoz mor velle
                1   2
failek.
  3

For each question in this group, select the one of the five suggested choices that correctly translates the italicized word or group of words into the Artificial Language.

Sample question

There is *the boy*.
      1

    a. bex kaplek
    b. wir kaplek
    c. wir ekaplek
    d. velle ekaplek
    e. bex ekaplek

Choice **c** is the correct translation of the underlined words, *the boy*. Now read the following paragraph and choose the correct translation for the words or groups of words that are italicized.

> The *men and women* who patrol and *guard the border* have a complex and difficult
>   21   22
>
> job. They have to deal with both friendly and *unfriendly aliens*, as well as with well-
>   23
>
> trained and *skillful spies*, who are often dangerous. *They have to inspect* and identify
>   24   25
>
> complex *governmental papers* that are written in various foreign languages, and
>   26
>
> they have to make difficult decisions, frequently alone and away from their *stations*.
>   27
>
> *This country's* borders are *skillfully guarded* and kept secure by *these loyal women*
>   28   29   30
>
> and these loyal men.

21. a. kaplekoz loa kaplekferoz
    b. kaplekoz loa kapleknefozc
    c. kaplekae loa kapleknefae
    d. kaplekae loa kaplekferae
    e. kaplekoz bex kaplekferoz

22. a. bonimoz wir reglek
    b. bonimoz wir reglekoz
    c. bonem wir reglek
    d. bonker wir reglek
    e. bonim wir reglek

23. a. ferkometlekkioz huslekoz
b. ferkometlekki huslekki
c. ferkometleoz huslekoz
d. ferkometlekoz huslekoz
e. ferkometlekkioz huslekkioz

24. a. janle tatlekoz
b. janle tatlek
c. janleoz tatlekoz
d. janleoz tatkeroz
e. janle tatkeroz

25. a. yevoz tulim zelkerim
b. yevoz tulem zelker
c. yevoz tulzotim zelker
d. yevoz tulzotim zelkerim
e. yevoz tulim zelker

26. a. almanleoz trenedlekoz
b. almanlek trenedlek
c. almanlek trenedlekoz
d. almanlekoz trenedlekoz
e. almanle trenedlekoz

27. a. lexkeroz
b. lexlekae
c. lexkerae
d. lexlekoz
e. lexleoz

28. a. volle failekae
b. volleae failekae
c. volle failek
d. volleae failek
e. volle faileae

29. a. janlekioz bonzotim
b. janleki bontooz
c. janleki bonto
d. janlekioz bonzotem
e. janleki bonlekki

30. a. volleoz inlenef kapleknefoz
b. vollenefoz inlenefoz kapleknefoz
c. volleoz inle kapleknefoz
d. vollenefoz inlenef kapleknefoz
e. vollenefoz inlenefoz kapleknefoz

Of the five suggested answers to questions 31–36, select the one that correctly translates the English word or words in parentheses into the Artificial Language. You should translate the entire sentence in order to determine what form should be used.

31. (This boy did not have) difficulty crossing the border.
a. Volle ekaplek pohtulremot
b. Velle ekaplek pohtulremot
c. Volle kaplek pohtulremot
d. Volle ekaplek tulremot
e. Velle kaplek pohtulremot

32. She is a spy of (that unfriendly government).
a. vollezof pohkometlek almanlekzof
b. velle pohkometle almanlek
c. volle pohkometlek almanlek
d. vellezof pohkometlezof almanlekzof
e. velle pohkometlek almanlek

33. He shot (an escaped girl).
a. bex pirremot ekaplekzof
b. bexzof pirlezof ekaplekzof
c. bex pirlezof ekaplekzof
d. bexzof pirremot ekaplekzof
e. bex pirle ekaplekzof

34. Two men escaped (from a border station).
a. quea bex regle lexlek
b. mor bex reglek lexlek
c. mor ric regle lexlek
d. mor bex reglekoe lexlek
e. mor bex regle lexlek

35. (The enemy spy) had to injure the loyal guard.
- **a.** Bex avelek tatbar
- **b.** Ric avele tatlek
- **c.** Ric avele tatbar
- **d.** Bex avelek tatlek
- **e.** Ric avelek tatot

36. (The river crossing) was near the station.
- **a.** Bex browlek chonlek
- **b.** Ric browlek chonlek
- **c.** Bex browle chonlek
- **d.** Ric browlekoe chonlek
- **e.** Ric browle chonlek

Select the one of the five suggested answers to questions 37–40 that is the correct form of the expression as it is used in the sentence. Mark on your answer sheet the letter of the correct translation.

At the end of the sentence, you will find instructions in parentheses telling you which grammatical form the answer will be. In some sentences, you will be asked to supply the correct form of *two or more* expressions. In this case, the instructions for these expressions are presented consecutively in the parentheses and are separated by a dash. Be sure to translate the entire sentence before selecting your answer.

37. Ric bonlekzofax synret *inleax*; *yev* synret tatlekax. (negative plural feminine adjective—plural feminine pronoun)
- **a.** inlezofax—yevzofax
- **b.** pohinleax—yevax
- **c.** pohinlezofax—yevax
- **d.** pohinlezofax—yevzofax
- **e.** inleax—yevax

38. Velle avele tatbar *tulremot chonlek* bex browlek. (past singular verb—infinitive)
- **a.** tulet—chonbar
- **b.** tulremet—chonlek
- **c.** tulremot—chonlek
- **d.** tulot—chonbar
- **e.** tulremot—chonbar

39. Ric *ekaplek* trenedlekax synret *pohcolle*. (masculine plural possessive noun—negative plural adjective)
- **a.** kaplekaxoe—pohcolleax
- **b.** ekaplekaxoe—pohcolleax
- **c.** ekaplekax—pohcolle
- **d.** kaplekax—pohcolleax
- **e.** ekaplekaxoe—pohcolle

40. Ric *zelbar* frigot *inle*. (masculine singular noun—adverb)
- **a.** zelot—inlede
- **b.** zellek—inle
- **c.** zellek—inlede
- **d.** zellekax—inlede
- **e.** zelot—inle

► Answers

Section 1: Logical Reasoning

1. b. The essential information from which the answer can be derived is contained in the third and fifth sentence. The third sentence tells us that "some substances found at a crime scene yield valuable clues under microscopic examination." The fifth sentence explains that ". . . all substances found at a crime scene are potential sources of evidence. Therefore, choice **b** can be validly concluded. Choices **a**, **c**, **d**, and **e** are incorrect because they are not supported by the passage.

2. a. Choice **a** (northeast) is the only possible choice. Using the information provided in the passage, it is recommended you draw a map while reading the passage.

3. c. We know from the second sentence that 90% of the people in this district have fingerprints that can be coded. Therefore, we know that 10% (100 − 90 = 10%) have fingerprints that cannot be coded. Choice **a** is incorrect because a probability of 10% is an underestimate of the probability that the fingerprints of a person from the district can be coded. Choice **b** is incorrect because it is also an estimate. Choice **d** is incorrect because it is an overestimate of the probability that the fingerprints of a person from this district cannot be coded. Choice **e** is incorrect because the probability that the fingerprints can be coded is known to be 90%.

4. e. We know from the third sentence that the Type A micro pattern exists in 70% of all Acme Model 200 printers and in some other models of printers. However, we know neither how many other models nor what percentage of other models produce the Type A micro pattern. Accordingly, the probability that the note was printed on the Acme Model 200 printer cannot be determined. Subsequently, choices **a**, **b**, **c**, and **d** are incorrect.

5. b. A specific rule contained in the procedures requires Agent Maguire to accompany the man to the hospital since the man refused to identify himself and was therefore unidentified.

6. d. The passage says that three of the four types of homicide are either *justifiable* or *excusable*, so we can infer that they are *legal* (supporting choice **d**), and if they are legal, logically they would be *exempt from punishment* (ruling out choice **e**). The passage says that homicide is a *neutral term*, but it does not say that it is a *neutral act* (which would be an illogical statement) (ruling out choice **a**). Only *criminal homicide* is listed as *felonious* (ruling out choice **b**). The passage lists a kind of homicide called *accidental homicide* (ruling out choice **c**).

7. b. The passage states that the actor who does not attempt to stop the crime he or she solicited is guilty *whether or not the crime is committed* (supporting choice **b** as not being in the passage). The other choices are in the passage and are therefore incorrect choices for this question. (Choice **d** is incorrect because of the phrase *by words or actions* in the first sentence, implying that there are nonverbal ways to suggest the committing of a crime.)

8. d. See the first sentence, in which slander is defined by *the speaking of false and defamatory statements* (supporting choice **d**). The term *only if* in the question rules out the other choices—all the choices constitute *slander*.

9. b. The passage speaks of two categories of deportable aliens, those who can be deported for committing prohibited acts before coming to the United States and those who can be deported for committing them since— therefore, logically, the alien need not have committed deportable offenses before entering the United States in order to be deported (supporting choice **b** and ruling out choices **a** and **c**). Choices **d** and **e** are examples—the word *only* at the beginning of the choice rules them out.

10. b. The passage states that an alien cannot hold *federal elective office;* it does not speak about other types of office (supporting choice **b**). The other choices are affirmed in the passage and are therefore the wrong answers to this question.

11. a. Logically, if a person is convicted of manslaughter rather than murder, that person will get a lighter sentence (supporting choice **a**). The word *only* in choices **b, c**, and **d** rules out those choices—all are used as examples of places where mitigating circumstances are looked at. Sentence 2 of the passage says that the term *mitigating circumstances does not constitute justification for the offense* (ruling out choice **e**).

12. b. The fact that no shots were fired is an important feature of the report (without incident). Neither choice **a** nor choice **c** mentions this fact. In addition, these choices fail to adequately locate the storage shed. Choice **d** confuses the names of participants. There is no information provided that even remotely supports **e**.

13. d. Choice **d** is clearly stated in the first and last sentences of the passage. The statement *the crime of arson is always divided into three degrees* rules out choices **a, c**, and **e**. The passage begins with the words *In several states,* implying that other states may not divide arson into three degrees. Similarly, the word *always* rules out choice **b**—examples of arson other than *the burning at night of an inhabited dwelling* are given in the passage.

14. b. It is true that hearsay is *a statement made outside of court and repeated in court,* but according to the passage, not every such statement is hearsay, only *some* such statements are hearsay (see sentence 6). This supports choice

b and rules out choices **a** and **d**. There is nothing in the passage about the truth or untruth of hearsay statements (ruling out choices **c** and **e**).

15. d. Sentence 3 states that if a third person is present, the attorney-client privilege is presumed waived *unless that third person is deemed helpful to the consultation.* (This supports choice **d** as the right answer to this *cannot* question, because it is contradicted in the passage.) The other choices are affirmed in the passage and are therefore wrong answers to this question.

16. d. Choice **d** is clearly supported by the fourth sentence in the paragraph. Choices **a** and **b** are not addressed in the paragraph. Although choice **c** regarding the legislature is mentioned in the paragraph, there is no support for the conclusion in this choice. Choice **e** draws a false conclusion not supported by the paragraph.

17. d. The passage states that, although eyewitness testimony is often unreliable, *judges generally presume that juries are intelligent enough to judge* that testimony (supporting choice **d** and ruling out choice **c**). Choices **a, b**, and **e** confuse *eyewitness testimony* with *expert testimony* and so make little sense.

18. a. Cross-examination involves asking questions of the witness, so choice **a** is illogical and is not in the passage. The other choices are in the passage, making them wrong answers to this question.

19. d. The passage gives examples of times when questioning a witness about a prior bad act is proper and when it isn't, supporting choice **d** and ruling out choices **a** and **b**. Choices **c** and **e** are contradicted in the passage.

20. b. The passage states that the testimony will not be allowed *unless the character trait bears directly upon the crime at issue* (supporting choice **b** and ruling out choices **c** and **e**).

There is no mention of proof in the passage (ruling out choice **a**). Choice **d** is wrong because the question asks about *any defendant,* not just Bob, and some crimes (for example, assault) do not have to do with truthfulness.

21. d. The passage says that A-3 visas *may be extended in increments* [regular additions] *of not more than two years.* Since the plural word (*increments*) is used, it is reasonable to assume more than one increment can be added (supporting choice **d** and ruling out choices **a** and **b**). Choice **c** applies to A-1 and A-2 visa holders. Choice **e** is not mentioned in the passage.

22. c. To find the right choice, it is necessary to make one's way through a maze of convoluted language. Choice **c** could be rewritten in the positive, to read *Videotapes . . . can be used if they have value as evidence and are not unfairly prejudicial.* Similarly, choice **a** could be rewritten in the positive, to read *Videotapes . . . can be used if they have probative value and are unfairly prejudicial,* which is wrong according to the passage. Choice **e** could not be rewritten in the same way, but it is illogical since it implies that videotapes are kept out of court *if* they have value as evidence. Choices **b** and **d** are wrong because there is no discussion in the passage of occasions on which videotapes *will always be used.*

23. d. The passage demonstrates that, *in this case,* the testimony of an expert who had sat through the trial listening was allowed (supporting choice **d**). The passage does not discuss when expert witness testimony is allowed generally (ruling out choices **a** and **b**). There is nothing in the passage about when an expert will be believed (ruling out choices **c** and **e**).

24. b. The passage says that the freedom to act on a belief is limited for the protection of society—choice **b** is another way of saying this. Put in a different way, choice **a** means society needs protection from beliefs that are not acted upon, which makes no sense. Regarding the other choices, in this passage, it is *society* that may need to be protected, not the *religious belief* (ruling out choices **c, d,** and **e**).

25. a. Choice **a** is a convoluted way of saying, in the negative, that *Ron is guilty of entrapment* if Sheryl were not intending to commit the crime until he suggested it. Choice **b** is wrong because it says that Sheryl was already contemplating committing the crime. Choices **c, d,** and **e** contradict the passage by saying that (1) there was no entrapment, and (2) Sheryl would not have committed the crime unless Ron suggested it or led her to think it was legal.

26. d. Only choice **d** matches the requirements for embezzlement. Choice **a** does not match criteria 1 or 3. Choices **b** and **c** do not match criterion 1. Choice **e** does not match criterion 4.

27. e. The judge has said it is Candi's choice whether to testify or not (supporting choice **e**). The passage says that Candi's marriage to Pete one month ago does not entitle them to spousal privilege (ruling out choice **a**). There is nothing in the passage about whether or not the judge could compel Candi to testify under any circumstances (ruling out choice **b**). There is nothing in the passage to suggest that Candi will be implicated if she testifies (ruling out choices **c** and **d**).

28. b. When the choices are worded in a convoluted way and filled with unnecessary negatives, it helps to rewrite them, taking out as many negatives as possible to clarify (for example, change "not irrelevant" to "relevant"). If choice **b** were rewritten, it would read *Irrelevant* *evidence has no probative value;* therefore, choice **b** is correct. Choice **a** would read *Relevant evidence has no probative value,* and is incorrect. Choice **c** would read *Evidence that has probative value is irrelevant,* and is incorrect. Choice **d** would read *Relevant evidence does not have probative value* (same as choice **a**), and is incorrect. Choice **e** would read *Evidence that has no probative value is relevant,* and is incorrect.

29. b. If choice **b** is reworded to clear out unnecessary negatives, it will read *Expatriation takes place only if the act of expatriating is voluntary;* therefore, choice **b** is correct. Choice **a** will read *No denaturalization takes place if the naturalization order is found to have been obtained illegally,* which is incorrect. Choice **c** is fairly clear and is incorrect, since expatriation must be a voluntary act. Choice **d** is fairly clear and is wrong—little words like *unless* are very important.

30. b. Probation is an act of clemency and is granted instead of imprisonment (supporting choice **b** and ruling out choice **a**). Probation is granted under judicial order; it is parole that is granted under executive order (ruling out choice **c**). The passage says that the probationer is *frequently* (not always) a juvenile or first offender (ruling out choice **d**). The passage calls the probationer a *convicted person,* which means that that person has committed a truly criminal act.

Section 2: Spanish Language

1. e. *Cultivaban* (cultivated) most nearly matches *labraban* (worked).

2. c. The choice that most nearly matches *entregó* (to surrender) in the proper person is *dio* (to give).

3. b. The best choice to match *Comienzo* (I start) is *Empiezo* (I begin).

4. c. *Alguien* (someone) means nearly the same thing as *alguna persona* (some person).

5. a. The best choice to match *entraron* (enter) is *venido adentro* (come in).

6. d. The best match for *El señor* (the gentleman) is *El hombre* (the man).

7. e. The only choice that matches *mercaré* (I shall buy) is *compraré* (I shall buy).

8. a. *La capacidad* (the ability) is the nearest to meaning *la derecha* (the right).

9. c. *Ropa nueva* (new clothing) is nearest in meaning to *vestido nuevo* (new dress).

10. b. *No podía cruzar* (could not cross) is the nearest in meaning to *no podía cruzar* (were not able).

11. a. The choice that most nearly matches *visitar* (to visit) is *viajar a* (to travel to).

12. b. The best choice for *¿Qué tal?* (how is it going?) is *¿Cómo estás?* (how are you?).

13. e. The best match for *aquella ciudad* (that city) is *aquel pueblo* (that town).

14. d. *Cocinaban* (were cooking) most nearly matches *preparaban* (were preparing).

15. c. *Policia* (police) most nearly means the same as *agentes* (agents).

16. e. *El tren* (the train) is the best match for *El ferrocarril* (the railroad) in this context. Choice **d**, *El funicular* (the funicular, or cable car, railroad), although close in meaning, could not be considered a principal means of transport.

17. a. The best match for *Caminamos* (we go about) is *Andamos* (we walk).

18. b. The best choice to match *arma* (weapon) is *cuchillo* (knife).

19. e. In this context, the choice that most nearly matches the meaning of *hablar* (to speak) is *usar* (to use).

20. a. The correct choice is *vete* (go away) because it most nearly matches the meaning of *quítate* (withdraw).

21. c. In this choice, there is agreement of tense, and the sentence makes logical sense.

22. b. In this choice, there is agreement of number and gender, and the sentence makes logical sense.

23. a. This is the right choice because of agreement of person and correct verb form.

24. c. In this choice, there is the correct command verb form and number.

25. d. This is the only choice that makes sense.

26. a. The other choices use an incorrect word, gender, or number.

27. b. In this choice, there is agreement in person, and the correct verb form is used.

28. c. Here, there is agreement of verb form and proper word usage.

29. e. Here, there is agreement of gender (*agua* takes *el* even though it is feminine).

30. c. The choice of verb and number and gender agreement are correct.

31. d. This is the only choice that has the correct word usage, verb form, and gender agreement.

32. b. The other choices have mismatched genders and verb forms.

33. d. This is the only choice that does not have a mistake in verb form, word usage, or gender agreement.

34. c. All the other choices have mistakes in spelling or verb form.

35. c. The other choices use a wrong word or incorrect verb form.

36. a. This is the only choice that does not have improper verb form, word usage, or mixed genders.

37. d. This is the only choice that does not have mistakes of word choice, verb form, or gender agreement.

38. c. This choice lacks the grammatical errors of incorrect verb form or word usage that the others have.

39. a. The other choices have mistakes in verb form or word usage.

40. a. The other choices use the wrong verb or an incorrect verb form.

41. a. *Autorizó* (to "authorize") easily replaces *aprobó* (to "approve") in the proper tense.

42. e. The sentence is correct as is.

43. d. This is the correct answer because the two verbs in the third-person plural, *abarcan* ("cover") and *abrevian* ("shorten"), agree with the masculine plural subject *manuales* ("manuals").

44. e. The sentence is correct as is.

45. b. *Viajamos* (we traveled) is correct because the other verb forms use an incorrect tense or word.

46. b. *Mucho calor* (much heat) is correct. The construction *hace + mucho + calor* is used to mean "it is hot."

47. b. The correct choice is *una* (a). The others do not agree in gender.

48. d. The appropriate choice to correctly complete the sentence is *Tú* (You) because it matches the verb form.

49. a. *El professor* (the professor) is correct. The other choices use the wrong gender and make no sense.

50. e. The sentence is correct as it is written.

Section 2: Artificial Language

1. d. The word numbered 1, *bonlek*, is the correct translation of the noun *guard*, formed according to Rule 8. The word numbered 2, *zelremot*, is incorrect because it is the past tense, *inspected*. It should be *zelot*, which is the present indicative, singular form of the verb formed according to Rule 6. The word numbered 3, *trenedlekax*, is the correct plural form of the noun *trenedlek*, *paper*, formed according to Rule 2.

2. b. The word numbered 1, *velle*, is incorrect; it is an adjective that must agree in number and gender with the noun it modifies, according to Rule 3. It should be translated as *velleax*. The word numbered 2, *arlekax*, is correctly translated; it is the plural noun formed from the infinitive *arbar*, *to drive*, following Rules 2 and 8. The word numbered 3, *huslek*, is an incorrect translation because it is a singular noun that should be a plural formed according to Rule 2.

3. d. The word numbered 1, *yevzof*, is correctly formed; it is the feminine *she* formed from the masculine *he* by attaching the feminine singular suffix according to Rule 1. The word numbered 2, *synet*, is, according to Rule 6, incorrectly translated; it is the plural form of the verb, but the singular form, *synot*, is required here. The word numbered 3, *almanlek*, is correct.

4. e. The word numbered 1, *autileax*, is incorrect because it should be the singular, *autile*, to agree with the noun it modifies, *inspector*, according to Rule 3. The word numbered 2, *zellekax*, is an incorrect translation of *inspector* because it is in the plural form in the Artificial Language; it should be translated *zellek*. The word numbered 3, *vellezof*, is incorrect because it has a feminine singular ending, but it should be in the masculine plural form (following Rule 3) to agree in number and gender with *trenedlekax*.

5. c. The word numbered 1, *volle*, is incorrect. It is an adjective that must agree in gender and number with the noun (Rules 1 and 3); the correct translation is *vollezof*. The word numbered 2, *synremot*, is incorrect because it is translated in the past tense; it should be *synot*, the present tense formed according to Rule 6. The word numbered 3, *tatlekzof*, is correctly translated taking the feminine end-

ing to agree with the female subject of the sentence, *girl* (Rule 1).

6. c. The word numbered 1, *bex*, is an incorrect translation of the word *the*; it should be *ric*. The word numbered 2, *synremet*, is incorrect because it is in the plural past tense, and the verb ending should be singular (*synremot*) following Rules 4, 5, and 7. The word numbered 3, *failek*, is a correct translation of the word *country*.

7. a. The word numbered 1, *ekaplekax*, is a correctly formed masculine plural noun (Rule 2). The word numbered 2, *regremet*, is incorrect; although it has the correctly formed past plural verb ending, it is the wrong verb (*bordered*). It should be *chonremot* (*crossed*). The word numbered 3, *ricax*, is incorrect; it is the definite article, *the*, with a masculine plural suffix attached; in the Artificial Language, the definite article applies to all genders and numbers without changing its form (see the note to the vocabulary list).

8. d. The word numbered 1, *ekaplek* (*boy*), is an incorrect translation of the word *man* (*kaplek*). The word numbered 2, *degremot*, is correct; it is the masculine singular past tense form of the verb *degbar* (*to shoot*), formed according to Rules 4, 5, and 7. The word numbered 3, *yev*, is a correct translation of the word *him*.

9. e. The word numbered 1, *vollezof*, is incorrect; it is a feminine singular adjective, but should be the feminine plural, *vollezofax*, to agree with the noun it modifies, *women* (Rules 2 and 3). The word numbered 2, *kaplekzof*, is incorrect because the noun is in feminine singular form, where it should be the feminine plural, *kaplekzofax*, to translate the noun *women* (Rule 2). The word numbered 3, *pohcolle*, is incorrect because it is used as an adverb in the sentence, and it is missing the adverbial ending (Rule 10); it should be *pohcollede*.

10. b. The word numbered 1, *kaplekzof*, while using the appropriate feminine ending, is an incorrect translation of the word *she*. It should be the word for *he*, *yev*, in its feminine form, *yevzof* (Rule 1). The word numbered 2, *synot*, is the correct present singular form of the verb *to be*, *synbar* (Rules 4, 5, and 6). The word numbered 3, *tatlekzof*, is incorrect. *Tatlekzof* is a feminine noun formed from the verb *tatbar* according to Rules 1 and 8; however, the phrase *to spy* should be translated as the unconjugated infinitive *tatbar*.

11. d. The word numbered 1, *avelekax*, is correct; it is the masculine plural noun formed according to Rule 2. The word numbered 2, *degremet*, is the correct past plural of the verb *degbar*, formed according to Rules, 4, 5, and 7. The word numbered 3, *arle*, is incorrect. It has the adjectival suffix *-le* (Rule 9); however, the word is used as an noun in the sentence, so it should take the noun suffix *lek* (Rule 8).

12. a. The word numbered 1, *mor*, is a correct translation of the word *from*. Because it is a preposition, it requires no special endings. The word numbered 2, *reglek*, is incorrect. The word *border* in the sentence is an adjective modifying the noun *station*; therefore, the correct translation requires the adjectival ending (Rule 9), and the correct translation would be *regle*. The word numbered 3, *lexot*, is incorrect because the word it translates is a masculine singular noun formed from the verb *to station*, but the translation incorrectly adds the masculine singular verb ending; the correct translation is *lexlek* (Rule 8).

13. e. The word numbered 1, *tulremot*, is incorrect because it is conjugated in the past tense; the correct translation is *tulot*, present tense singular (Rules 4 and 6). The word numbered 2,

bonot, is incorrect because the verb is conjugated in the present tense; the phrase it translates, *to guard*, requires the unconjugated infinitive, *bonbar*, for correct translation. The word numbered 3, *browlekoe*, is incorrect because the noun has the possessive suffix, *-oe* (Rule 11); the word it translates is not a possessive noun, so the correct translation is *browlek*.

14. b. The word numbered 1, *zelbremot*, is an incorrectly formed conjugation of the verb *zelbar*. To conjugate the verb, the verb stem *bar* must be removed from the infinitive (Rule 4); the incorrect *zelbremot* retains the *b* from the stem. The correct form of the verb is *zelremot*. The word numbered 2, *yevoe*, is correct; it is the possessive form (*his*) of the pronoun *he*, formed correctly by adding the possessive ending (Rule 11). The word numbered 3, *trenedlek*, is incorrectly formed; it requires the plural ending *-ax* to correctly translate the word *papers* (Rule 2).

15. c. The word numbered 1, *velleax*, *those*, is an incorrect translation of the word *these*. The word numbered 2, *piret*, is incorrectly translated; it is the plural present conjugation of the verb *pirbar*, *to escape*. The correct translation is the plural past tense, *piremet* (Rules 4, 5, and 7). The word numbered 3, *lexlek*, is the correct form of a noun formed from a verb (Rule 8).

16. d. The word numbered 1, *cre*, is a correct translation of the word *and*. The word numbered 2, *pohcolleax*, is correctly formed, attaching the negative prefix *poh-* to the word for *legal*, *colle*, to form the adjective *illegal* (*pohcolle*), and adding *ax* to make it plural (Rule 12). The word numbered 3, *trenedlekax*, is the correctly formed plural of the noun *trenedlek*, taking the plural ending *-ax* according to Rule 2.

17. d. The word numbered 1, *synet*, is the correct present plural form of the verb *synbar* (Rules 4, 5, and 6). The word numbered 2, *quea*, is a correct translation of the word *of*. The word numbered 3, *inle*, is an incorrect translation of the adjective *disloyal*; it is lacking the negative prefix *poh-* to form the word *disloyal*, *pohinle*, from the adjective *loyal*, *inle* (Rule 12).

18. b. The word numbered 1, *volleoz*, is incorrect. *Volleoz* (these) is in the masculine form. Since the sentence is about a feminine subject (*women*), you must apply Rules 1 and 3, according to which adjectives (such as *these*) modifying a feminine noun (such as *women*) must take the ending *-nef* before taking the plural ending *-oz* (see Rule 2). Accordingly, the correct form for these in this sentence would be *vollenefoz*.

    The word numbered 2, *frigim*, is correct. According to Rules 4 and 6, the present tense of a verb is formed by adding the suffix *-im* to the stem of the infinitive when the verb has a plural subject (as is the case in this sentence: women work). The word numbered 3, *fercollekinef*, is incorrect. According to Rule 11, in order to form an adverb from an adjective, you should add the suffix *-ki* to the adjectival form. Thus, the adverb *colleki* (*legally*) is formed by adding the suffix *-ki* to the adjective *colle* (*legal*). Next, when the word is negative, it takes the prefix *fer* (see Rule 13); accordingly, the adverb *colleki* must take the prefix *fer*, thus becoming the negative adverb *fercolleki* (*illegally*). Finally, the word *fercolleki*, being an adverb, must never take the feminine ending *-nef*. As stated in Rule 11, adverbs do not change their form according to gender. The reason is that adverbs, by definition, modify verbs, which are, also by definition, genderless (see the discussion on verbs and adverbs in the glossary).

19. c. The word numbered 1, *fercolle*, is incorrect. According to the vocabulary lists, *colle* means *legal*. According to Rule 13, the negative form *fercolle* (*illegal*) is formed by adding the negative prefix *fer* to the affirmative. However, the adjective *illegal* is modifying a plural noun (*aliens*) in the sentence. Consequently, the adjective *fercolle* must take the plural ending *-oz*, thus forming the word *fercolleoz* (Rules 2 and 3). The word numbered 2, *synimfer*, is incorrect. *Synim* is the present tense plural *are*, whereas the sentence has the verb in the past tense, *were*. According to Rules 4 and 7, the past tense is formed by adding the suffix *zot* to the stem of the infinitive and then adding the suffix *im* when the verb is in the plural form. Accordingly, the correct translation of were would be *synzotim*. Lastly, since the sentence has this verb in the negative form, *were not*, the prefix *fer* must be added to the verb (Rule 13), thus forming *fersynzotim*. (Note that the sentence in question 19 incorrectly uses *fer* as a suffix, rather than as a prefix.) The word numbered 3, *liatooz*, is correct. In this sentence, *liatooz* is a past participle, which is formed according to Rule 8. First, the suffix *-to* should be added to the stem of the infinitive to make the verb a past participle. Next, the suffix *-oz* should be added to the past participle because the participle is used as a predicate to modify the masculine plural noun aliens.

20. c. The word numbered 1, *fersynem*, is incorrect. The verb (*are*) is a plural verb and, consequently, according to Rule 6, it must take the suffix *-im*, rather than the suffix *-em*. On the other hand, the use of the negative prefix (*fer*) is correct, since according to Rule 13, the prefix *fer-* should be added to the affirmative form in order to make a word negative. Accordingly, the correct word for *are not* is *fersynim*. The word numbered 2, *huslekoz*, is incorrect. According to the vocabulary lists, *huslek* means *alien*, and according to Rule 2, the plural of a noun is formed by adding the suffix *oz*, but since the subject of the sentence is *feminine* (*women*), the suffix *-nef* must be added to the noun before making it plural (see Rules 1 and 2). Accordingly, the correct word is *husleknefoz*. The word numbered 3, *failek*, is correct. *Failek* is the word that appears in the vocabulary lists for *country*.

21. b. First, the plural noun *men* is formed, according to Rule 2, by adding the suffix *-oz* to the singular form of the noun *kaplek*. Accordingly, the correct word is *kaplekoz*. Second, the word *and* (*loa*) is found in the vocabulary lists. Third, the plural noun *women* is formed, according to Rules 1 and 2, by first adding the feminine suffix *nef* to the singular masculine form of the noun (*kaplek*) and then adding the suffix *-oz* for the plural. Accordingly, the correct word is *kapleknefoz*. Among the incorrect choices, choice **a** incorrectly uses the negative *fer* instead of the feminine *nef*; choice **c** incorrectly uses the possessive form *ae* instead of the plural form *oz*; choice **d** incorrectly uses both the negative *fer* and the possessive *ae*; and choice **e** incorrectly uses the negative *fer* and the article *bex* (a, an).

22. e. First, you must form the present tense of the verb to guard (*bonker*). According to Rules 4 and 6, the present tense of a verb is formed by omitting the infinitive suffix *-ker* and replacing it with the suffix *-im* when the subject is plural. Since the subject of this sentence is plural (*men and women*, i.e., they), the verb should take the plural suffix. Accordingly, the correct form is *bonim*. Second, the article *the* is translated as *wir,* according to the vocabulary lists. Third, the noun *border*

(*reglek*) is formed according to Rule 9 by adding the suffix *-lek* to the stem of the verb. Among the incorrect choices, choice **a** incorrectly applies Rule 2 to the verb by adding the suffix *-oz* to the plural verb *bonim*. Rule 2 is only used to form the plurals of nouns, pronouns, adjectives, and articles, not verbs. Choice **b** also incorrectly applies Rule 2 to the verb and, in addition, applies Rule 2 to the noun *reglek* (*border*), thus incorrectly making it the plural *reglekoz* (*borders*). Choice **c** incorrectly uses the singular form of the verb (*bonem*), and choice **d** incorrectly uses the infinitive form of the verb (*bonker*).

23. c. First, the word *ferkometleoz* (*unfriendly* in the plural form) is formed by applying Rules 10, 13, 3, and 2. Rule 10 tells you that to form an adjective from a noun you should use the suffix *-le*, instead of the suffix *-lek*. Hence, you change the noun *kometlek* (*friend*), which appears in the vocabulary lists, to the adjective *kometle*. However, since the adjective is negative in the sentence, and since it is modifying the plural noun *aliens*, you must also apply Rule 13 (thus adding the negative prefix *fer*) and Rules 3 and 2, thus adding the plural suffix *-oz*. Second, the word *huslekoz* (*aliens*) is formed by applying Rule 2, according to which you must add the suffix *-oz* to form the plural of a noun. Among the incorrect choices, choices **a**, **b**, and **e** erroneously apply the rule to form adverbs (Rule 11) to the noun *kometlek*. In addition, choices **b** and **e** make the same error with the noun *huslek*. Choice **d** erroneously applies the plural *-oz* to the noun form *ferkometlek* (*non-friend*), rather than to the correct adjectival form (*ferkometle*).

24. c. First, the word *janleoz* (*skillful* in the plural form) is formed by applying Rules 2 and 3, according to which the suffix *-oz* must be added to the adjective *janle* (*skillful*) because it is modifying the plural noun *spies*. Second, the word *tatlekoz* (*spies*) is formed by applying Rules 2, 4, and 9, according to which in order to form a noun from a verb, you should add the suffix *-lek* to the stem of the infinitive, and next, you should add the suffix *-oz* to make the noun plural. Among the incorrect choices, choices **a**, **b**, and **e** incorrectly neglect Rules 2 and 3 by using the singular adjective *janle*. In addition, choice **b** fails to use the correct plural for *spies*; and choices **d** and **e** neglect Rule 9 to form a noun and instead use the infinitive *to spy* (*tatker*) with the plural ending *-oz* (which, according to Rule 2, is only for nouns, pronouns, adjectives, and articles).

25. e. First, the pronoun *yevoz* (*they*) is formed according to Rule 2 by adding the plural suffix to the singular pronoun *yev* (*he*). (Remember that all nouns and pronouns, unless referring to a specifically feminine subject, are assumed to be masculine.) Second, the verb *tulim* (*have in the plural present tense*) is formed according to Rules 4 and 6 by adding the plural suffix *-im* to the stem of the infinitive. Third, the infinitive *zelker* (*to inspect*) is found in the vocabulary lists. Among the incorrect choices, choice **a** erroneously adds the plural verb form *-im* to the infinitive *zelker*, choice **b** erroneously uses the verb in its singular form *tulem*, and choices **c** and **d** erroneously use the past tense *tulzotim*; in addition, choice **d** erroneously adds the plural verb ending *-im* to the infinitive *zelker*.

26. e. First, the adjective *almanleoz* is formed by changing the suffix *-lek* in the noun *almanlek* (*government*) to the adjectival suffix *le*, thus transforming the noun into the adjective *almanle* (*governmental*), and then adding the plural suffix *-oz* to the adjective, since adjectives modifying plural nouns must take plural

endings (see Rules 2, 3, and 10). Second, the plural noun *trenedlekoz* (*papers*) is formed, according to Rule 2, by adding the plural suffix *-oz* to the singular form of the noun. Among the incorrect choices, choices **b** and **c** erroneously use the singular noun *almanlek* (*government*), and in addition, choice **b** also erroneously uses the singular noun *trenedlek* (*paper*); choice **d** erroneously uses the plural noun *almanlekoz* (*governments*); and choice **e** erroneously uses the singular form of the adjective *almanle* (*governmental*).

27. d. The plural noun *lexlekoz* (*stations*) is formed by first applying Rule 9, according to which in order to form a noun from a verb, you should add the suffix *-lek* to the stem of the verb. Then, apply Rule 2, according to which you must add the suffix *-oz* to form the plural of a noun. Among the incorrect choices, choice **a** incorrectly applies Rule 2 and adds the suffix *-oz* to the infinitive *lexker*, choice **b** incorrectly applies Rule 12 and adds the possessive suffix *-ae* to the noun *lexlek*, choice **c** incorrectly applies the possessive suffix *-ae* to the infinitive *lexker*, and choice **e** incorrectly applies Rule 10 to form the adjectival form *lexle* instead of the noun *lexlek*.

28. d. First, the word *volle* means *this* and is found in the vocabulary lists. Second, the word *failekae* is a possessive form, which is formed according to Rule 12 by adding the suffix *ae* to the noun *failek* (*country*), also found in the vocabulary lists.

Among the incorrect choices, choices **b** and **d** erroneously add the possessive *ae* to the adjective *volle*, choices **c** and **d** erroneously omit the possessive in *failek*, and choice **e** erroneously uses an adjectival form (*faile*) instead of the noun *failek*.

29. b. First, the adverb *janleki* (*skillfully*) is formed, according to Rule 11, by adding the suffix *-ki* to the masculine form of the adjective *janle* (which appears in the vocabulary lists). Second, the verb *bontooz* is in the form of a past participle (*guarded*). According to Rule 8, the past participle of a verb is formed by adding the suffix *-to* to the stem of the verb. Also, according to Rule 8, when the participle is used as a predicate with the verb *to be*, it must take the plural form if the noun it modifies is plural. Among the incorrect choices, choices **a** and **d** erroneously add the plural suffix *-oz*, which is NOT used for adverbs; in addition, choices **a** and **d** erroneously use the past tense of the verb rather than the participle. Choice **c** uses the correct adverb (*janleki*), but fails to add the plural ending to the participle. Choice **e** erroneously uses the adverbial ending *-ki* with the noun *guard* (*bonlek*), rather than using the participle.

30. **b.** First, the adjective *vollenefoz* (*these*) is formed, according to Rules 1, 2, and 3, by adding the feminine suffix *-nef* and then the plural suffix *-oz* to the masculine singular form (*volle*). Second, the adjective *inlenefoz* (*loyal*) is formed, according to the same rules, by adding the same suffixes, *-nef* and *-oz*, to the masculine singular form (*inle*). Third, the noun *kapleknefoz* (*women*) is formed, according to Rules 1 and 2, by adding the suffix *-nef* to the masculine noun *kaplek* (*man*) and then adding the suffix *-oz* to *kapleknef* (*woman*) to make it plural. Among the incorrect choices, choices **a** and **c** incorrectly omit the feminine suffix in the adjective *volleoz*; in addition, choice **a** incorrectly omits the plural suffix in the adjective *inlenef*, and choice **c** incorrectly omits both the feminine suffix and the plural suffix in the adjective *inle*. Choice **d** incorrectly omits the plural suffix in the

adjective *inlenef*, and choice **e** incorrectly omits both the feminine suffix and the plural suffix in the adjective *inle*.

31. **a.** *Volle ekaplek pohtulremot* is the only one of these expressions that means *this boy did not have*.

32. **b.** *Velle pohkometle almanlek* is the only one of these expressions that properly translates *that unfriendly government*. The adjectives, *velle* and *pohkometle*, are in the correct form, agreeing with the masculine noun, *almanlek* (Rule 3), and the adjective, *pohkometle*, has the correct negative prefix (Rule 12).

33. **c.** The expression *bex pirlezof ekaplekzof* correctly translates the phrase *an escaped girl*, because the adjective, *escaped*, is correctly formed from the infinitive, *to escape* (*pirbar*), following Rules 8 and 9; and it also has the correct feminine suffix to agree with the noun, *girl* (Rules 1 and 3).

34. **e.** *Mor bex regle lexlek* is the only one of these expressions that properly translates *from a border station* because the adjective, *regle* (*border*), is correctly formed from the infinitive, *regbar*, following Rules 8 and 9, and the noun, *lexlek* (*station*), is correctly formed from the infinitive, *lexbar*, following Rule 8.

35. **b.** *Ric avele tatlek* is the only one of these expressions that properly translates *the enemy spy*, where the adjective, *enemy* (*avele*), is correctly formed from the noun, *avelek* (Rule 9), and the noun, *spy* (*tatlek*), is correctly formed from the infinitive, *tatbar*, using Rule 8.

36. **e.** *Ric browle chonlek* is the only one of these expressions that properly translates *the river crossing* because the word *the* is correctly translated; the adjective *browle* has the correct adjectival ending (Rule 9); and the noun, *chonlek*, is correctly formed from the infinitive *chonbar* (Rule 8).

37. d. Choices **a** and **e** are incorrect because the adjective is lacking the negative prefix, *poh-* (Rule 12). Choice **b** is incorrect because both the adjective and the pronoun are in the masculine form. Choice **c** is incorrect because the pronoun is in the masculine plural form. In choice **d,** the adjective has the negative prefix (Rule 12), and both the adjective and the pronoun have the feminine plural endings (Rule 2).

38. e. Choices **a** and **d** are incorrect because the verbs, *tulet* and *tulot*, are in the present tense. Choices **b** and **c** are incorrect because *chonlek* is the noun, not the infinitive. In choice **e**, the verb, *tulremot (had)* is in the correct past singular form, and the verb, *chonbar (to cross)*, is in the infinitive form.

39. b. In choices **a** and **d**, the noun is misspelled. In choices **c** and **e**, the adjective is singular, but it should be plural. In choice **b**, the possessive noun *ekaplekaxoe* has the proper plural ending (Rule 2), and the correct possessive suffix; *pohcolleax* has the proper negative prefix (Rule 12).

40. c. Choices **a** and **e** are incorrect because the word *zelot* is a conjugation of the verb, not the noun form. Choice **b** is incorrect because *inle* is the adjectival, not the adverbial, form. Choice **d** is incorrect because *zellekax* is the plural form of the noun. In choice **c**, the noun, *zellek*, is in the correct masculine form of the noun, and is properly formed from the infinitive, *zelbar* (Rule 8); further, the adverb, *inlede*, has been formed properly with the adverbial ending according to Rule 10.

► Scoring

A passing score of 70% on the reasoning and language sections of the test is necessary to be considered for the oral interview. Each question on the test is weighted according to DHS standards. It is a good idea to total the number of correct answers to get a complete picture of your strengths and weaknesses.

You have probably seen improvement between your first practice exam score and this one, but if you didn't improve as much as you'd like, here are some options:

- **If 60% of your answers were incorrect**, reconsider taking the Border Patrol Exam at this time. A good idea would be to take some brush-up courses, either at a university or community college or through correspondence. If you don't have time for a course, you might try private tutoring.
- **If 60–70% of your answers were correct**, you need to work as hard as you can to improve your skills. Check out the LearningExpress book *501 Challenging Logic and Reasoning Problems*. If your difficulty is with Spanish, try some of the books from the "Resources" part of Chapter 9, "Checking Your Spanish Proficiency." If you have trouble with the Artificial Language, review Chapter 8, "Using the Artificial Language Manual" and the Artificial Language Manual itself in Chapter 7. It might also be helpful to ask friends and family to make up mock test questions and quiz you on them.
- **If 70–85% of your answers were correct**, you could still benefit from additional work by going back to the instructional chapters and by brushing up your reading comprehension and general language skills before the exam.
- **If 85% of your answers were correct**, that's great! That kind of score should make you a good candidate for a Border Patrol Agent job. Don't lose your edge, though; keep studying right up to the day before the exam.

There's an old joke that goes like this: In New York City, a man stops a second man on the street and asks, "How do I get to Carnegie Hall?" The second man answers, "Practice."

The key to success in almost any pursuit is to prepare for all you're worth. By taking the practice exams in this book, you've made yourself better prepared than other people who may be taking the exam with you. You've diagnosed where your strengths and weaknesses lie and learned how to deal with the various kinds of questions that will appear on the test. So go into the exam with confidence, knowing that you're ready and equipped to do your best.

NOTES

NOTES

NOTES

NOTES

NOTES

Special FREE Offer from LearningExpress!

**LearningExpress will help you be better prepared for,
and get higher scores on, the Border Patrol Exam**

Go to the LearningExpress Practice Center at www.LearningExpressFreeOffer.com,
an interactive online resource exclusively for LearningExpress customers.

Now that you've purchased LearningExpress's *Border Patrol Exam, 3rd Edition*, you
have FREE access to:

- **A full-length Border Patrol practice test** that mirrors the official Border Patrol Exam
- **Immediate scoring** and **detailed answer explanations**
- Benchmark your skills and focus your study with our **customized diagnostic report**

Follow the simple instructions on the scratch card in your copy of *Border Patrol Exam, 3rd Edition*. Use
your individualized access code found on the scratch card and go to www.LearningExpressFreeOffer.com
to sign in. Start practicing online for the Border Patrol Exam right away!

Once you've logged on, use the spaces below to write in your access code and newly created password for easy reference:

Access Code: _____   Password: _____